The NYSTROM ATLAS of CANADA AND THE WORLD

NYSTROM

HERFF JONES EDUCATION DIVISION

CREDITS

Educational Consultants	Angelo Bolotta, Curriculum Coordinator Ontario Institute for Catholic Education, Toronto, Ontario
	John R. Chalk, Lecturer, Faculty of Education University of British Columbia, Vancouver, British Columbia
	Walter Donovan, Professor, Faculty of Education (retired) University of Toronto, Toronto, Ontario
	John Lohrenz, Social Studies and Sustainable Development Consultant, K–12 (retired) Manitoba Education, Winnipeg, Manitoba

2006 Update of Names and Boundaries
Copyright © 2003, 1995 **NYSTROM** Herff Jones Education Division
3333 N. Elston Avenue
Chicago, Illinois 60618
**For information about ordering this atlas,
call toll-free 800-621-8086.**

All rights reserved. No part of this book may be reproduced or transmitted in any form or by any means, electronic or mechanical, including photocopying, recording, or by any information storage and retrieval system, without permission in writing from the publisher.

10 9 8 7 6   09 08 07 06

ISBN: 0-7825-0895-2   Printed in Canada   9ACW

CONTENTS

THEMATIC MAPS AND GRAPHS

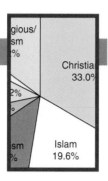

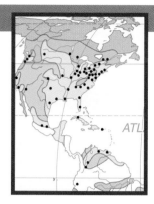

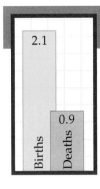

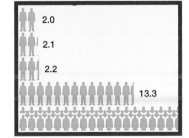

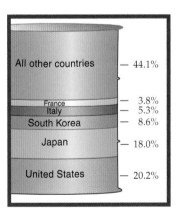

INTRODUCTION

The Nystrom Atlas of Canada and the World includes physical and political maps of large areas, regional maps of smaller areas, thematic maps, graphic presentations of data, and illustrative photographs. Each map, graph, and photo is best suited to providing specific kinds of information.

Physical Maps

Physical maps in this atlas are designed so that the names and relative locations of natural features can be seen at a glance. Colours represent water depths and land elevations. Although the emphasis is on natural features, countries and key cities also are named.

Political Maps

Political maps are coloured by state, province, or country, making it as easy as possible to tell where one ends and another begins. The names of capitals and other major cities are quickly found because the maps are carefully edited to keep them uncluttered.

Thematic Maps

Thematic maps focus on single topics or themes, and the subject can be anything that is mappable. Among the thematic maps in this atlas are maps of rainfall, land use, and population. Often the patterns on one thematic map become more meaningful when compared to the patterns on another.

Regional Maps

Regional maps in this atlas offer close-up views of areas on the political maps. Because regional maps enlarge the areas shown, they can name more cities while remaining highly readable. Other details also are added, such as the names of landforms, including some not given on the physical maps.

Legends

Legends are provided for all maps. For most of the thematic maps, the legends are simple keys showing what the map colours stand for. The legends for the physical, political, and regional maps are lengthier. To save space, the complete legend for these maps is given only once, on the facing page.

Graphs

Graphs summarize facts in a visual way, making it easier to see trends and make comparisons. Many different topics are presented in a variety of graphic styles. Some topics are graphed only once, while others form strands that run through the whole book.

Photographs

Photographs can portray the characteristics of a place like nothing else can. The photos in this atlas were carefully chosen to illustrate the natural setting and cultural aspects of places around the world. Photographic realism is the perfect complement to the abstract symbolism of maps.

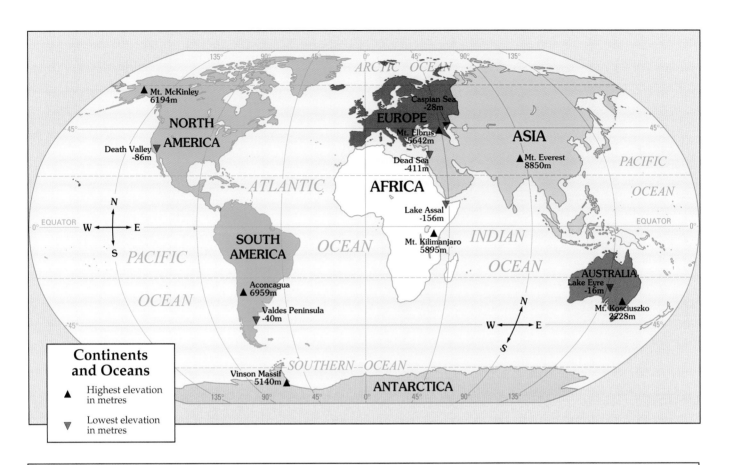

Continents and Oceans

▲ Highest elevation in metres

▼ Lowest elevation in metres

Complete Legend

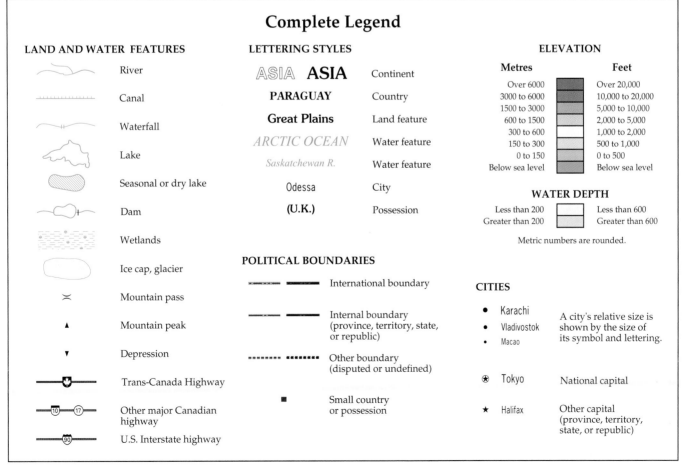

LAND AND WATER FEATURES

- River
- Canal
- Waterfall
- Lake
- Seasonal or dry lake
- Dam
- Wetlands
- Ice cap, glacier
- Mountain pass
- ▲ Mountain peak
- ▼ Depression
- Trans-Canada Highway
- Other major Canadian highway
- U.S. Interstate highway

LETTERING STYLES

ASIA **ASIA**	Continent
PARAGUAY	Country
Great Plains	Land feature
ARCTIC OCEAN	Water feature
Saskatchewan R.	Water feature
Odessa	City
(U.K.)	Possession

POLITICAL BOUNDARIES

- International boundary
- Internal boundary (province, territory, state, or republic)
- Other boundary (disputed or undefined)
- Small country or possession

ELEVATION

Metres	Feet
Over 6000	Over 20,000
3000 to 6000	10,000 to 20,000
1500 to 3000	5,000 to 10,000
600 to 1500	2,000 to 5,000
300 to 600	1,000 to 2,000
150 to 300	500 to 1,000
0 to 150	0 to 500
Below sea level	Below sea level

WATER DEPTH

Less than 200	Less than 600
Greater than 200	Greater than 600

Metric numbers are rounded.

CITIES

- ● Karachi
- ● Vladivostok
- · Macao

A city's relative size is shown by the size of its symbol and lettering.

- ⊛ Tokyo — National capital
- ★ Halifax — Other capital (province, territory, state, or republic)

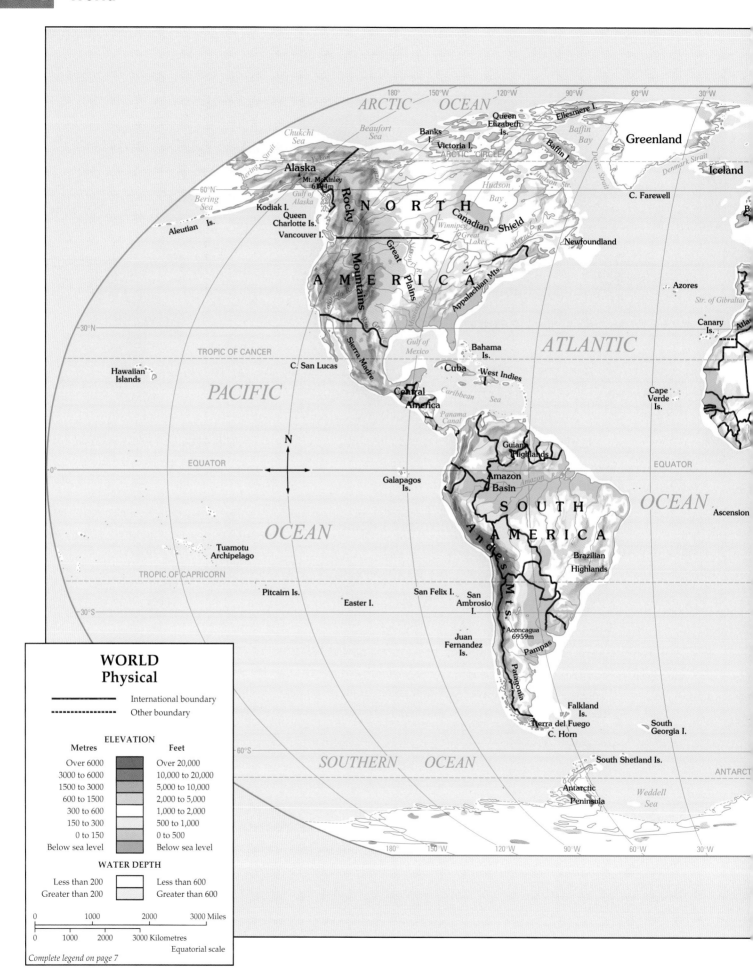

ARCTIC OCEAN

Chukchi Sea

Beaufort Sea

Queen Elizabeth Is.

Banks I.

Victoria I.

ARCTIC CIRCLE

Baffin Bay

Baffin I.

Ellesmere I.

Greenland

Iceland

Denmark Strait

Davis Strait

Bering Strait

Alaska

Yukon

Mt. McKinley 6194m

Gulf of Alaska

Bering Sea

Kodiak I.

Queen Charlotte Is.

Vancouver I.

Aleutian Is.

Rocky

NORTH

Hudson Bay

Hudson Str.

C. Farewell

Mackenzie R.

Canadian Shield

L. Winnipeg

Great Lakes

St. Lawrence

Newfoundland

AMERICA

Mountains

Great Plains

Colorado R.

Rio Grande

Mississippi R.

Missouri R.

Appalachian Mts.

Azores

Str. of Gibraltar

30°N

TROPIC OF CANCER

C. San Lucas

Sierra Madre

Gulf of Mexico

Bahama Is.

Cuba

West Indies

Canary Is.

Cape Verde Is.

Atla

B.

Hawaiian Islands

PACIFIC

Central America

Caribbean Sea

Panama Canal

ATLANTIC

Cape Verde Is.

N

EQUATOR

Galapagos Is.

Guiana Highlands

Amazon Basin

Amazon R.

SOUTH

EQUATOR

OCEAN

Ascension

OCEAN

Tuamotu Archipelago

AMERICA

Andes Mts.

Brazilian Highlands

TROPIC OF CAPRICORN

Pitcairn Is.

Easter I.

San Felix I.

San Ambrosio I.

Aconcagua 6959m

Pampas

30°S

Juan Fernandez Is.

Patagonia

Falkland Is.

South Georgia I.

Tierra del Fuego

C. Horn

60°S

SOUTHERN OCEAN

South Shetland Is.

ANTARCT

Antarctic Peninsula

Weddell Sea

180°   150°W   120°W   90°W   60°W   30°W

WORLD
Physical

————————	International boundary
- - - - - - - - - -	Other boundary

ELEVATION

Metres	Feet
Over 6000	Over 20,000
3000 to 6000	10,000 to 20,000
1500 to 3000	5,000 to 10,000
600 to 1500	2,000 to 5,000
300 to 600	1,000 to 2,000
150 to 300	500 to 1,000
0 to 150	0 to 500
Below sea level	Below sea level

WATER DEPTH

Less than 200	Less than 600
Greater than 200	Greater than 600

0   1000   2000   3000 Miles

0   1000   2000   3000 Kilometres

Equatorial scale

Complete legend on page 7

RCTIC   OCEAN
30°E   60°E   90°E   120°E   150°E   180°

Svalbard
North Cape
Novaya
Zemlya
Severnaya
Zemlya
New Siberian
Is.
East
Siberian
Sea
Laptev
Sea
Kara
Sea
Barents
Sea
egian
Sea
Scandinavian
Peninsula
West
Siberian
Plain
Central
Siberian
Plateau
ARCTIC   CIRCLE
Verkhoyansk Range
Kolyma Range
Ural Mountains
Ob
Siberia
60°N
S I B E R I A
EUROPE
Northern
European   Plain
Alps
Steppes
A S I A
Kamchatka
Peninsula
Sea
of
Okhotsk
Sakhalin
Manchurian
Plain
Kuril
Is.
Aral
Sea
L. Balkhash
Altai Mts.
Gobi
Hokkaido
Caucasus
Mts.
Mt. Elbrus
5642m
Black Sea
Caspian Sea
Tien Shan
Huang
Sea of
Japan
(East Sea)
Honshu
Sicily
Mediterranean
Sea
Pamirs
Kunlun Mts.
Plateau
of Tibet
North
China
Plain
Yellow
Sea
Kyushu
PACIFIC
30°N
ahara
RICA
Iranian
Plateau
Himalayas
Mt. Everest
8848m
Yunnan
Plateau
East
China
Sea
Ryukyu
Is.
nagar
Mts.
Tibesti
Mts.
Arabian
Peninsula
Red
Sea
Mt. Everest
8848m
Taiwan
TROPIC OF CANCER
OCEAN
ahel
Arabian Sea
Deccan
Plateau
Bay
of
Bengal
Philippine
Is.
Mariana
Is.
Ethiopian
Highlands
Sri
Lanka
South
China
Sea
Philippine
Sea
Caroline Is.
L. Victoria
Maldives
Sumatra
Borneo
Celebes
Sea
EQUATOR
0°
Congo
Basin
Mt. Kilimanjaro
5895m
INDIAN
Chagos
Archipelago
Sulawesi
(Celebes)
New Guinea
Solomon Is.
Zanzibar I.
Seychelles
Java
Timor
Bie
Plateau
Comoros
OCEAN
Arafura
Sea
Fiji Is.
Madagascar
Mauritius
Timor Sea
Coral
Sea
New
Caledonia
Kalahari
Desert
Mozambique Channel
TROPIC OF CAPRICORN
Great Sandy
Desert
Drakensberg
AUSTRALIA
Great Dividing Range
30°S
C. of Good Hope
Amsterdam I.
St. Paul I.
C. Leeuwin
Mt. Kosciuszko
2228m
Darling
Tasman
Sea
North I.
New
Zealand
Bass Strait
Tasmania
South I.
Kerguelen I.
Stewart I.
Auckland
I.
60°S
CLE
SOUTHERN   OCEAN
ANTARCTICA
30°E   60°E   90°E   120°E   150°E   180°

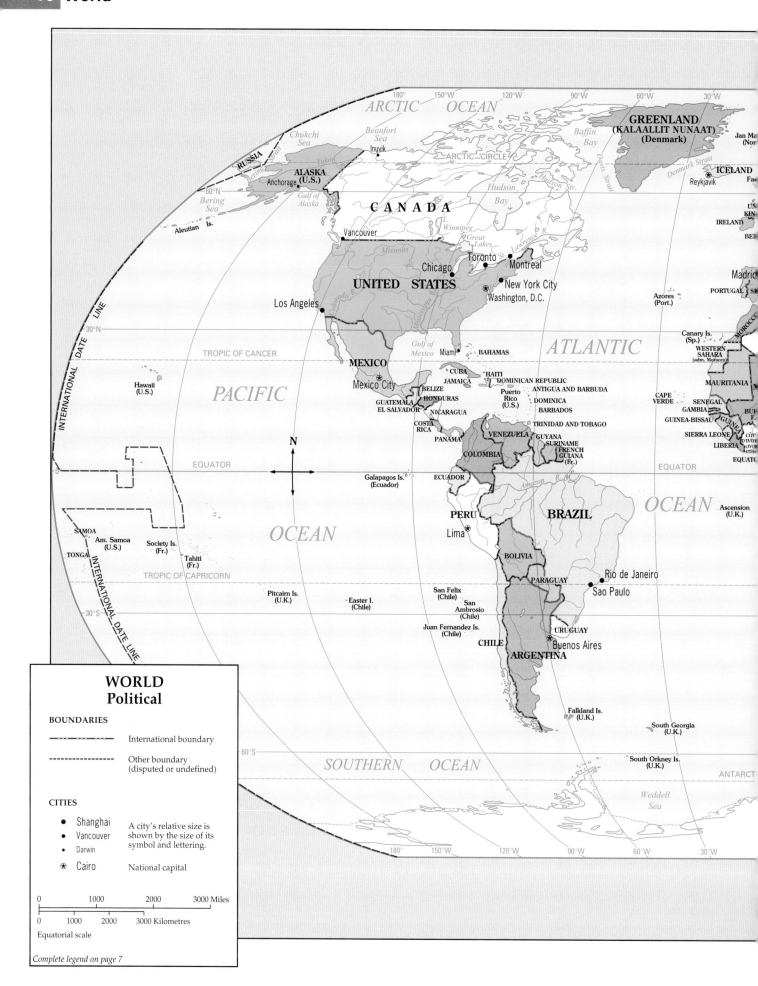

ARCTIC   OCEAN

GREENLAND
(KALAALLIT NUNAAT)
(Denmark)

Jan Ma
(Nor

Chukchi
Sea

Beaufort
Sea

Baffin
Bay

RUSSIA

Inuvik

ARCTIC CIRCLE

ICELAND

Reykjavik

Fa

ALASKA
(U.S.)

Anchorage

60°N

Hudson
Bay

Denmark Strait

Davis Strait

Hudson Str.

UN
KIN

Bering
Sea

Gulf of
Alaska

C A N A D A

IRELAND

BE

Aleutian Is.

Vancouver

Winnipeg

Toronto

Montreal

Madrid

UNITED   STATES

Chicago

New York City

PORTUGAL   S

30°N

Los Angeles

Washington, D.C.

Azores
(Port.)

TROPIC OF CANCER

Canary Is.
(Sp.)

MOROCCO

MEXICO

Gulf of
Mexico

Miami

BAHAMAS

WESTERN
SAHARA
(adm. Morocco)

Hawaii
(U.S.)

PACIFIC

Mexico City

CUBA

HAITI

DOMINICAN REPUBLIC

MAURITANIA

JAMAICA

BELIZE

ANTIGUA AND BARBUDA

HONDURAS

Puerto
Rico
(U.S.)

DOMINICA

CAPE
VERDE

SENEGAL

GUATEMALA

NICARAGUA

BARBADOS

GAMBIA

EL SALVADOR

COSTA
RICA

TRINIDAD AND TOBAGO

GUINEA-BISSAU

GUINEA

F.

N

PANAMA

VENEZUELA

GUYANA

SIERRA LEONE

CÔT
DIVO
COAS

SURINAME

LIBERIA

EQUATOR

COLOMBIA

FRENCH
GUIANA
(Fr.)

EQUATO

Galapagos Is.
(Ecuador)

ECUADOR

Amazon   R.

ATLANTIC

EQUATOR

Ascension
(U.K.)

PERU

BRAZIL

OCEAN

Lima

OCEAN

SAMOA

Am. Samoa
(U.S.)

Society Is.
(Fr.)

Tahiti
(Fr.)

BOLIVIA

Rio de Janeiro

TONGA

TROPIC OF CAPRICORN

PARAGUAY

Sao Paulo

Pitcairn Is.
(U.K.)

Easter I.
(Chile)

San Felix
(Chile)

San
Ambrosio
(Chile)

URUGUAY

30°S

Juan Fernandez Is.
(Chile)

CHILE

Buenos Aires

ARGENTINA

Falkland Is.
(U.K.)

South Georgia
(U.K.)

60°S

South Orkney Is.
(U.K.)

SOUTHERN   OCEAN

ANTARCT

Weddell
Sea

INTERNATIONAL DATE LINE

Bering Strait

Yukon

Bering
Sea

Colorado R.

Missouri

Great
Lakes

L.

St. Lawrence R.

Mississippi

WORLD
Political

BOUNDARIES

International boundary

Other boundary
(disputed or undefined)

CITIES

• Shanghai

• Vancouver

· Darwin

⊛ Cairo

A city's relative size is
shown by the size of its
symbol and lettering.

National capital

| 0 | 1000 | 2000 | 3000 Miles |

| 0 | 1000 | 2000 | 3000 Kilometres |

Equatorial scale

Complete legend on page 7

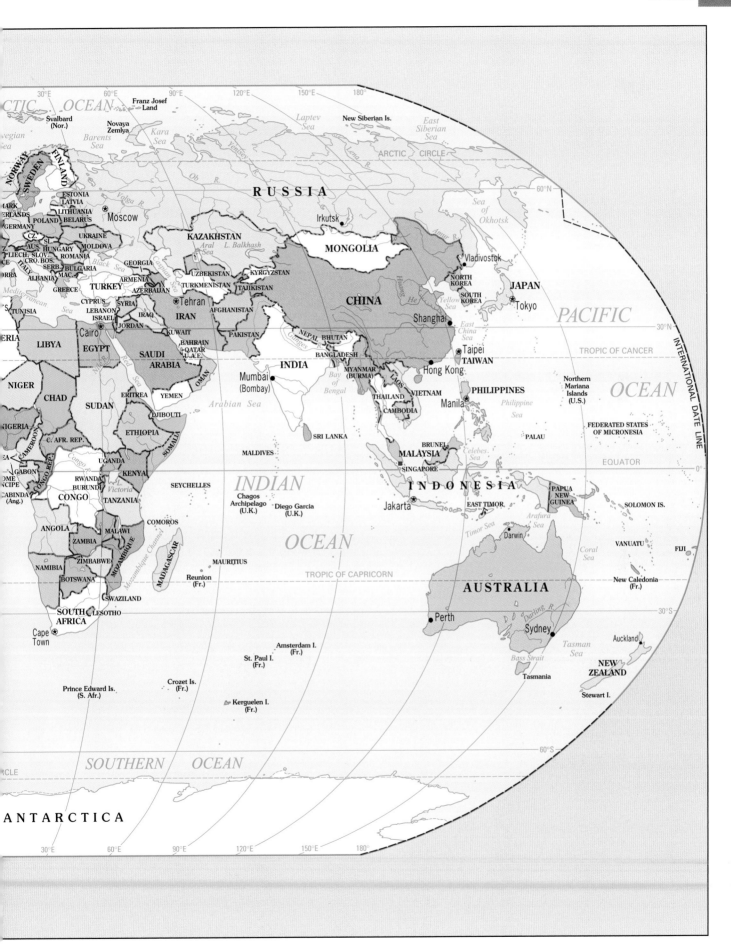

CTIC OCEAN

Svalbard (Nor.)

Franz Josef Land

Novaya Zemlya

New Siberian Is.

Laptev Sea

East Siberian Sea

Kara Sea

Barents Sea

gian Sea

NORWAY FINLAND SWEDEN

ARCTIC CIRCLE

R U S S I A

DMARK ESTONIA LATVIA LITHUANIA ERLANDS BELARUS GERMANY POLAND

Moscow

Irkutsk

Sea of Okhotsk

60°N

CZ. SL. UKRAINE IECH. SLOV. HUNGARY MOLDOVA CE CRO. BOS. ROMANIA RRA SERB. BULGARIA ITALY MAC. ALBANIA

Volga R.

KAZAKHSTAN

Aral Sea

L. Balkhash

MONGOLIA

Vladivostok

Amur R.

GEORGIA *Black Sea* ARMENIA TURKEY AZERBAIJAN GREECE

Caspian Sea

UZBEKISTAN KYRGYZSTAN TURKMENISTAN TAJIKISTAN

NORTH KOREA

JAPAN

Huang He

SOUTH KOREA

Tokyo

rranean Sea CYPRUS LEBANON SYRIA ISRAEL IRAQ

Tehran

IRAN

AFGHANISTAN

CHINA

Yellow Sea

Shanghai

East China Sea

PACIFIC

30°N

TUNISIA JORDAN KUWAIT BAHRAIN QATAR U.A.E.

Cairo

PAKISTAN

NEPAL BHUTAN

Ganges R.

Taipei

TROPIC OF CANCER

TAIWAN

Hong Kong

ERIA LIBYA EGYPT

Red Sea

SAUDI ARABIA OMAN

INDIA

BANGLADESH

MYANMAR (BURMA)

OCEAN

INTERNATIONAL DATE LINE

NIGER CHAD SUDAN ERITREA YEMEN

Mumbai (Bombay)

Bay of Bengal

LAOS

VIETNAM

Northern Mariana Islands (U.S.)

THAILAND

PHILIPPINES

Manila

Philippine Sea

DJIBOUTI

Arabian Sea

CAMBODIA

NIGERIA C. AFR. REP. ETHIOPIA SOMALIA

SRI LANKA

MALDIVES

BRUNEI

MALAYSIA

FEDERATED STATES OF MICRONESIA

CAMEROON EA UGANDA OME GABON CIPE RWANDA CONGO REP. BURUNDI ABINDA (Ang.) **CONGO** TANZANIA KENYA

SEYCHELLES

INDIAN

L. Victoria

SINGAPORE

Celebes Sea

PALAU

EQUATOR 0°

Chagos Archipelago (U.K.)

Diego Garcia (U.K.)

I N D O N E S I A

PAPUA NEW GUINEA

SOLOMON IS.

ANGOLA ZAMBIA MALAWI

COMOROS

Jakarta

EAST TIMOR

Arafura Sea

MADAGASCAR

Timor Sea

Darwin

Coral Sea

VANUATU

FIJI

NAMIBIA ZIMBABWE BOTSWANA MOZAMBIQUE

Mozambique Channel

MAURITIUS

Reunion (Fr.)

TROPIC OF CAPRICORN

New Caledonia (Fr.)

AUSTRALIA

30°S

SWAZILAND SOUTH AFRICA LESOTHO

Perth

Cape Town

Amsterdam I. (Fr.)

Darling R.

Sydney

Auckland

St. Paul I. (Fr.)

Tasman Sea

Prince Edward Is. (S. Afr.)

Crozet Is. (Fr.)

Bass Strait

NEW ZEALAND

Tasmania

Kerguelen I. (Fr.)

Stewart I.

60°S

SOUTHERN OCEAN

RCLE

ANTARCTICA

30°E 60°E 90°E 120°E 150°E 180°

Earthquakes and Volcanoes

The "ring of fire" is the belt of frequent volcanic and seismic activity that encompasses the Pacific Ocean.

Major earthquakes
Major volcanoes

Ocean Depths and Surface Currents

Metres	Depth	Feet
0 to 200		0 to 600
200 to 4000		600 to 12,000
4000 to 6000		12,000 to 18,000
More than 6000		More than 18,000

Surface ocean current

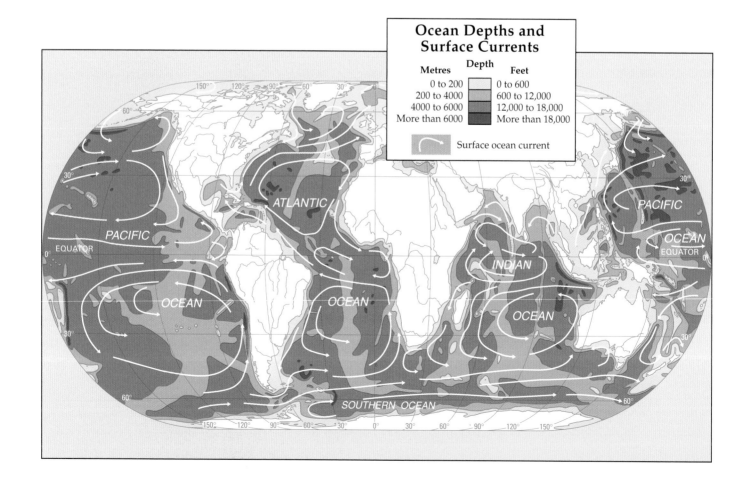

Notable Earthquakes

Earthquake	Date	Magnitude (Richter Scale)	Deaths
Southern India	January 26, 2001	7.7	19 988
Northwestern Turkey	August 17, 1999	7.4	17 118
Central India	Sept. 30, 1993	6.4	22 000
Northwestern Iran	June 21, 1990	7.7	40 000+
Loma Prieta, CA, U.S.	October 17, 1989	6.9	62
Northwestern Armenia	December 7, 1988	6.8	55 000+
Mexico City, Mexico	Sept. 19-21, 1985	8.1	4 200+
Tangshan, China	July 28, 1976	7.6	242 000
Guatemala	February 4, 1976	7.5	22 778
Northern Peru	May 31, 1970	7.8	66 794
Kenai Pen., AK, U.S.	March 28, 1964	8.6	131
Nan-Shan, China	May 22, 1927	8.3	200 000
Yokohama, Japan	September 1, 1923	8.3	143 000
Gansu, China	December 16, 1920	8.6	100 000
Messina, Italy	December 28, 1908	7.5	83 000
San Francisco, CA, U.S.	April 18, 1906	8.3	700
New Madrid, MO, U.S.	December 16, 1811-February 7, 1812	8.7	unknown
Shemaka, Azerbaijan	November 1667	---	80 000
Shaanxi, China	January 24, 1556	---	830 000
Antioch, Syria	May 20, 526	---	250 000

Notable Volcanic Eruptions

Volcano	Place	Year	Deaths
Kilauea	Hawaii, U.S.	1983-present	1
Nyiragongo	Goma, Congo	2002	147
Pinatubo	Philippines	1992	200+
Redoubt	Alaska, U.S.	1989-1990	0
Nevada del Ruiz	Colombia	1985	22 940
El Chichon	Mexico	1982	100+
St. Helens	Washington, U.S.	1980	57
Erebus	Ross I., Antarctica	1970-1980	0
Surtsey	N. Atlantic Ocean	1963-1967	0
Paricutin	Mexico	1943-1952	1 000
Kelud	Java, Indonesia	1919	5 000
Pelee	Martinique	1902	26 000
Krakatoa	Sumatra, Indonesia	1883	36 000
Tambora	Sumbawa, Indonesia	1815	56 000
Unzen	Japan	1792	10 400
Etna	Sicily, Italy	1669	20 000
Kelud	Java, Indonesia	1586	10 000
Etna	Sicily, Italy	1169	15 000
Vesuvius	Italy	79	16 000
Thera (Santorini)	Aegean Sea	1645 B.C.	thousands

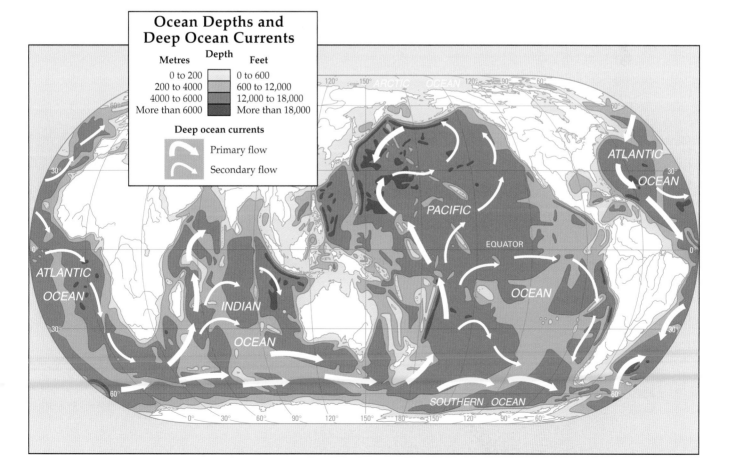

World Climates

Tropical Climates
- Tropical rain forest
- Savanna

Dry Climates
- Steppe (semi-desert)
- Desert

Mild Climates
- Mediterranean
- Humid subtropical
- Marine

Continental Climates
- Hot summer
- Cool summer
- Subarctic

Polar Climates
- Tundra
- Ice cap

Highland Climate
- (Varies greatly with elevation and latitude.)

Climographs

Letters refer to locations on the map.
Colors correspond to climate regions.
Curved lines show temperatures in Celsius and Fahrenheit degrees.
Bars show rainfall in inches and millimetres.

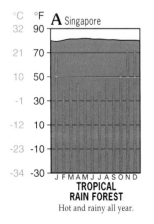

A Singapore

TROPICAL RAIN FOREST

Hot and rainy all year.

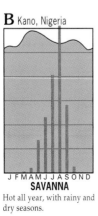

B Kano, Nigeria

SAVANNA

Hot all year, with rainy and dry seasons.

C Kimberley, South Africa

STEPPE

Semi-desert with occasional rain.

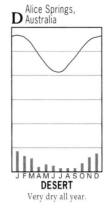

D Alice Springs, Australia

DESERT

Very dry all year.

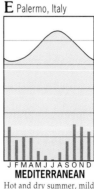

E Palermo, Italy

MEDITERRANEAN

Hot and dry summer, mild and rainy winter.

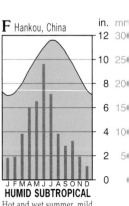

F Hankou, China

HUMID SUBTROPICAL

Hot and wet summer, mild and damp winter.

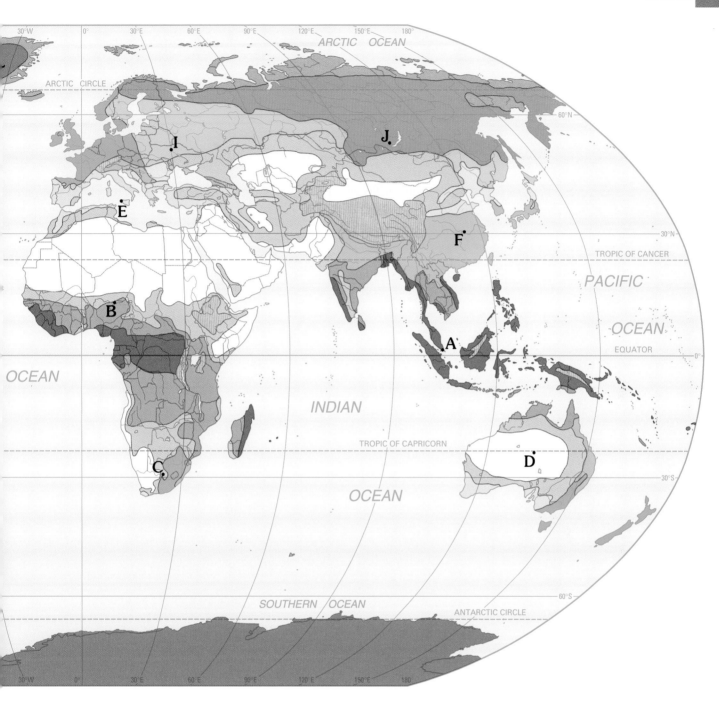

ARCTIC OCEAN

ARCTIC CIRCLE

60°N

I

J

E

TROPIC OF CANCER

F

PACIFIC

OCEAN

B

A

EQUATOR

OCEAN

INDIAN

TROPIC OF CAPRICORN

C

D

30°S

OCEAN

SOUTHERN OCEAN

ANTARCTIC CIRCLE

60°S

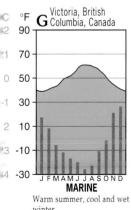

G Victoria, British Columbia, Canada

MARINE

Warm summer, cool and wet winter.

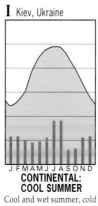

H Omaha, Nebraska, United States

CONTINENTAL: HOT SUMMER

Hot and wet summer, cold and snowy winter.

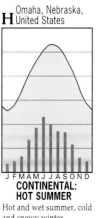

I Kiev, Ukraine

CONTINENTAL: COOL SUMMER

Cool and wet summer, cold and very snowy winter.

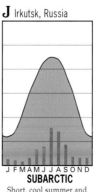

J Irkutsk, Russia

SUBARCTIC

Short, cool summer and very cold, snowy winter.

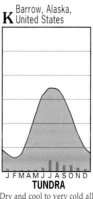

K Barrow, Alaska, United States

TUNDRA

Dry and cool to very cold all year.

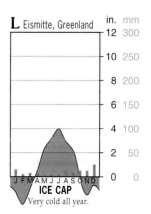

L Eismitte, Greenland

ICE CAP

Very cold all year.

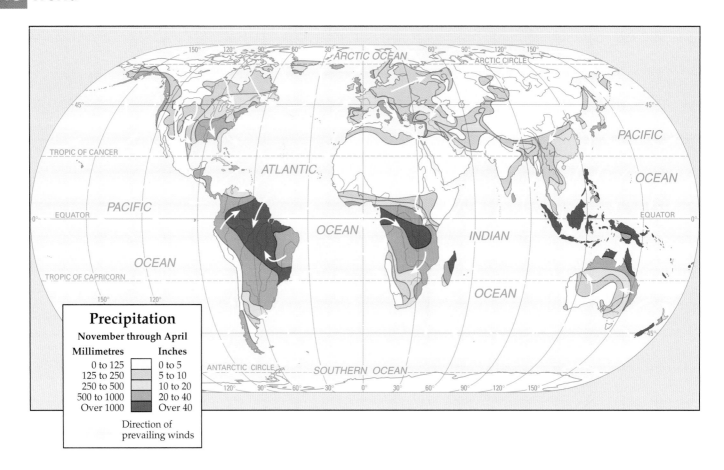

Precipitation

November through April

Millimetres	Inches
0 to 125	0 to 5
125 to 250	5 to 10
250 to 500	10 to 20
500 to 1000	20 to 40
Over 1000	Over 40

Direction of prevailing winds

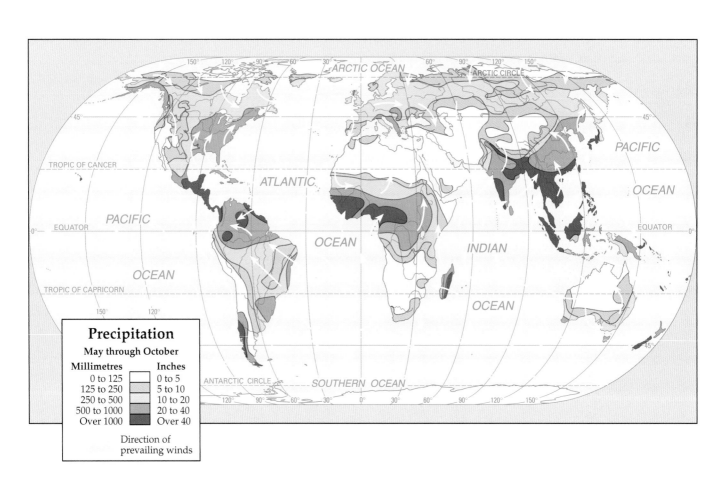

Precipitation

May through October

Millimetres	Inches
0 to 125	0 to 5
125 to 250	5 to 10
250 to 500	10 to 20
500 to 1000	20 to 40
Over 1000	Over 40

Direction of prevailing winds

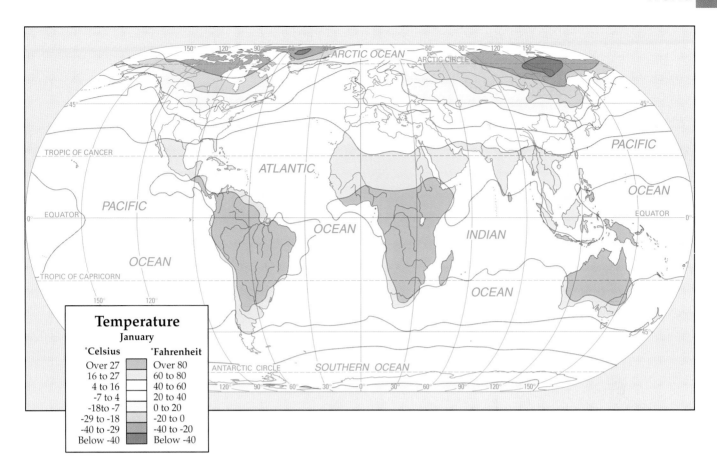

Temperature
January

°Celsius		°Fahrenheit
Over 27		Over 80
16 to 27		60 to 80
4 to 16		40 to 60
-7 to 4		20 to 40
-18 to -7		0 to 20
-29 to -18		-20 to 0
-40 to -29		-40 to -20
Below -40		Below -40

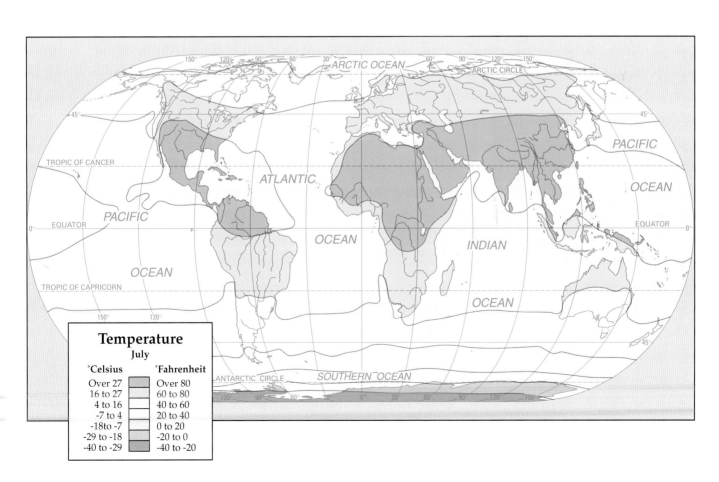

Temperature
July

°Celsius		°Fahrenheit
Over 27		Over 80
16 to 27		60 to 80
4 to 16		40 to 60
-7 to 4		20 to 40
-18 to -7		0 to 20
-29 to -18		-20 to 0
-40 to -29		-40 to -20

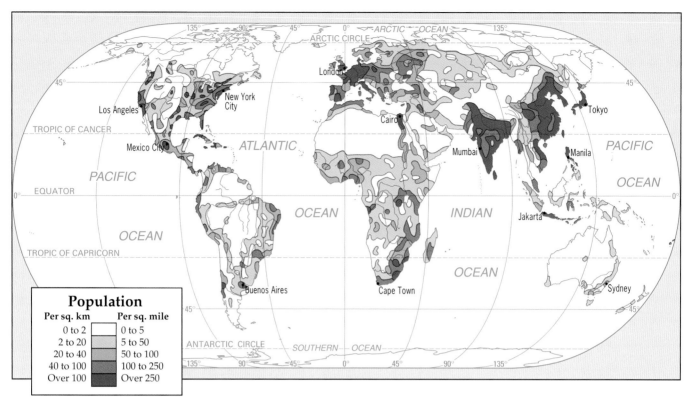

Population

Per sq. km		Per sq. mile
0 to 2		0 to 5
2 to 20		5 to 50
20 to 40		50 to 100
40 to 100		100 to 250
Over 100		Over 250

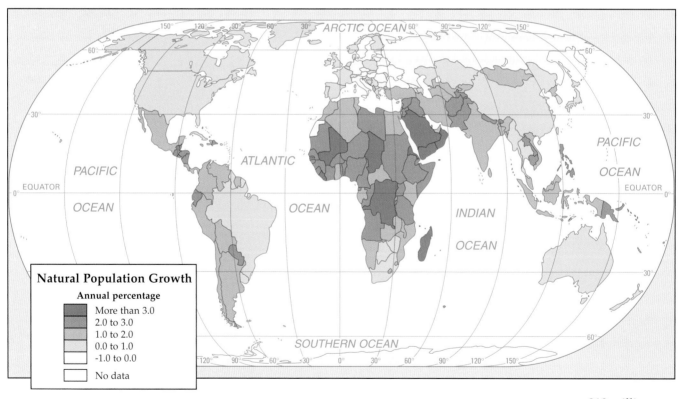

Natural Population Growth

Annual percentage

	More than 3.0
	2.0 to 3.0
	1.0 to 2.0
	0.0 to 1.0
	-1.0 to 0.0
	No data

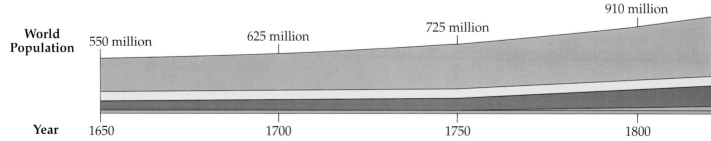

World Population

550 million   625 million   725 million   910 million

Year   1650   1700   1750   1800

AFRICA Population Profile

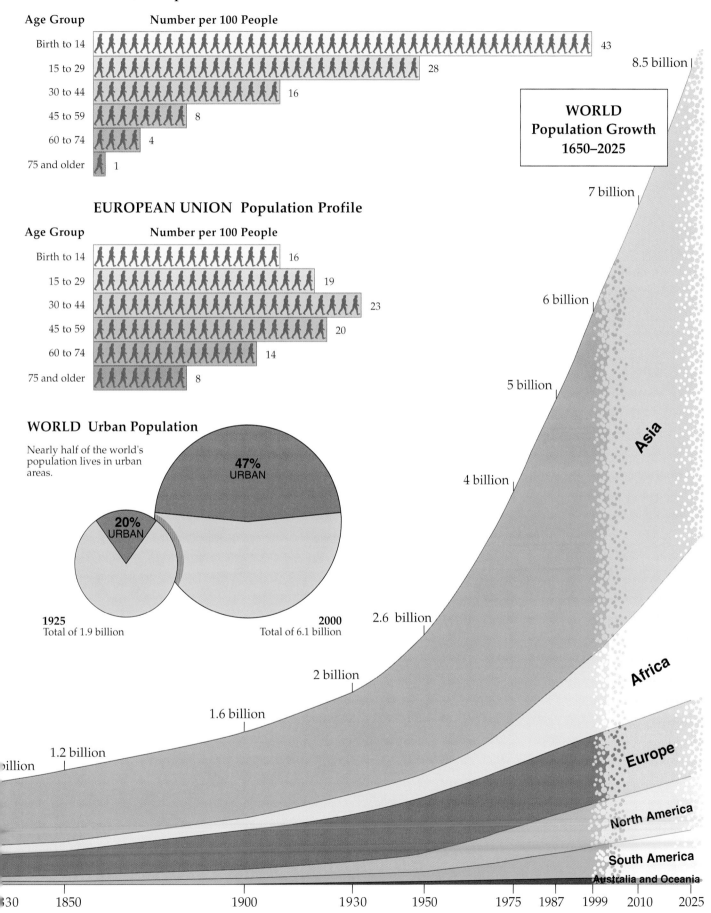

Age Group	Number per 100 People
Birth to 14	43
15 to 29	28
30 to 44	16
45 to 59	8
60 to 74	4
75 and older	1

EUROPEAN UNION Population Profile

Age Group	Number per 100 People
Birth to 14	16
15 to 29	19
30 to 44	23
45 to 59	20
60 to 74	14
75 and older	8

WORLD Urban Population

Nearly half of the world's population lives in urban areas.

20% URBAN

1925
Total of 1.9 billion

47% URBAN

2000
Total of 6.1 billion

WORLD Population Growth 1650–2025

8.5 billion

7 billion

6 billion

5 billion

4 billion

Asia

2.6 billion

Africa

2 billion

Europe

1.6 billion

North America

1.2 billion

South America

...illion

Australia and Oceania

30   1850   1900   1930   1950   1975   1987   1999   2010   2025

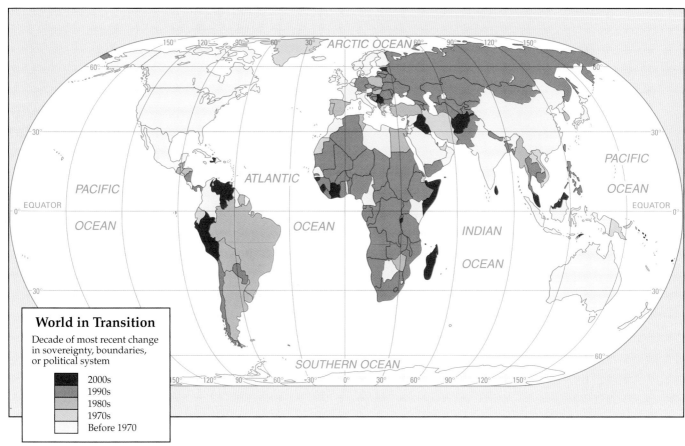

World in Transition

Decade of most recent change in sovereignty, boundaries, or political system

- 2000s
- 1990s
- 1980s
- 1970s
- Before 1970

Worldwide Immigration to Canada

Primary migration 1991–1996

Place of origin

- Australia and Oceania
- Asia
- Europe
- Africa
- Americas (except United States)
- Other countries*
- United States

* "Other countries" includes the Soviet Union through 1991 and Africa and Latin America through 1981.

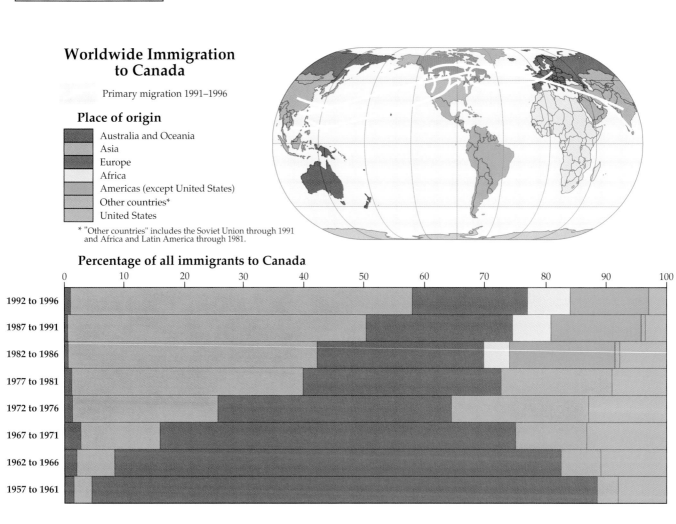

Percentage of all immigrants to Canada

	0	10	20	30	40	50	60	70	80	90	100
1992 to 1996											
1987 to 1991											
1982 to 1986											
1977 to 1981											
1972 to 1976											
1967 to 1971											
1962 to 1966											
1957 to 1961											

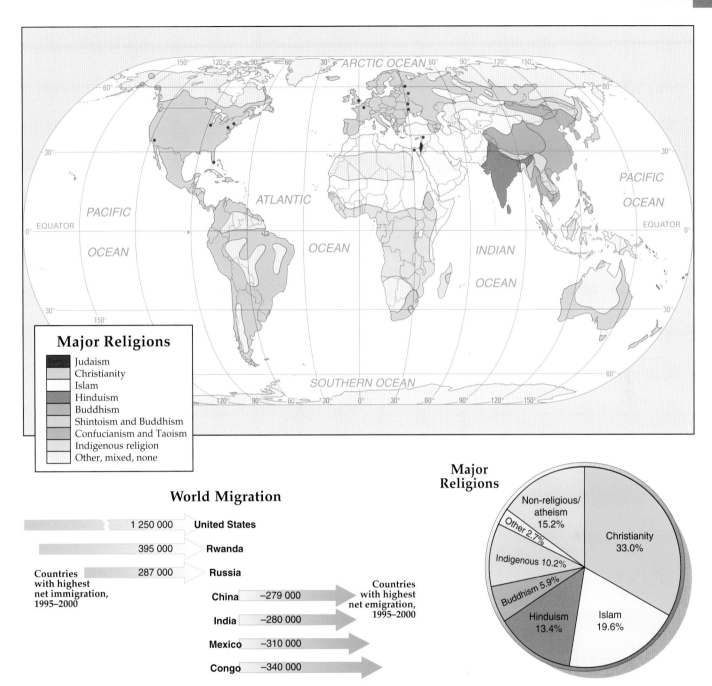

Major Religions

- Judaism
- Christianity
- Islam
- Hinduism
- Buddhism
- Shintoism and Buddhism
- Confucianism and Taoism
- Indigenous religion
- Other, mixed, none

World Migration

Countries with highest net immigration, 1995–2000

1 250 000	United States
395 000	Rwanda
287 000	Russia

Countries with highest net emigration, 1995–2000

China	−279 000
India	−280 000
Mexico	−310 000
Congo	−340 000

Major Religions

- Christianity 33.0%
- Islam 19.6%
- Hinduism 13.4%
- Buddhism 5.9%
- Indigenous 10.2%
- Other 2.7%
- Non-religious/atheism 15.2%

Until recently Quebec was the principal port of entry for immigration into Canada. In every year until 1971, most immigrants came from Europe.

Today most Canadian cities have growing communities of immigrants from Latin America and Asia. In recent years nearly as many people have emigrated from Hong Kong alone as from all of Europe.

World's Fastest Growing Urban Areas

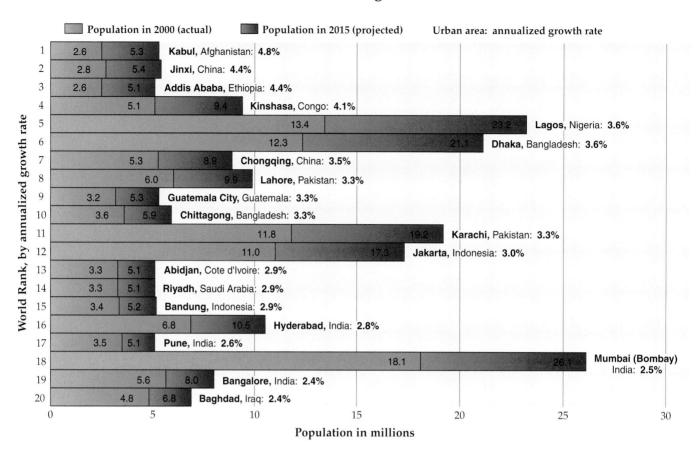

Legend: Population in 2000 (actual) · Population in 2015 (projected) · Urban area: annualized growth rate

World Rank, by annualized growth rate:

Rank	Urban area	2000	2015	Growth
1	Kabul, Afghanistan	2.6	5.3	4.8%
2	Jinxi, China	2.8	5.4	4.4%
3	Addis Ababa, Ethiopia	2.6	5.1	4.4%
4	Kinshasa, Congo	5.1	9.4	4.1%
5	Lagos, Nigeria	13.4	23.2	3.6%
6	Dhaka, Bangladesh	12.3	21.1	3.6%
7	Chongqing, China	5.3	8.9	3.5%
8	Lahore, Pakistan	6.0	9.9	3.3%
9	Guatemala City, Guatemala	3.2	5.3	3.3%
10	Chittagong, Bangladesh	3.6	5.9	3.3%
11	Karachi, Pakistan	11.8	19.2	3.3%
12	Jakarta, Indonesia	11.0	17.3	3.0%
13	Abidjan, Cote d'Ivoire	3.3	5.1	2.9%
14	Riyadh, Saudi Arabia	3.3	5.1	2.9%
15	Bandung, Indonesia	3.4	5.2	2.9%
16	Hyderabad, India	6.8	10.5	2.8%
17	Pune, India	3.5	5.1	2.6%
18	Mumbai (Bombay) India	18.1	26.1	2.5%
19	Bangalore, India	5.6	8.0	2.4%
20	Baghdad, Iraq	4.8	6.8	2.4%

Population in millions

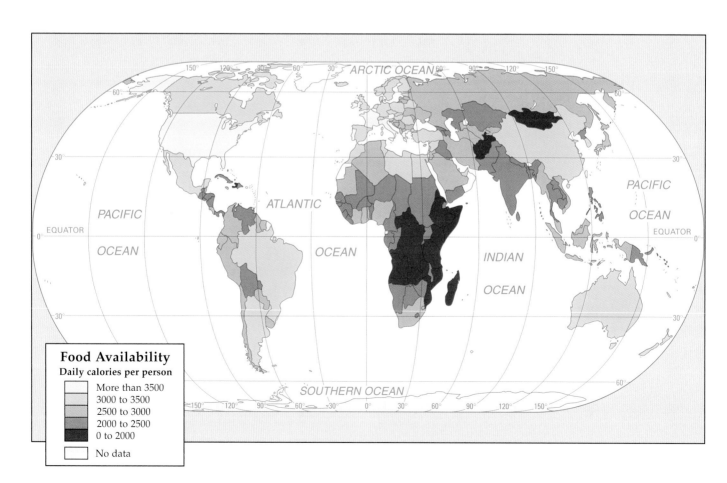

Food Availability
Daily calories per person

- More than 3500
- 3000 to 3500
- 2500 to 3000
- 2000 to 2500
- 0 to 2000
- No data

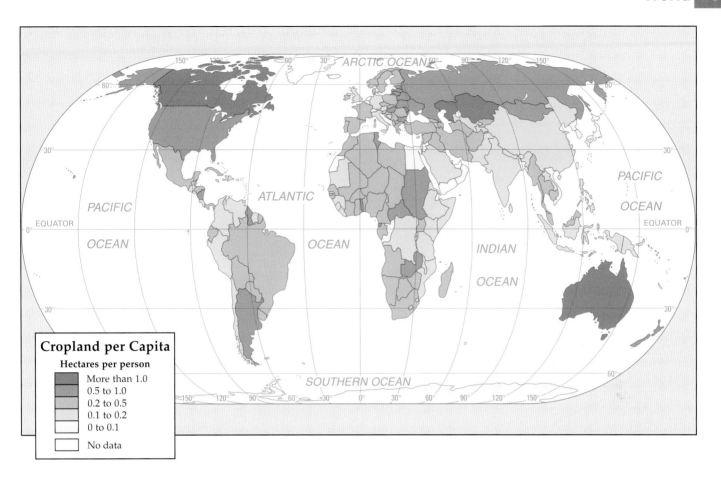

Cropland per Capita

Hectares per person

- More than 1.0
- 0.5 to 1.0
- 0.2 to 0.5
- 0.1 to 0.2
- 0 to 0.1
- No data

Staple Food Production

Grains are the main source of food for most of the world's population. Many grains are also used in processed foods and livestock feed. Grain producers range from large commercial farms that export their harvest to small farms that grow grains for regional consumption.

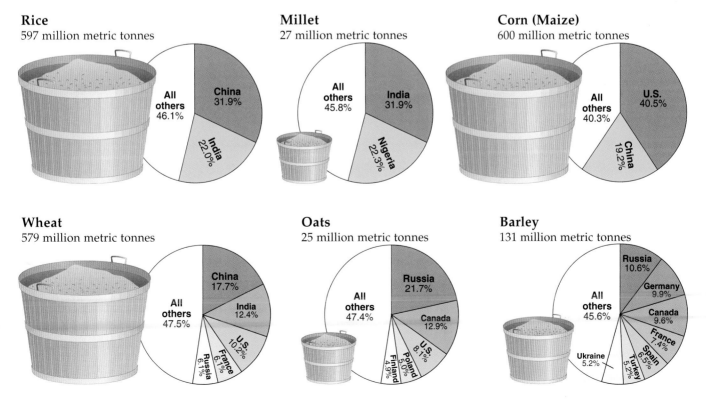

Rice
597 million metric tonnes

- China 31.9%
- India 22.0%
- All others 46.1%

Millet
27 million metric tonnes

- India 31.9%
- Nigeria 22.3%
- All others 45.8%

Corn (Maize)
600 million metric tonnes

- U.S. 40.5%
- China 19.2%
- All others 40.3%

Wheat
579 million metric tonnes

- China 17.7%
- India 12.4%
- U.S. 10.2%
- France 6.1%
- Russia 6.1%
- All others 47.5%

Oats
25 million metric tonnes

- Russia 21.7%
- Canada 12.9%
- U.S. 8.1%
- Poland 5.0%
- Finland 4.9%
- All others 47.4%

Barley
131 million metric tonnes

- Russia 10.6%
- Germany 9.9%
- Canada 9.6%
- France 7.4%
- Spain 6.5%
- Turkey 5.2%
- Ukraine 5.2%
- All others 45.6%

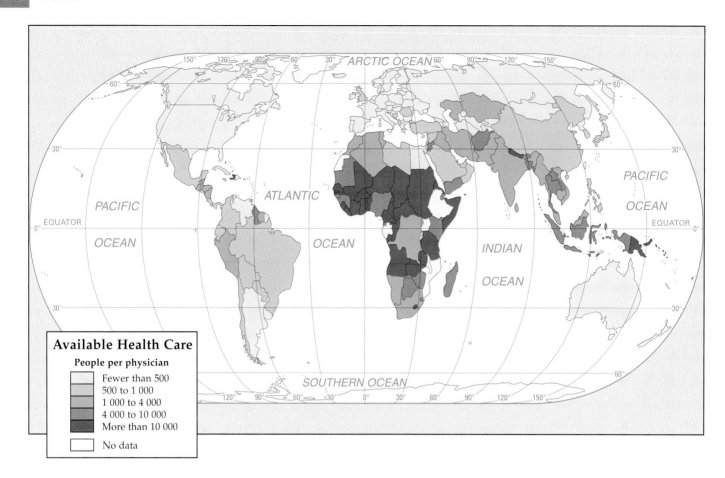

Available Health Care

People per physician

- Fewer than 500
- 500 to 1 000
- 1 000 to 4 000
- 4 000 to 10 000
- More than 10 000
- No data

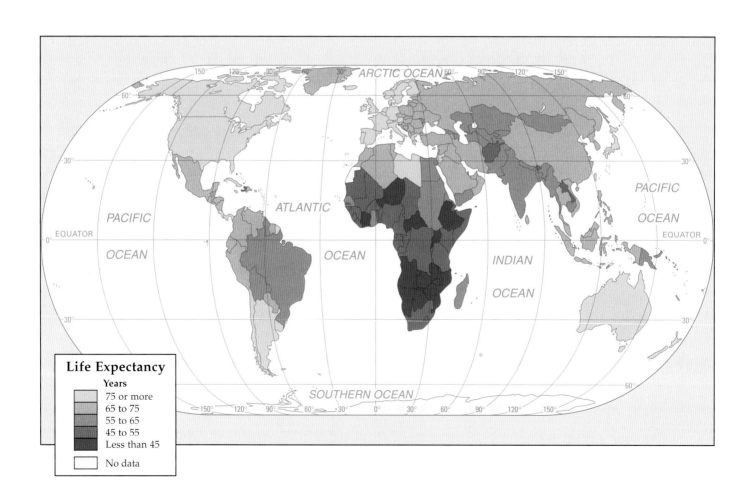

Life Expectancy

Years

- 75 or more
- 65 to 75
- 55 to 65
- 45 to 55
- Less than 45
- No data

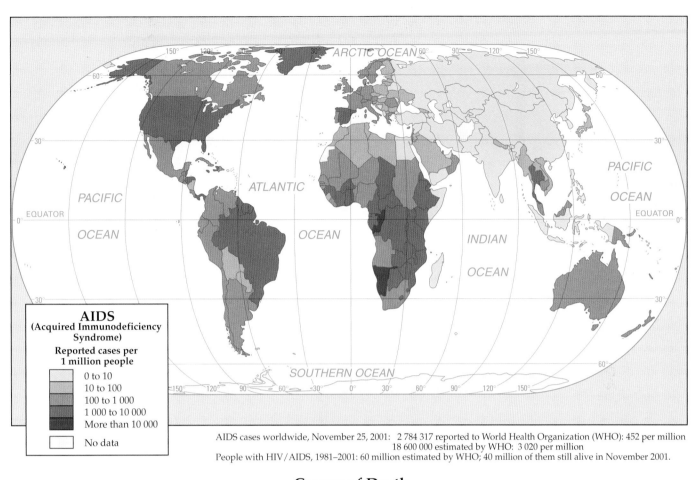

AIDS
(Acquired Immunodeficiency Syndrome)
Reported cases per
1 million people

- 0 to 10
- 10 to 100
- 100 to 1 000
- 1 000 to 10 000
- More than 10 000
- No data

AIDS cases worldwide, November 25, 2001: 2 784 317 reported to World Health Organization (WHO): 452 per million
18 600 000 estimated by WHO: 3 020 per million
People with HIV/AIDS, 1981–2001: 60 million estimated by WHO; 40 million of them still alive in November 2001.

Causes of Death

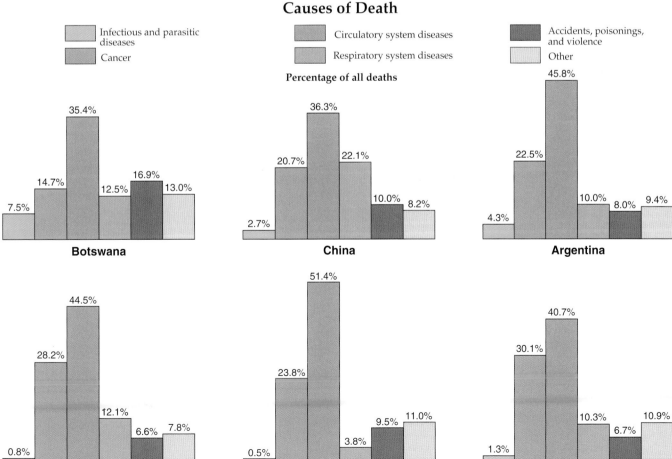

- Infectious and parasitic diseases
- Cancer
- Circulatory system diseases
- Respiratory system diseases
- Accidents, poisonings, and violence
- Other

Percentage of all deaths

Botswana
7.5% 14.7% 35.4% 12.5% 16.9% 13.0%

China
2.7% 20.7% 36.3% 22.1% 10.0% 8.2%

Argentina
4.3% 22.5% 45.8% 10.0% 8.0% 9.4%

New Zealand
0.8% 28.2% 44.5% 12.1% 6.6% 7.8%

Hungary
0.5% 23.8% 51.4% 3.8% 9.5% 11.0%

Canada
1.3% 30.1% 40.7% 10.3% 6.7% 10.9%

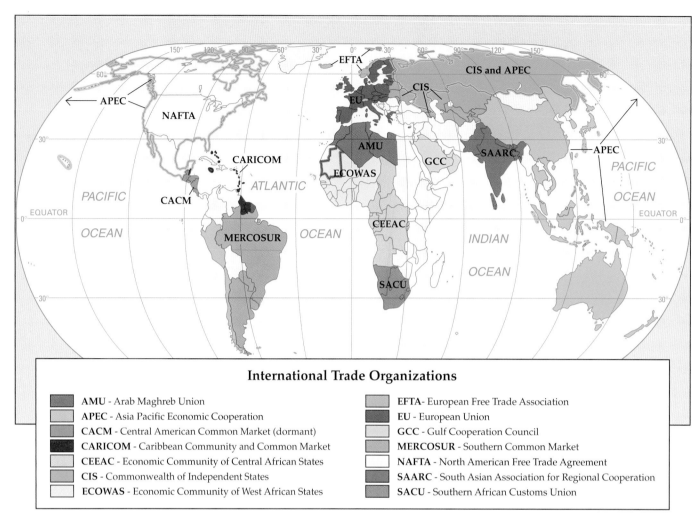

International Trade Organizations

AMU - Arab Maghreb Union		**EFTA**- European Free Trade Association
APEC - Asia Pacific Economic Cooperation		**EU** - European Union
CACM - Central American Common Market (dormant)		**GCC** - Gulf Cooperation Council
CARICOM - Caribbean Community and Common Market		**MERCOSUR** - Southern Common Market
CEEAC - Economic Community of Central African States		**NAFTA** - North American Free Trade Agreement
CIS - Commonwealth of Independent States		**SAARC** - South Asian Association for Regional Cooperation
ECOWAS - Economic Community of West African States		**SACU** - Southern African Customs Union

Single-Commodity Economies

Many countries rely on only one natural resource to support 70% or more of their export economies.

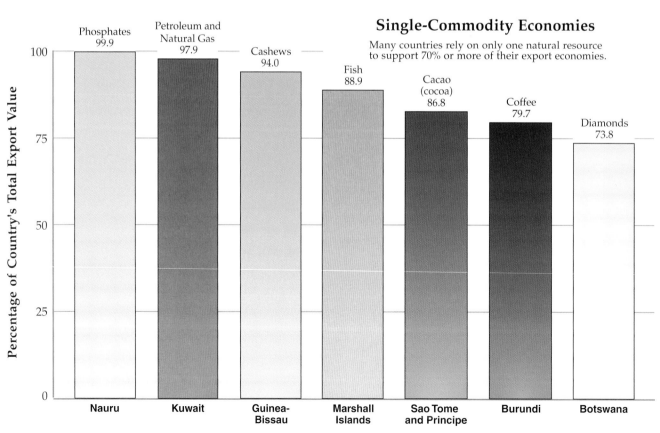

Percentage of Country's Total Export Value

- Phosphates 99.9 — **Nauru**
- Petroleum and Natural Gas 97.9 — **Kuwait**
- Cashews 94.0 — **Guinea-Bissau**
- Fish 88.9 — **Marshall Islands**
- Cacao (cocoa) 86.8 — **Sao Tome and Principe**
- Coffee 79.7 — **Burundi**
- Diamonds 73.8 — **Botswana**

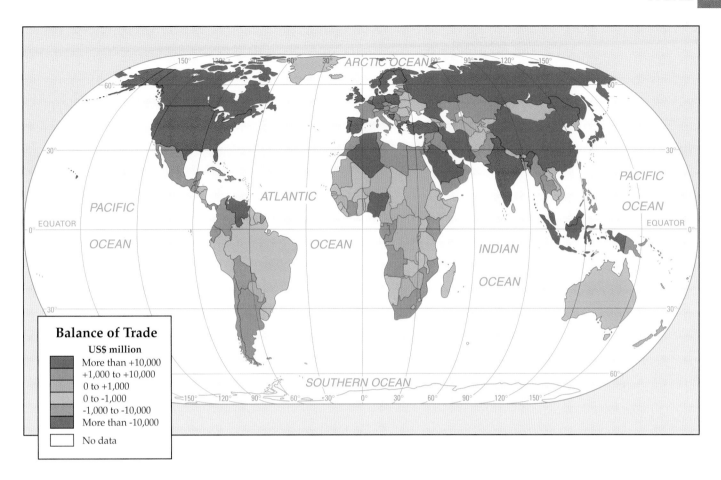

Balance of Trade

US$ million

- More than +10,000
- +1,000 to +10,000
- 0 to +1,000
- 0 to -1,000
- -1,000 to -10,000
- More than -10,000
- No data

Disparity of Income

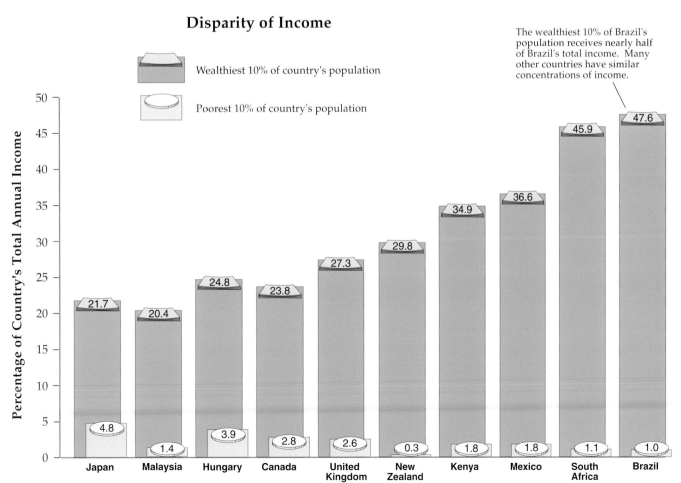

- Wealthiest 10% of country's population
- Poorest 10% of country's population

The wealthiest 10% of Brazil's population receives nearly half of Brazil's total income. Many other countries have similar concentrations of income.

Percentage of Country's Total Annual Income

Country	Wealthiest 10%	Poorest 10%
Japan	21.7	4.8
Malaysia	20.4	1.4
Hungary	24.8	3.9
Canada	23.8	2.8
United Kingdom	27.3	2.6
New Zealand	29.8	0.3
Kenya	34.9	1.8
Mexico	36.6	1.8
South Africa	45.9	1.1
Brazil	47.6	1.0

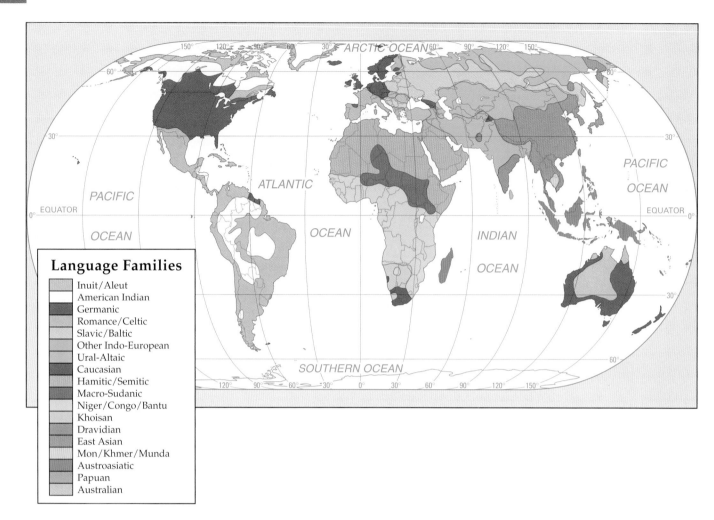

Language Families

- Inuit/Aleut
- American Indian
- Germanic
- Romance/Celtic
- Slavic/Baltic
- Other Indo-European
- Ural-Altaic
- Caucasian
- Hamitic/Semitic
- Macro-Sudanic
- Niger/Congo/Bantu
- Khoisan
- Dravidian
- East Asian
- Mon/Khmer/Munda
- Austroasiatic
- Papuan
- Australian

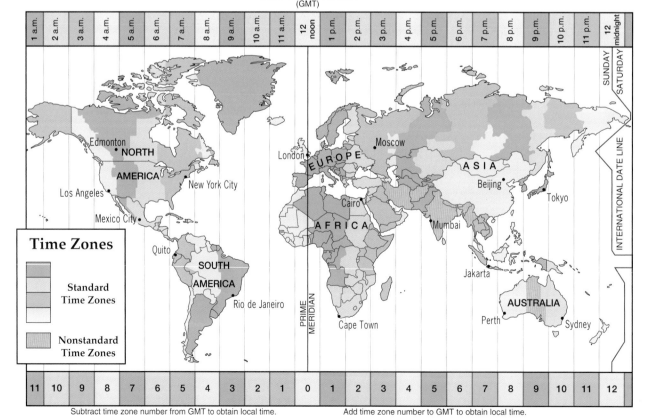

GREENWICH MEAN TIME
(GMT)

| 1 a.m. | 2 a.m. | 3 a.m. | 4 a.m. | 5 a.m. | 6 a.m. | 7 a.m. | 8 a.m. | 9 a.m. | 10 a.m. | 11 a.m. | 12 noon | 1 p.m. | 2 p.m. | 3 p.m. | 4 p.m. | 5 p.m. | 6 p.m. | 7 p.m. | 8 p.m. | 9 p.m. | 10 p.m. | 11 p.m. | 12 midnight |

Time Zones

- Standard Time Zones
- Nonstandard Time Zones

| 11 | 10 | 9 | 8 | 7 | 6 | 5 | 4 | 3 | 2 | 1 | 0 | 1 | 2 | 3 | 4 | 5 | 6 | 7 | 8 | 9 | 10 | 11 | 12 |

Subtract time zone number from GMT to obtain local time.   Add time zone number to GMT to obtain local time.

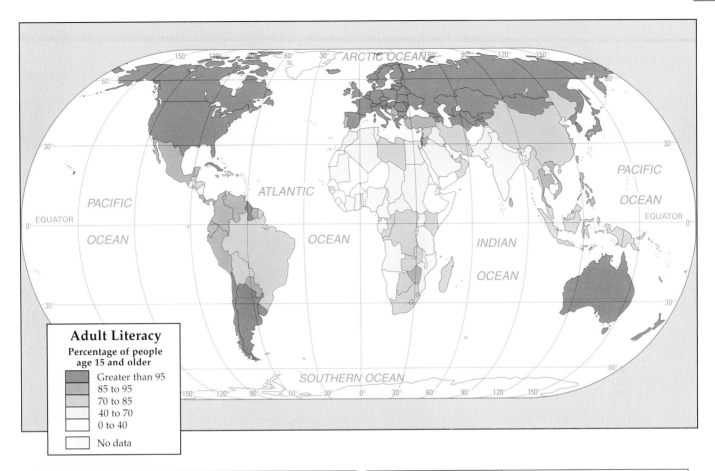

Adult Literacy
Percentage of people age 15 and older

- Greater than 95
- 85 to 95
- 70 to 85
- 40 to 70
- 0 to 40
- No data

Persons per Newspaper

Daily circulation		
2 578 000	Norway	1.7
4 718 000	Canada	6.3
9 030 000	Mexico	10.3
18 800 000	India	50.2

Persons per Telephone

Telephones owned		
18 500 000	Canada	1.6
17 039 000	Brazil	9.6
500 000	Nigeria	227.7
500 000	Bangladesh	274.9

Persons per Radio

Radios owned		
575 000 000	United States	0.5
32 300 000	Canada	0.9
8 200 000	Vietnam	9.2
370 000	Burkina Faso	29.0

Persons per Television

Televisions owned		
21 500 000	Canada	1.4
86 500 000	Japan	1.5
900 000	Bolivia	8.6
103 000	Tanzania	316.8

Speed of Travel

Route	Year	Means of travel	Length of time
North America to Europe via air	1978	Concorde SST — supersonic jet	3.5 hours
	1950	Intercontinental jet — twin engine jet	10 hours
	1927	*Spirit of St. Louis* — single engine aircraft	33.5 hours
North America to Europe via ocean	1898	*Lucania* — ocean liner	5.5 days
	1838	*Sirius* — steamship	18 days
	1497	John Cabot — sailing vessel	35 days

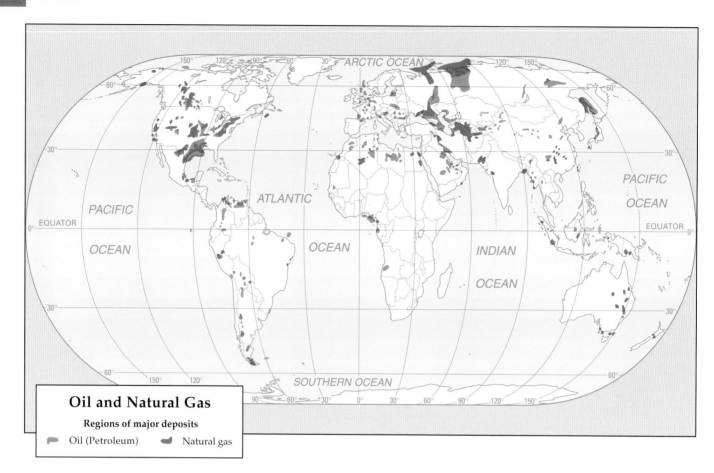

Oil and Natural Gas

Regions of major deposits

Oil (Petroleum)   Natural gas

Oil Production and Consumption

Leaders in World Production

11.9%	**Saudi Arabia**
9.2%	**Russia**
8.9%	**United States**
5.4%	**Iran**
4.8%	**China**
All other countries	59.8%

Leaders in World Consumption

25.4%	**United States**
7.5%	**Japan**
6.5%	**China**
3.7%	**Germany**
3.3%	**Russia**
All other countries	53.6%

Natural Gas Production and Consumption

Leaders in World Production

23.4%	**United States**
20.4%	**Russia**
7.1%	**Canada**
5.2%	**Algeria**
3.3%	**United Kingdom**
All other countries	40.6%

Leaders in World Consumption

25.7%	**United States**
16.6%	**Russia**
3.8%	**United Kingdom**
3.6%	**Canada**
3.6%	**Germany**
All other countries	46.7%

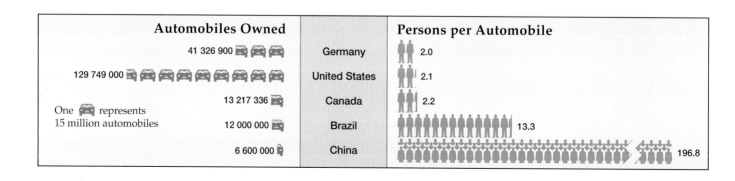

Automobiles Owned		**Persons per Automobile**	
41 326 900	Germany		2.0
129 749 000	United States		2.1
13 217 336	Canada		2.2
12 000 000	Brazil		13.3
6 600 000	China		196.8

One represents
15 million automobiles

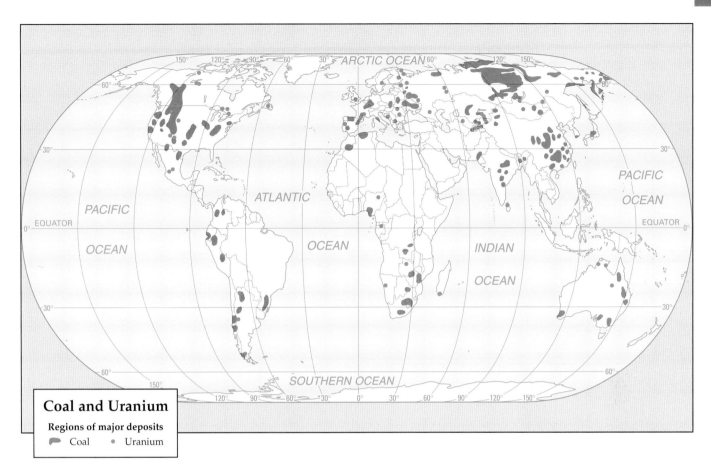

Coal and Uranium

Regions of major deposits

- Coal
- Uranium

Coal Production and Consumption

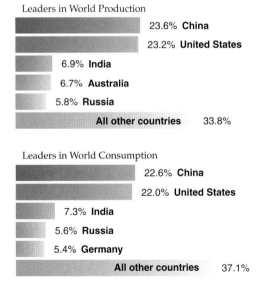

Leaders in World Production

23.6%	**China**
23.2%	**United States**
6.9%	**India**
6.7%	**Australia**
5.8%	**Russia**
All other countries	33.8%

Leaders in World Consumption

22.6%	**China**
22.0%	**United States**
7.3%	**India**
5.6%	**Russia**
5.4%	**Germany**
All other countries	37.1%

Uranium Production and Consumption*

Leaders in World Production

30.7%	**Canada**
21.8%	**Australia**
8.3%	**Niger**
7.8%	**Namibia**
6.8%	**Uzbekistan**
24.6%	**All other countries**

Leaders in World Consumption

32.0%	**United States**
15.6%	**France**
11.4%	**Japan**
5.7%	**Germany**
5.3%	**Russia**
30.0%	**All other countries**

*Includes only uranium used to generate electricity.

Lifetime of Fossil Fuels	Initial World Supply	Supply Consumed To Date	Remaining Known Reserves	Estimated Unknown Reserves	Estimated Year of Depletion*
Coal	7 600 000 million tonnes	190 000 million tonnes	7 410 000 million tonnes (known and unknown)		2200 to 5500
Oil (petroleum)	1 721 000 million barrels	560 320 million barrels	535 380 million barrels	525 300 million barrels	2035
Natural gas	255 400 000 million cubic metres	36 400 000 million cubic metres	97 300 000 million cubic metres	121 800 000 million cubic metres	2050

*given present rates of use

KITASKINAW SCHOOL

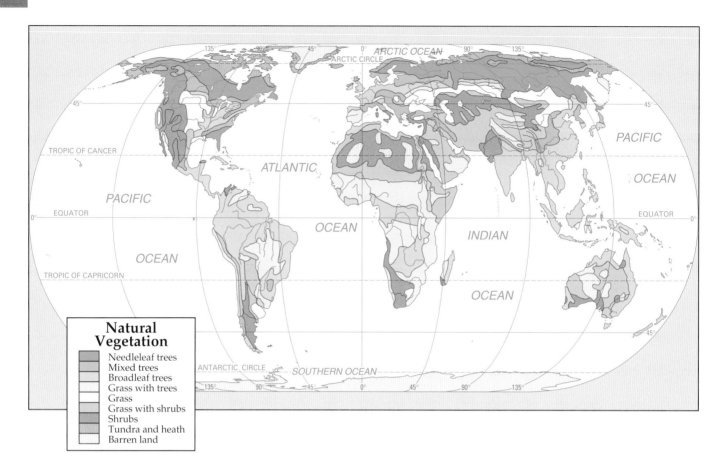

Natural Vegetation

	Needleleaf trees
	Mixed trees
	Broadleaf trees
	Grass with trees
	Grass
	Grass with shrubs
	Shrubs
	Tundra and heath
	Barren land

Natural Vegetation

The world can be divided into zones of natural vegetation. Several categories of vegetation are mapped above.

Most of the categories can be sub-divided. For example, there are several kinds of broadleaf trees: maples, oaks, birches, sycamores, cottonwoods, and so on.

Seven types of vegetation listed in the map key are shown here.

needleleaf trees

mixed trees

broadleaf trees

grass with trees

grass

shrubs

tundra and heath

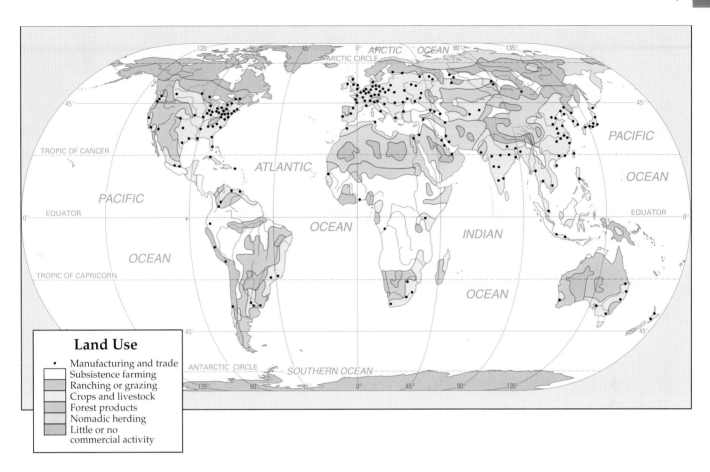

Land Use

- Manufacturing and trade
- Subsistence farming
- Ranching or grazing
- Crops and livestock
- Forest products
- Nomadic herding
- Little or no commercial activity

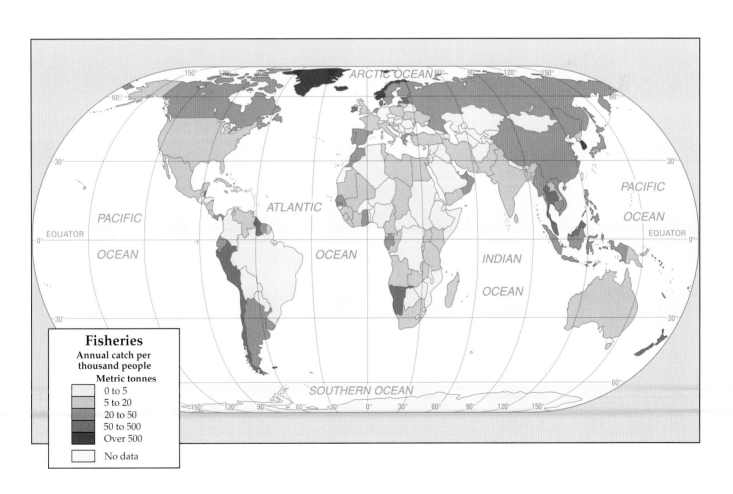

Fisheries

Annual catch per thousand people

Metric tonnes

- 0 to 5
- 5 to 20
- 20 to 50
- 50 to 500
- Over 500
- No data

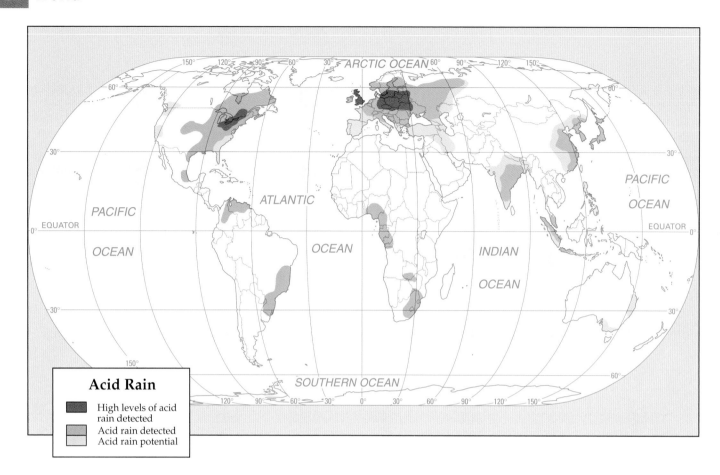

Acid Rain

- High levels of acid rain detected
- Acid rain detected
- Acid rain potential

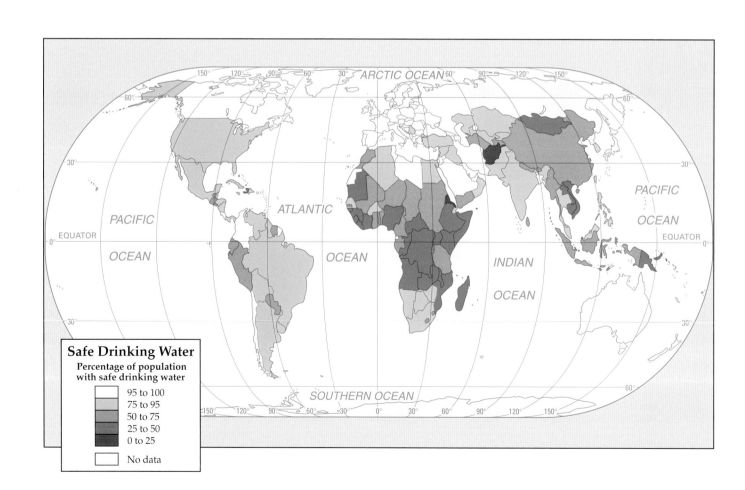

Safe Drinking Water

Percentage of population with safe drinking water

- 95 to 100
- 75 to 95
- 50 to 75
- 25 to 50
- 0 to 25

No data

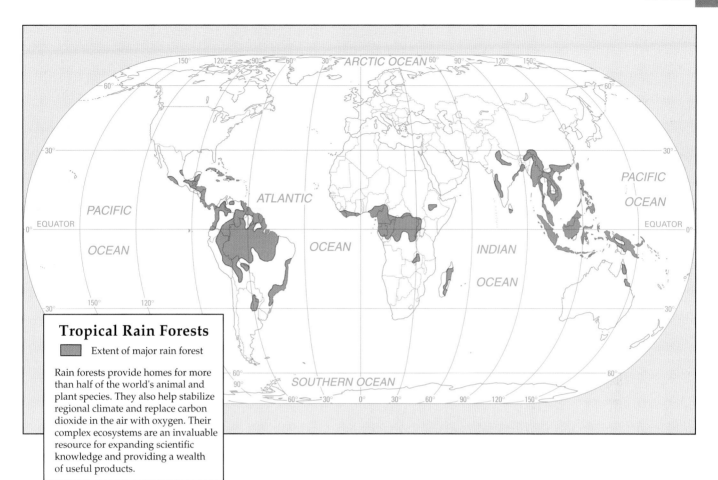

Tropical Rain Forests

Extent of major rain forest

Rain forests provide homes for more than half of the world's animal and plant species. They also help stabilize regional climate and replace carbon dioxide in the air with oxygen. Their complex ecosystems are an invaluable resource for expanding scientific knowledge and providing a wealth of useful products.

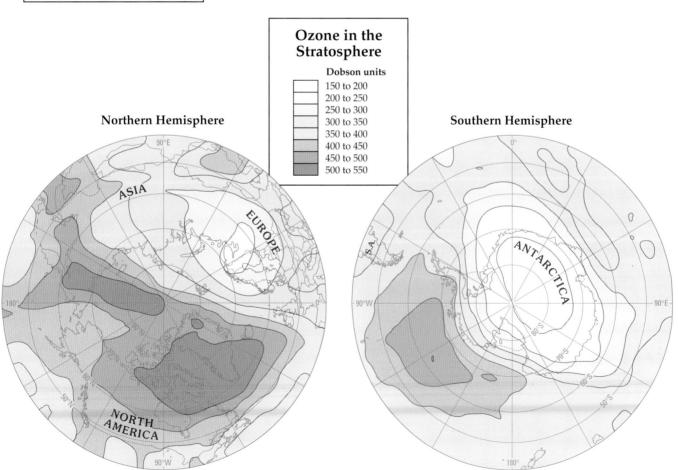

Ozone in the Stratosphere

Dobson units
150 to 200
200 to 250
250 to 300
300 to 350
350 to 400
400 to 450
450 to 500
500 to 550

Northern Hemisphere

Southern Hemisphere

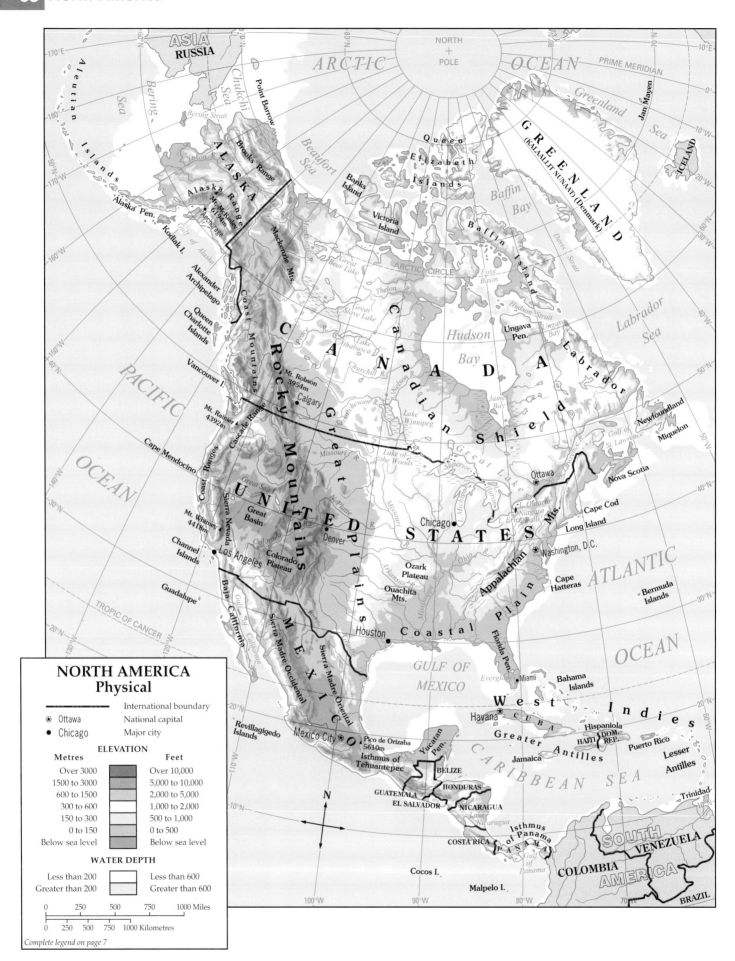

NORTH AMERICA
Physical

————	International boundary
⊛ Ottawa	National capital
● Chicago	Major city

ELEVATION

Metres		Feet
Over 3000		Over 10,000
1500 to 3000		5,000 to 10,000
600 to 1500		2,000 to 5,000
300 to 600		1,000 to 2,000
150 to 300		500 to 1,000
0 to 150		0 to 500
Below sea level		Below sea level

WATER DEPTH

Less than 200		Less than 600
Greater than 200		Greater than 600

0   250   500   750   1000 Miles

0   250   500   750   1000 Kilometres

Complete legend on page 7

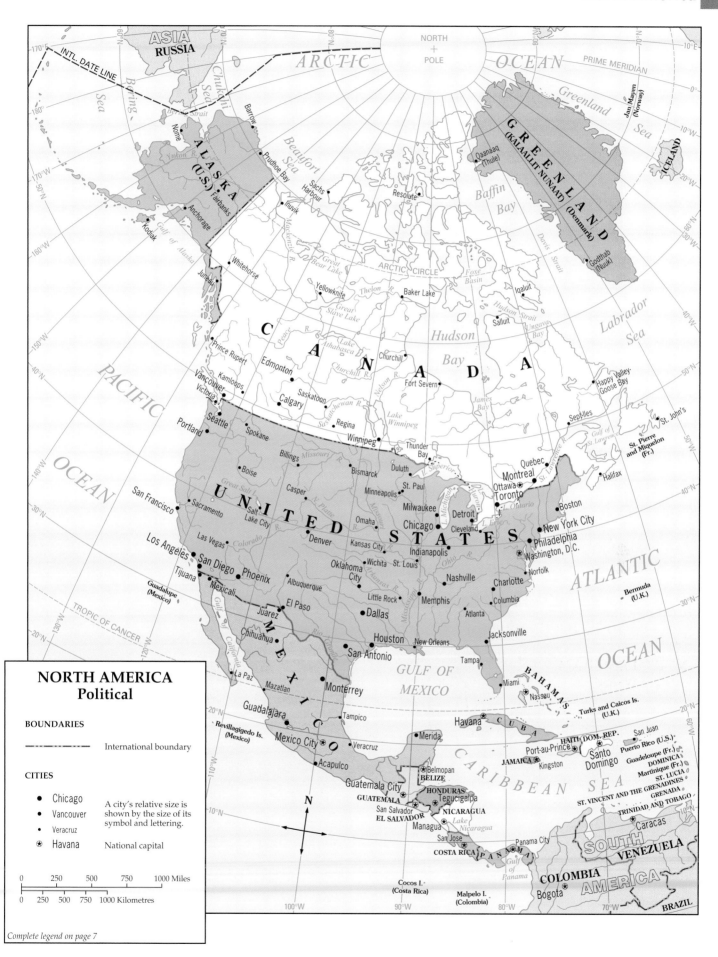

NORTH AMERICA
Political

BOUNDARIES

---·---·--- International boundary

CITIES

● Chicago — A city's relative size is shown by the size of its symbol and lettering.
• Vancouver
· Veracruz
⊛ Havana — National capital

| 0 | 250 | 500 | 750 | 1000 Miles |
| 0 | 250 | 500 | 750 | 1000 Kilometres |

Complete legend on page 7

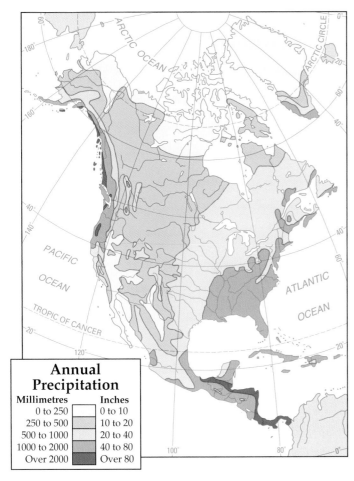

Annual Precipitation

Millimetres	Inches
0 to 250	0 to 10
250 to 500	10 to 20
500 to 1000	20 to 40
1000 to 2000	40 to 80
Over 2000	Over 80

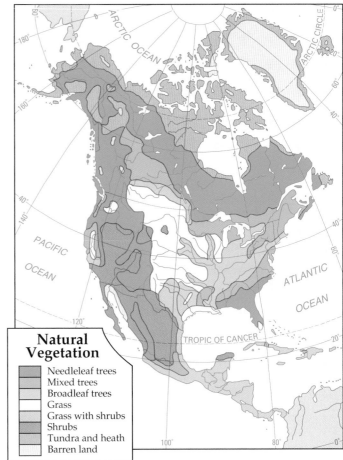

Natural Vegetation

Needleleaf trees
Mixed trees
Broadleaf trees
Grass
Grass with shrubs
Shrubs
Tundra and heath
Barren land

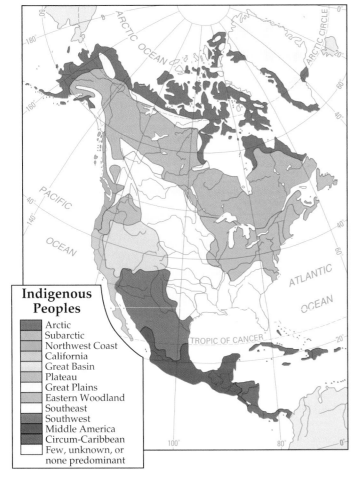

Indigenous Peoples

Arctic
Subarctic
Northwest Coast
California
Great Basin
Plateau
Great Plains
Eastern Woodland
Southeast
Southwest
Middle America
Circum-Caribbean
Few, unknown, or none predominant

The Canadian Rockies stretch across British Columbia and Alberta. They are part of the Rocky Mountain chain, which extends from the southwestern United States to northern Alaska.

Yellowstone National Park in the western United States preserves over 809 400 hectares of evergreen forests and mountain meadows. Its natural wonders include 3000 geysers and hot springs.

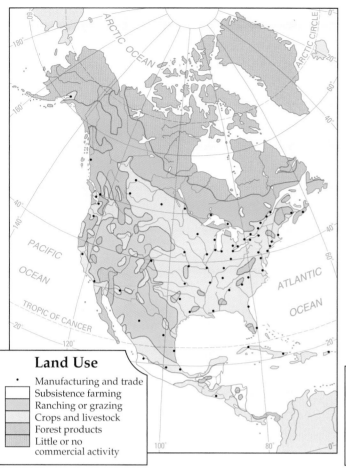

Land Use

- • Manufacturing and trade
- ☐ Subsistence farming
- ☐ Ranching or grazing
- ☐ Crops and livestock
- ☐ Forest products
- ☐ Little or no commercial activity

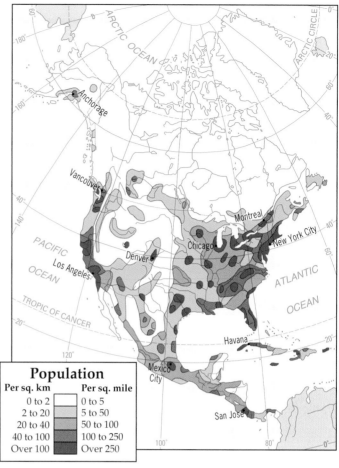

Population

Per sq. km	Per sq. mile
0 to 2	0 to 5
2 to 20	5 to 50
20 to 40	50 to 100
40 to 100	100 to 250
Over 100	Over 250

Canadian Trade in North America

Canadian trade is important, but not dominant, in many North American countries.

(See pages 128-129 for more about trade within NAFTA and the rest of the Pacific Rim.)

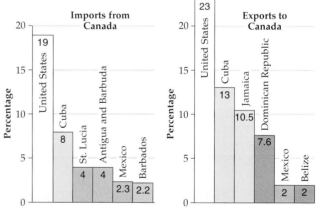

Imports from Canada

United States	19
Cuba	8
St. Lucia	4
Antigua and Barbuda	4
Mexico	2.3
Barbados	2.2

Exports to Canada

United States	23
Cuba	13
Jamaica	10.5
Dominican Republic	7.6
Mexico	2
Belize	2

MEXICO
Area Comparison

Mexico has about one-fourth the area of Canada but its population is three times as large.

| Mexico | 1 958 201 km² |
| Canada | 9 970 610 km² |

North America—the world's breadbasket—is a major producer and the leading exporter of wheat.

ASIA

RUSSIA

Bering Strait

Bering Sea

A L A S K A (U.S.)

ARCTIC CIRCLE

Yukon R.

• Anchorage

Gulf of Alaska

P A C I F I C

O C E A N

ARCTIC OCEAN

Beaufort Sea

Mackenzie Bay

• Inuvik

Banks Island

M'Clure Str.

Prince Patrick I.

Melville I.

Viscount Melville Sound

Ellef Ringnes I.

Queen Is

Bat

Amundsen Gulf

Coronation Gulf

Victoria Island

Queen Mau Gulf

W

W

YUKON TERRITORY

Mt. Logan 5959m

★ Whitehorse

Fairweather Mt. 4663m

Mackenzie Mts.

N O R T H W E S T

Great Bear Lake

• Yellowknife

Great Slave Lake

T E R R I T O R I E S

Dubawnt L.

C a n a d i a n

L. Athabasca

Wollaston Lake

Reindeer L.

Lac La Ronge

MA

Dixon Entrance

Queen Charlotte Is.

Hecate Str.

Skeena R.

Queen Charlotte Sound

R o c k y   M o u n t a i n s

Williston Lake

Peace R.

Liard R.

B R I T I S H

C O L U M B I A

Fraser R.

Coast Mountains

Vancouver I.

Victoria ★

Str. of Juan de Fuca

• Vancouver

• Seattle

Mt. Robson 3954m

I n t e r i o r

A L B E R T A

Edmonton ★

• Calgary

Bow R.

N. Saskatchewan R.

Athabasca R.

S A S K A T C H E W A N

P l a i n s

• Saskatoon

S. Saskatchewan R.

Regina ★

L. Manitoba

L. Winnipegosis

Winnip

Winni

Lesser Slave L.

U N I T E D

CANADA
Physical

————	International boundary
———	Province or territory boundary
⊛ Ottawa	National capital
★ Winnipeg	Provincial capital
• Vancouver	Major city

ELEVATION

Metres		Feet
Over 3000		Over 10,000
1500 to 3000		5,000 to 10,000
600 to 1500		2,000 to 5,000
300 to 600		1,000 to 2,000
150 to 300		500 to 1,000
0 to 150		0 to 500

WATER DEPTH

Less than 200		Less than 600
Greater than 200		Greater than 600

1 cm represents 200 km

| 0 | 200 | 400 | 600 Kilometres |

Complete legend on page 7

G R E E N L A N D
(KALAALLIT NUNAAT) (Denmark)

ICELAND

Denmark Strait

ARCTIC CIRCLE

ATLANTIC

OCEAN

Kane
Basin

Island

Ellesmere

eth

Devon Island

Lancaster Sound

rset

*Gulf of
Boothia*

*Baffin
Bay*

Cape Farewell

**Baffin
Island**

Davis Strait

*Labrador
Sea*

NUNAVUT

**Melville
Peninsula**

*Foxe
Basin*

Cumberland Sd.

★ Iqaluit

Trobisher Bay

*Foxe
Channel*

**Foxe
Peninsula**

**Southampton
I.**

*Hudson
Strait*

Cape
Chidley

*Chesterfield
Inlet*

**Coats
I.**

**Mansel
I.**

**Ungava
Peninsula**

*Ungava
Bay*

*Torngat
Mts.*

George R.

**NEWFOUNDLAND
AND
LABRADOR**

Hudson

Bay

**Belcher
Is.**

• Happy Valley-
Goose Bay

Labrador

Feuilles R.

*Smallwood
Res.*

Churchill R.

Strait of Belle Isle

*James
Bay*

S h i e l d

Newfoundland

★ St. John's

Nipigon

*L.
Mistassini*

*Manicouagan
Lake*

Cape Race

BA

**Anticosti
I.**

Miquelon
(Fr.)

St.-Pierre
(Fr.)

a n

QUEBEC

*Gulf of
St. Lawrence*

ONTARIO

*L.
Nipigon*

Gaspe Pen.

St. Lawrence R.

Cape
Breton
Island

Lake of
the Woods

Thunder
Bay

*L.
Superior*

Sault Ste.
Marie

Quebec
★

**PRINCE
EDWARD
ISLAND**

**NEW
BRUNSWICK** Fredericton
★

Sable I.

**NOVA
SCOTIA**

★ Halifax

*L.
Nipissing*

Montreal
•

Bay of Fundy

*L.
Michigan*

*Georgian
Bay*

*L.
Huron*

Ottawa
⊛

*L.
Simcoe*

Cape Sable

Toronto
★

L. Ontario

Detroit
•

Windsor
•

L. Erie

Niagara
Falls

ATLANTIC

OCEAN

S T A T E S

ASIA
RUSSIA

INTERNATIONAL DATE LINE

Bering Strait

Bering Sea

ARCTIC OCEAN

ALASKA

ARCTIC CIRCLE

Yukon

Beaufort Sea

Old Crow

Inuvik

Sachs Harbour

Banks I.

Ellef Ringnes I.

Prince Patrick I.

Melville I.

Queen Is

Viscount Melville Sound

Victoria Island

Cambridge Bay

Coronation Gulf

Queen Mau Gulf

Anchorage

YUKON TERRITORY

Dawson

Pelly Crossing

Yukon R.

Whitehorse

Norman Wells

Great Bear Lake

Mackenzie R.

NORTHWEST TERRITORIES

Dubawnt L.

Juneau

Fort Simpson

Yellowknife

Great Slave Lake

Hay River

Slave R.

Fort Smith

Liard

Watson Lake

PACIFIC OCEAN

Gulf of Alaska

N

Dixon Entrance

Queen Charlotte Is.

Prince Rupert

Skeena

Hecate Str.

Kitimat

Queen Charlotte Sound

BRITISH COLUMBIA

Williston Lake

Dawson Creek

Prince George

Fraser R.

Fort Nelson

Peace R.

Peace River

Athabasca R.

Lesser Slave L.

Fort McMurray

Athabasca

Wollaston Lake

Reindeer L.

Grande Prairie

ALBERTA

Edmonton

N. Saskatchewan R.

Lac La Ronge

Buffalo Narrows

MA

Thompson

Flin Flon

Winn

SASKATCHEWAN

Prince Albert

Vancouver I.

Victoria

Vancouver

Seattle

Str. of Juan de Fuca

Fraser R.

Kamloops

Columbia R.

Red Deer

Calgary

Bow R.

Saskatchewan R.

Medicine Hat

Lethbridge

Saskatoon

Moose Jaw

Regina

Winnipegosis

Manitoba L.

Winnip

Portland

UNITED

Brandon

CANADA
Political

BOUNDARIES

———————— International boundary

———————— Province or territory boundary

CITIES

● Montreal

● Saskatoon

· Resolute   A city's relative size is
                  shown by the size of
                  its symbol and lettering.

⊛ Ottawa   National capital

★ Winnipeg   Provincial capital

1 cm represents 200 km

0   200   400   600 Kilometres

Complete legend on page 7

G R E E N L A N D
(KALAALLIT NUNAAT) (Denmark)

ICELAND

Denmark Strait

ARCTIC CIRCLE

70°N

ATLANTIC

OCEAN

Ellesmere Island

eth

Devon I.

Lancaster Sound

Baffin Bay

Gulf of Boothia

Clyde River

Baffin Island

Davis Strait

Cape Farewell

NUNAVUT

ugaaruk

Foxe Basin

Cumberland Sd.

Godthåb (Nuuk)

Foxe Channel

Iqaluit

Frobisher Bay

Southampton I.

Chesterfield Inlet

Coats I.

Salluit

Hudson Strait

Labrador Sea

Mansel I.

Ungava Bay

Churchill

Fort Severn

Hudson Bay

Belcher Is.

Kuujjuarapik

George R.

Kuujjuaq

Feuilles R.

NEWFOUNDLAND AND LABRADOR

Happy Valley Goose Bay

Smallwood Res.

Churchill R.

James Bay

BA

Severn R.

Winisk R.

Labrador City

St. John's

Corner Brook

Newfoundland

Kenora

Lake of the Woods

ONTARIO

Albany R.

Moosonee

L. *Mistassini*

Manicouagan Lake

Sept-Îles

Anticosti I.

QUEBEC

Gulf of St. Lawrence

Strait of Belle Isle

Cape Breton I.

ST-PIERRE AND MIQUELON (France)

Sable I. (Nova Scotia)

Thunder Bay

L. *Nipigon*

Val-d'Or

St. Lawrence R.

Quebec

PRINCE EDWARD ISLAND

Charlottetown

NEW BRUNSWICK

Fredericton

NOVA SCOTIA

Halifax

Minneapolis

L. *Superior*

Sault Ste. Marie

Sudbury

L. *Nipissing*

Montreal

Saint John R.

Saint John

Bay of Fundy

Yarmouth

ATLANTIC

OCEAN

L. *Michigan*

L. *Huron*

Georgian Bay

L. *Simcoe*

Ottawa

Kingston

L. *Ontario*

Boston

Chicago

Detroit

Windsor

London

Hamilton

Toronto

Buffalo

Niagara Falls

L. *Erie*

New York City

S T A T E S

BRITISH COLUMBIA
Political

BOUNDARIES

— · — · — International boundary

— — — — Internal boundary (province, territory, or state)

CITIES

● Vancouver

● Richmond

• Penticton

★ Victoria

A city's relative size is shown by the size of its symbol and lettering.

Provincial, territorial, or state capital

1 cm represents 75 km

0   50   100   150   200   250 Kilometres

Complete legend on page 7

YUKON TERRITORY

NORTHWEST TERRITORIES

ALASKA (U.S.)

BRITISH COLUMBIA

ALBERTA

Rocky Mountains

Columbia Mountains

PACIFIC OCEAN

Vancouver Island

UNITED STATES

WASHINGTON

IDAHO

MONT.

Kluane National Park

St. Elias Mts.

Tatshenshini-Alsek Wilderness Provincial Park

Whitehorse

Logan Mts. 2773m

Nahanni National Park

Fort Simpson

Horn Plateau

Yellowknife

Great Slave Lake

Skagway

Atlin

Atlin L.

Atlin Provincial Park

Mt. Nesselrode 2470m

Watson Lake

Fort Liard

Hay River

Fairweather Mt. 4663m

Juneau

Sitka

Dease Lake

Muncho Lake

Fort Nelson

Wood Buffalo National Park

Caribou Mts.

Fort Vermilion

Alexander Archipelago

Prince of Wales I.

Mt. Ratz 3136m

Mount Edziza Provincial Park

Spatsizi Plateau Wilderness Provincial Park

Kwadacha Wilderness P.P.

Northern Rocky Mts. P.P.

Mt. Lloyd George 2972m

Fort St. John

Peace River

Fort

Stewart

Tatlatui Provincial Park

Hazelton

Williston L.

Dawson Creek

Grande Prairie

Slave Lake

Swan Hills

Terrace

Smithers

Omineca Mts.

Whitecourt

Naikoon Provincial Park

Masset

Prince Rupert

Kitimat

Vanderhoof

Prince George

Willmore Wilderness P.P.

Jasper

Hinton

Queen Charlotte Islands

Sandspit

Pitt I.

Banks I.

Princess Royal I.

Tweedsmuir Provincial Park

Bella Coola

Quesnel

Bowron Lake P.P.

Mt. Robson 3954m

Jasper National Park

Gwaii Haanas National Park

Queen Charlotte Sound

Williams Lake

Fraser Plateau

Wells Gray P.P.

Mt. Columbia 3747m

Banff National Park

Red Deer

Mt. Waddington 4016m

Mt. Queen Bess 3313m

Mt. Revelstoke N.P.

Glacier N.P.

Revelstoke

Kootenay N.P.

Yoho N.P.

Banff

Calgary

Port Hardy

Gott Peak 2957m

Kamloops

Mt. Assiniboine 3618m

Campbell River

Garibaldi P.P.

Mt. Garibaldi 2678m

Powell River

Vernon

Mt. Lyell 3504m

Strathcona P.P.

Sechelt

Vancouver

Burnaby

Surrey

Kelowna

Kimberley

Tofino

Port Alberni

Richmond

Chilliwack

Abbotsford

Penticton

Nelson

Cranbrook

Fernie

Pacific Rim National Park

Nanaimo

Saanich

Victoria

Gulf Islands N.P.

Trail

Olympic Mts.

Seattle

Spokane

Olympia

Tacoma

Mt. Rainier 4392m

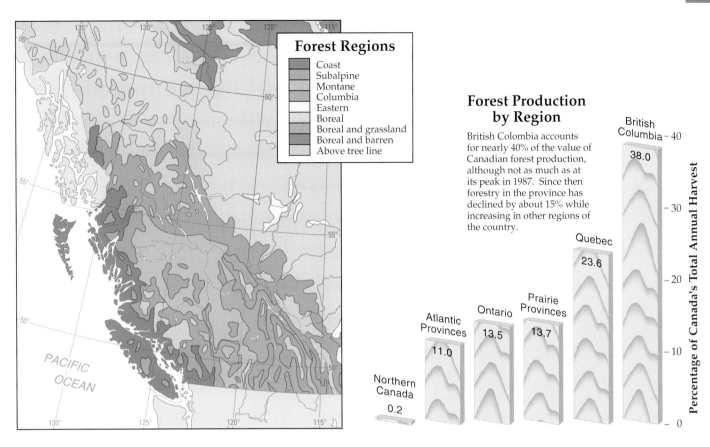

Forest Regions

- Coast
- Subalpine
- Montane
- Columbia
- Eastern
- Boreal
- Boreal and grassland
- Boreal and barren
- Above tree line

PACIFIC OCEAN

Forest Production by Region

British Colombia accounts for nearly 40% of the value of Canadian forest production, although not as much as at its peak in 1987. Since then forestry in the province has declined by about 15% while increasing in other regions of the country.

Percentage of Canada's Total Annual Harvest

- Northern Canada 0.2
- Atlantic Provinces 11.0
- Ontario 13.5
- Prairie Provinces 13.7
- Quebec 23.6
- British Columbia 38.0

Energy in British Columbia

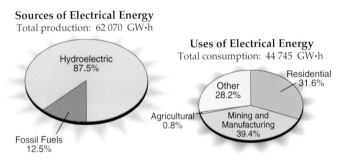

Sources of Electrical Energy
Total production: 62 070 GW·h

- Hydroelectric 87.5%
- Fossil Fuels 12.5%

Uses of Electrical Energy
Total consumption: 44 745 GW·h

- Residential 31.6%
- Mining and Manufacturing 39.4%
- Agricultural 0.8%
- Other 28.2%

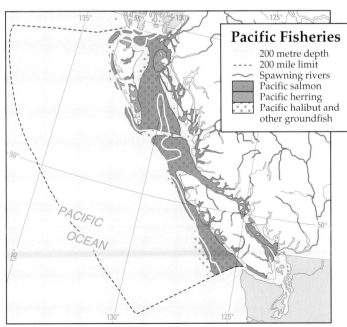

Pacific Fisheries

- 200 metre depth
- 200 mile limit
- Spawning rivers
- Pacific salmon
- Pacific herring
- Pacific halibut and other groundfish

PACIFIC OCEAN

Forests in the coastal mountains of British Columbia are valuable both as rich ecosystems and as sources of prized logs and lumber.

Vancouver is Canada's busiest port for exports. Half of all shipments from Canada to foreign countries depart from Vancouver or other ports in British Columbia.

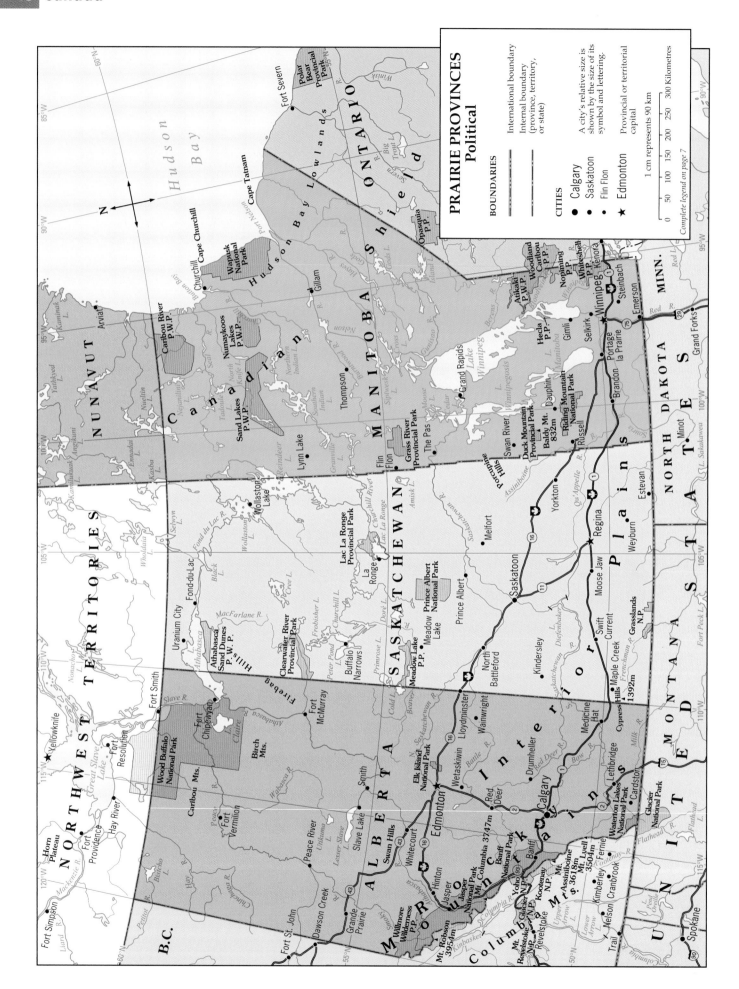

PRAIRIE PROVINCES
Political

BOUNDARIES
International boundary
Internal boundary
(province, territory,
or state)

CITIES
A city's relative size is
shown by the size of its
symbol and lettering.
● Calgary
● Saskatoon
● Flin Flon
★ Edmonton   Provincial or territorial
capital

1 cm represents 90 km
0   50 100 150 200 250 300 Kilometres

Complete legend on page 7

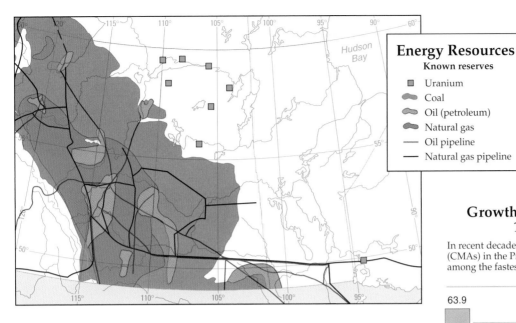

Energy Resources
Known reserves

- ▪ Uranium
- ⬮ Coal
- ⬮ Oil (petroleum)
- ⬮ Natural gas
- — Oil pipeline
- ━ Natural gas pipeline

Growth of Prairie Cities
1981–2001

In recent decades, Census Metropolitan Areas (CMAs) in the Prairie Provinces have been among the fastest growing places in Canada.

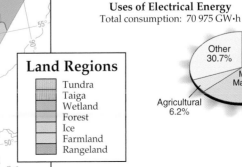

City	%
Calgary	63.9
Saskatoon	49.5
Edmonton	45.6
Vancouver	63.9
Toronto	62.8
Halifax	29.3
Montreal	24.2
St. John's	13.8

Prairie CMAs   Other Canadian CMAs

Percentage Increase in Population

Canola, which is grown mainly for its oil, has become both valuable and widespread. The canola grown each year is now worth about 70% as much as Canada's entire annual wheat crop.

Wheat Production by Province

The Prairie Provinces account for about 93% of Canada's wheat harvest each year.

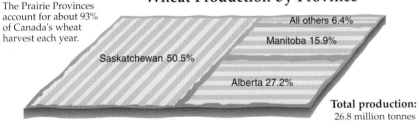

- Saskatchewan 50.5%
- Alberta 27.2%
- Manitoba 15.9%
- All others 6.4%

Total production:
26.8 million tonnes

Energy in the Prairie Provinces

Sources of Electrical Energy
Total production: 96 283 GW·h

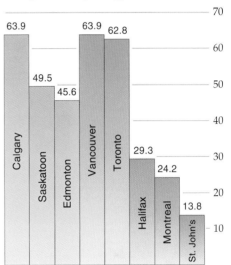

- Fossil Fuels 65.4%
- Hydroelectric 34.6%

Uses of Electrical Energy
Total consumption: 70 975 GW·h

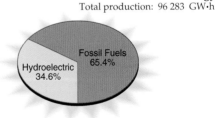

- Residential 19.8%
- Mining and Manufacturing 43.3%
- Agricultural 6.2%
- Other 30.7%

Land Regions

- Tundra
- Taiga
- Wetland
- Forest
- Ice
- Farmland
- Rangeland

**ONTARIO
Political**

BOUNDARIES

International boundary

Internal boundary (province, territory, or state)

CITIES

● Mississauga

● Thunder Bay

• Kenora

A city's relative size is shown by the size of its symbol and lettering.

⊛ Ottawa — National capital

★ Toronto — Provincial or state capital

1 cm represents 90 km

0 50 100 150 200 250 300 Kilometres

Complete legend on page 7

NUNAVUT

MANITOBA

Caribou River P.W.P.

Netaminw Lake

Seal R.

North Knife Lake

Numaykoos Lakes P.W.P.

Sand Lakes P.W.P.

Churchill R.

Button Bay

Churchill

Cape Churchill

Wapusk National Park

Port Nelson

Cape Tatnam

Gillam

Nelson R.

Stephens L.

Hayes R.

Gods R.

Fort Severn

Hudson Bay Lowlands

Wabuk Point

Cape Henrietta Maria

Long I.

Polar Bear Provincial Park

Bear I.

Pointe Louis-XIV

H u d s o n

B a y

Ottawa Islands

Winisk R.

Sutton L.

Ekwan R.

Gods L.

Sachigo R.

Sachigo L.

Big Trout L.

Winisk River P.P.

Winisk L.

Attawapiskat

Akimiski I.

J a m e s

B a y

Chisasibi

Rés. de La Grande 4

Rés. de La Grande 2

La Grande R.

Rés. de La Grande 3

R. Kanaaupscow

Rés. Opinaca

R. Opinaca

R. Eastmain

Island L.

Opasquia P.P.

Sandy L.

Berens R.

Winisk R.

Attawapiskat R.

Kapiskau R.

Charlton I.

Eastmain

Rés. de Eastmain Un

R. de Rupert

L. Sakami

Woodland Caribou P.P.

Trout L.

Central Patricia

Otoskwin R.

Albany R.

Moosonee

L. Mistassini

C a n a d i a n

Balmertown

St. Joseph L.

Ogoki R.

Ogoki Res.

Albany R.

Moose R.

Nopiming P.P.

L. Seul

Wabakimi P.P.

Armstrong

Kenogami R.

Missinaibi R.

Kesagami L.

Abitibi R.

S h i e l d

QUEBEC

Chibougamau

Whiteshell P.P.

Kenora

Dryden

Lake of the Woods

Longlac

Hearst

Kapuskasing

Oba

Cochrane

Matagami

R. Bell

R. Harricana

R. Nottaway

Evans L.

Rés. Gouin

71

17

Fort Frances

Rainy L.

Atikokan

Nipigon

Thunder Bay

Schreiber

White River

Kabinakagami L.

Timmins

Kirkland Lake

Rouyn-Noranda

Senneterre

Parent

11

11

Quetico P.P.

International Falls

Rainy R.

Red L.

Pigeon R.

St. Ignace I.

Pukaskwa National Park

17

Wawa

Chapleau

Kapuskasing R.

Mattagami R.

Cobalt

117

Val-d'Or

Rés. Cabonga

MINNESOTA

Isle Royale

Michipicoten I.

Lake Superior P.P.

Ramsey L.

Biscotasi L.

Ishpatina Ridge 693m

Temagami L.

Indian

Montreal R.

Abitibi L.

11

Témiscaming

Rés. Kipawa

Rés. Décelles

Simard

Rés. Kempt

Rés. Baskatong

Mont-Tremblant P.P.

L a k e   S u p e r i o r

Mississagi R.

Sudbury

Maniwaki

Duluth

Marquette

Whitefish Bay

Sault Ste. Marie

Blind River

North Channel

Killarney P.P.

North Bay

Algonquin P.P.

Pembroke

Gatineau

Laval

17

Superior

M I C H I G A N

Upper Peninsula

Sault Ste. Marie

Manitoulin I.

Cockburn I.

Bruce Peninsula N.P.

Georgian Bay Islands N.P.

Georgian Bay

Parry Sound

Huntsville

Bancroft

Ottawa R. (R. des Outaouais)

Ottawa

Cornwall

St. Lawrence Seaway

20

69

St. Cloud

35

WISCONSIN

Alpena

75

Nipissing L.

11

L. Simcoe

7

Brockville

Kingston

417

Minneapolis

St. Paul

94

L a k e   M i c h i g a n

Green Bay

Traverse City

Owen Sound

Barrie

Kawartha Lakes

Belleville

St. Lawrence Islands N.P.

81

Wausau

Saginaw

L a k e   H u r o n

Richmond Hill

Peterborough

Oshawa

401

Lake Ontario

Rochester

Rochester

La Crosse

43

Lower Peninsula

Waterloo

Kitchener

Toronto

Mississauga

Niagara Falls

90

Syracuse

Mason City

Milwaukee

94

London

Hamilton

St. Catharines

Buffalo

Susquehanna R.

IOWA

Madison

96

Sarnia

402

401

Welland Canal

NEW   YORK

Waterloo

Dubuque

Rock R.

Rockford

69

75

Lansing

L. St. Clair

Thames R.

Chatham

L a k e   E r i e

Erie

STATES

79

81

Cedar Rapids

Des Moines R.

Iowa R.

80

Davenport

Moline

88

90

INDIANA

Gary

85°W

OHIO

Detroit

Windsor

Pt. Pelee N.P.

Toledo

Cleveland

PENNSYLVANIA

Des Moines

35

UNITED

Chicago

ILLINOIS

60°N

55°N

50°N

45°N

95°W

90°W

85°W

80°W

75°W

N

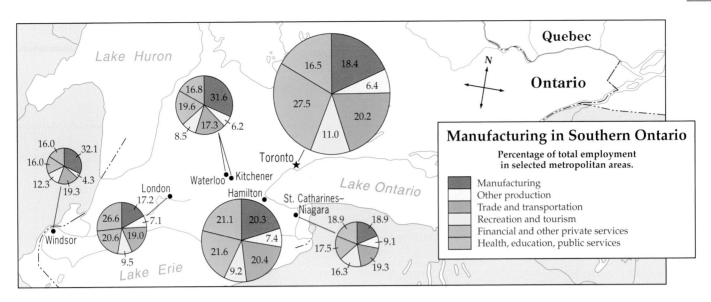

Manufacturing in Southern Ontario

Percentage of total employment
in selected metropolitan areas.

- Manufacturing
- Other production
- Trade and transportation
- Recreation and tourism
- Financial and other private services
- Health, education, public services

Value of Manufacturing by Province

Ontario accounts for more than one half of Canada's manufacturing production each year.

Ontario	52.4%
Quebec	23.8%
British Columbia	8.1%
Alberta	7.8%
All others combined	7.9%

Total manufacturing $420.9 billion

Energy in Ontario

Sources of Electrical Energy
Total production: 152 429 GW·h

- Hydroelectric 25.6%
- Nuclear 59.7%
- Fossil Fuels 14.7%

Uses of Electrical Energy
Total consumption: 127 844 GW·h

- Other 34.0%
- Residential 33.5%
- Mining and Manufacturing 30.3%
- Agricultural 2.2%

Great Lakes and St. Lawrence Seaway

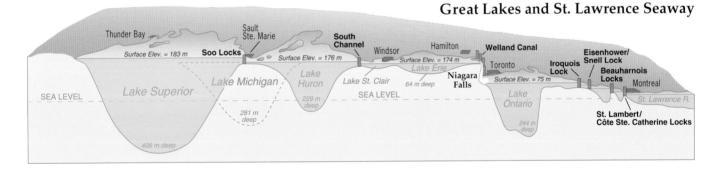

Nearly 20% of all Canadian shipping occurs on the Great Lakes. The Soo Locks, between Ontario and Michigan at Sault Ste. Marie, permit freighters to reach Lake Superior from the lower Great Lakes.

Surface mines in the vicinity of Sudbury yield ore from one of the world's richest deposits of nickel.

NUNAVUT

Southampton Island

Salisbury Island
Nottingham Island

Baffin Island

Coats Island

Mansel Island

Frobisher Bay

Salluit

Hudson Strait

Resolution Island

QUEBEC Political

BOUNDARIES

International boundary

Internal boundary (province, territory, or state)

CITIES

● Montreal
● Longueuil
● Kuujjuaq

A city's relative size is shown by the size of its symbol and lettering.

⊛ Ottawa — National capital
★ Quebec — Provincial, territorial or state capital

1 cm represents 100 km

0 50 100 150 200 250 300 Kilometres

Complete legend on page 7

Ungava Peninsula

Akpatok Island

Killiniq Island

Cape Chidley

Hudson Bay

Povungnituk

R. de Povungnituk

R. Vachon

Ungava Bay

Ottawa Islands

L. Payne

Torngat Mts.

Inukjuak

Mt. d'Iberville (Mt. Caubvick) 1652m

Kuujjuaq

R. aux Feuilles

R. George

R. de la Baleine

Sleeper Is.

King George Is.

L. Minto

R. aux Mélèzes

ATLANTIC OCEAN

Belcher Islands

L. à l'Eau Claire

R. Caniapiscau

N

Cape Henrietta Maria

Long I.

Kuujjuarapik

Grande R. de la Baleine

L. Bienville

Schefferville

Rigolet

Polar Bear P.P.

Pointe Louis-XIV

R. Kanaaupscow

QUEBEC

Rès. de Caniapiscau

Menihek Lakes

Smallwood Res.

Lake Melville

Mealy Mts.

Bear I.

de la Grande 2

Grande R.

Rès. de la Grande 4

Churchill Falls

Happy Valley-Goose Bay

Chisasibi

Labrador

Shield

Churchill R.

NEWFOUNDLAND AND LABRADOR

James Bay

Rès. de la Grande 3

Ross Bay Junction

Twin Falls

Churchill Falls

Akimiski I.

L. Sakami

Rès. Opinaca

L. Opiscotéo

Labrador City

Ashuanipi

L. Brûlé

Charlton I.

R. Opinaca

R. Eastmain

Otish Mts.

R. Ste-Marguerite

R. Magpie

R. Romaine

R. Natashquan

L. Musquaro

Strait of Belle Isle

Moosonee

Eastmain

Rès. de Eastmain Un

R. de Rupert

Gagnon

R. aux Outardes

R. Aguanish

R. Natashquan

R. du Petit Mécatina

Moose R.

R. Broadback

L. Evans

L. Naococane

R. Manicouagan

Canadian

R. Nottaway

L. Mistassini

Rès. Manicouagan

Mingan Archipelago N.P. Reserve

Havre-Saint-Pierre

Gros Morne National Park

Kesagami L.

R. Harricana

Rès. Opinaca

R. Mégiscane

L. Manouane

Rès. Pipmuacan

Sept-Îles

Anticosti Island

Grand Lake

Matagami

Chibougamau

Baie-Comeau

Pointe des Monts

Chic-Choc Mts.

Gulf of St. Lawrence

Corner Brook

Stephenville

Cochrane

Rès. Gouin

Alma

Matane

Gaspésie P.P.

Forillon N.P.

Newfoundland

Timmins

L. Abitibi

Rouyn-Noranda

Senneterre

L. St-Jean

Saguenay R.

Rimouski

Gaspé

Gaspe Peninsula

Chandler

Channel-Port aux Basques

Val-d'Or

Rès. Cabonga

Parent

St-Maurice

Saguenay

Tadoussac

Rivière-du-Loup

Chaleur Bay

Campbellton

Magdalen Is.

Cabot Strait

Cobalt

Simard Decelles

L. Kipawa

Kempt

La Tuque

Notre Dame Mts.

Edmundston

Bathurst

Cape Breton Highlands N.P.

L. Temagami

Témiscaming

Rès. Baskatong

Laurentian

St. John R.

Grand Falls

NEW BRUNSWICK

Kouchibouguac N.P.

PRINCE EDWARD ISLAND

Cape Breton Island

Sydney

Maniwaki

Mont-Tremblant P.P.

La Mauricie National Park

Quebec

Montmagny

Lévis

Charlottetown

New Glasgow

Port Hawkesbury

North Bay

Algonquin P.P.

Pembroke

Gatineau

Joliette

Trois-Rivières

UNITED

Fredericton

Moncton

Amherst

Canso

L. Nipissing

Parry Sound

ONTARIO

Huntsville

Laval

Drummondville

Longueuil

Granby

Sherbrooke

STATES

Saint John

Fundy N.P.

Truro

NOVA SCOTIA

Barrie

Bancroft

Ottawa

Montreal

MAINE

Moosehead L.

Bay of Fundy

Halifax

Richmond Hill

Kawartha Lakes

Peterborough

Kingston

St. Lawrence Seaway

Grand Manan I.

Digby

Kejimkujik National Park

Lunenburg

Sable I.

Toronto

Mississauga

Oshawa

Brockville

St. Lawrence Islands N.P.

Montpelier

VERMONT

NEW YORK

Augusta

Yarmouth

Cape Sable

ATLANTIC OCEAN

Niagara Falls

Buffalo

Lake Ontario

Syracuse

Champlain

NEW HAMPSHIRE

Portland

Concord

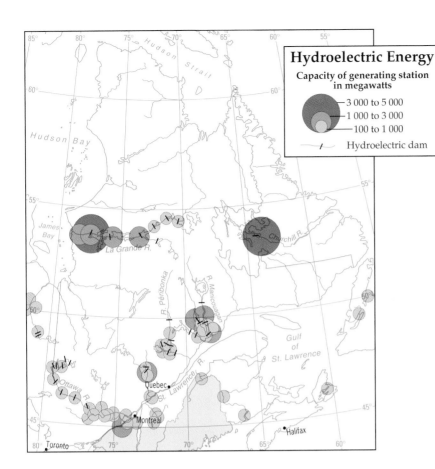

Hydroelectric Energy

Capacity of generating station
in megawatts

- 3 000 to 5 000
- 1 000 to 3 000
- 100 to 1 000
- Hydroelectric dam

Quebec's growing industrial strength is partly due to its hydroelectric power. High-voltage lines carry electricity from dams in the north to cities near the St. Lawrence River.

Manufacturing in Quebec

Percentage of total value	
24.0	Transportation equipment, machinery, electronics
21.4	Wood, furniture, paper, publishing
14.5	Food, beverages, tobacco
14.1	Metals
12.7	Chemicals, fuels, minerals
3.3	Clothing, textiles
10.0	Other

Annual value:
$96.4 billion

Manufacturing in Quebec is not dominated by any one sector. As a result, the province has a more flexible economy.

Energy in Quebec

Sources of Electrical Energy
Total production: 163 601 GW·h

- Hydroelectric 96.5%
- Nuclear 3.3%
- Fossil Fuels 0.2%

Uses of Electrical Energy
Total consumption: 144 128 GW·h

- Agricultural 1.2%
- Other 21.2%
- Residential 34.6%
- Mining and Manufacturing 43.0%

Ethnic Composition of Quebec

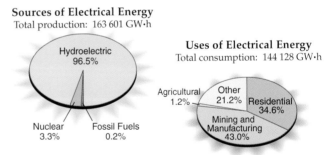

Quebec	Remainder of Canada
29.3%	2.9%
56.4%	21.7%
8.9%	18.5%
3.0%	8.4%
2.4%	48.5%

- French
- British
- Other European
- Asian
- Other, mixed

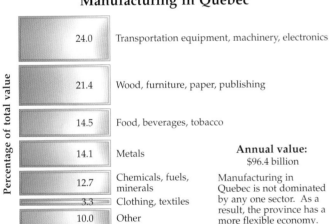

Founded in 1642, Montreal is one of the oldest and largest cities in Canada. Today Montreal remains a major financial centre and the principal city of French-speaking Canada.

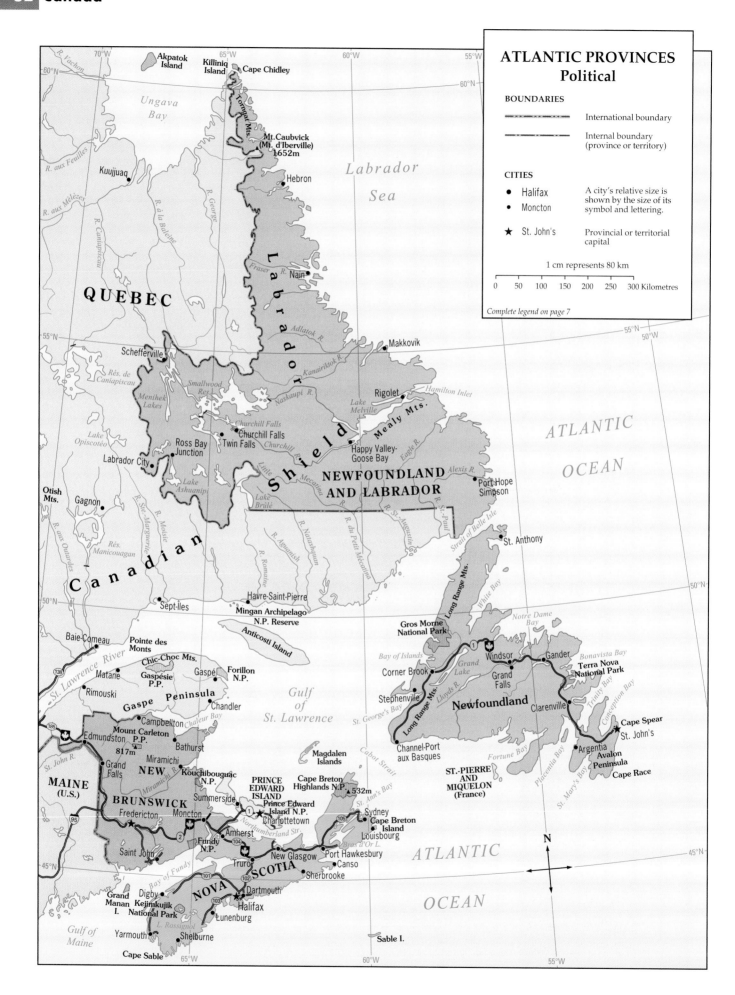

ATLANTIC PROVINCES
Political

BOUNDARIES

International boundary

Internal boundary
(province or territory)

CITIES

● Halifax

● Moncton

A city's relative size is
shown by the size of its
symbol and lettering.

★ St. John's

Provincial or territorial
capital

1 cm represents 80 km

| 0 | 50 | 100 | 150 | 200 | 250 | 300 Kilometres |

Complete legend on page 7

Akpatok
Island

Killiniq
Island

Cape Chidley

*Ungava
Bay*

Torngat Mts.

*Labrador
Sea*

R. Vachon

70°W
65°W
60°W
55°W

60°N

R. aux Feuilles

R. aux Mélèzes

Kuujjuaq

Mt.Caubvick
(Mt. d'Iberville)
1652m

Hebron

R à la Baleine

R. George

Nain

Fraser R.

QUEBEC

Labrado**r**

Adlatok R.

Makkovik

55°N
50°W

Schefferville

*Rés. de
Caniapiscau*

R. Caniapiscau

Smallwood
Res.

Kanairiktok R.

Rigolet

Hamilton Inlet

*Lake
Melville*

*Menihek
Lakes*

Naskaupi R.

Mealy Mts.

Shield

Churchill Falls

Churchill Falls

Twin Falls

Churchill R.

Happy Valley-
Goose Bay

Eagle R.

*Lake
Opiscotéo*

Ross Bay
Junction

Little Mecatina R.

**NEWFOUNDLAND
AND LABRADOR**

Alexis R.

ATLANTIC

Labrador City

*Lake
Ashuanipi*

*Lake
Brûlé*

R. Natashquan

Port Hope
Simpson

OCEAN

Otish
Mts.

Gagnon

R. Ste-Marguerite

R. Moisie

R. Romaine

R. Aguanish

R. du Petit Mécatina

R. St-Augustin

R. St-Paul

Strait of Belle Isle

St. Anthony

50°N

Canadia**n**

*Rés.
Manicouagan*

Havre-Saint-Pierre

Mingan Archipelago
N.P. Reserve

Anticosti Island

Island of Belle Isle

Long Range Mts.

White Bay

Gros Morne
National Park

*Notre Dame
Bay*

50°N

Baie-Comeau

Pointe des
Monts

Chic-Choc Mts.

St. Lawrence River

Matane

Gaspésie
P.P.

Gaspé

Forillon
N.P.

*Gulf
of
St. Lawrence*

Bay of Islands

Windsor

Gander

Bonavista Bay

138

Rimouski

Gaspe Peninsula

Chaleur Bay

Chandler

Corner Brook

*Grand
Lake*

Terra Nova
National Park

185

Campbellton

Grand
Falls

Lloyds R.

Long Range Mts.

Newfoundland

Clarenville

Trinity Bay

Mount Carleton
P.P.
817m

Bathurst

Stephenville

Cape Spear
St. John's

Edmundston

Miramichi

Magdalen
Islands

St. George's Bay

Channel-Port
aux Basques

Fortune Bay

Argentia

Grand
Falls

NEW

Kouchibouguac
N.P.

Cabot Strait

**ST.-PIERRE
AND
MIQUELON
(France)**

Avalon
Peninsula

Cape Race

**MAINE
(U.S.)**

BRUNSWICK

Miramichi R.

**PRINCE
EDWARD
ISLAND**

Cape Breton
Highlands N.P.

532m

Placentia Bay

Conception Bay

95

Fredericton

Summerside

Prince Edward
Island N.P.

St. Ann's Bay

St. Mary's Bay

Moncton

Charlottetown

106

Sydney

Cape Breton
Island

2

Amherst

Louisbourg

Fundy
N.P.

104

Bras d'Or L.

Port Hawkesbury

ATLANTIC

Saint John

New Glasgow

Bay of Fundy

Truro

SCOTIA

Canso

OCEAN

45°N

101

102

Sherbrooke

N

Digby

103

Dartmouth

45°N

Grand
Manan
I.

Kejimkujik
National Park

NOVA

Halifax

L. Rossignol

Lunenburg

*Gulf of
Maine*

Yarmouth

Shelburne

Sable I.

Cape Sable

65°W

60°W

55°W

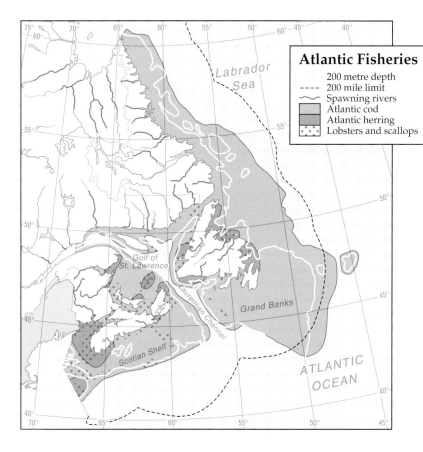

Atlantic Fisheries

- — 200 metre depth
- ---- 200 mile limit
- ～ Spawning rivers
- Atlantic cod
- Atlantic herring
- Lobsters and scallops

Productivity in the Atlantic Provinces

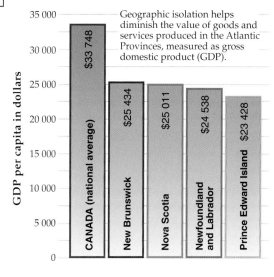

Geographic isolation helps diminish the value of goods and services produced in the Atlantic Provinces, measured as gross domestic product (GDP).

GDP per capita in dollars

- CANADA (national average) $33 748
- New Brunswick $25 434
- Nova Scotia $25 011
- Newfoundland and Labrador $24 538
- Prince Edward Island $23 428

Recent drops in fish populations have led many fishing villages to adopt new ways to survive. Some attract tourists. Many others have turned to *aquaculture* (growing fish domestically, often in offshore enclosures).

Atlantic Cod

In 1993, to protect fish stocks, cod fishing was banned in Canada. In 1997 fishing reopened in some areas, although stocks of cod continue to decline.

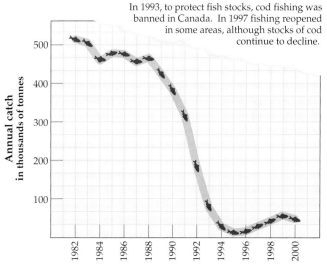

Annual catch in thousands of tonnes

Energy in the Atlantic Provinces

Sources of Electrical Energy
Total production: 64 181 GW·h

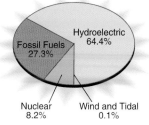

- Hydroelectric 64.4%
- Fossil Fuels 27.3%
- Nuclear 8.2%
- Wind and Tidal 0.1%

Uses of Electrical Energy
Total consumption: 31 365 GW·h

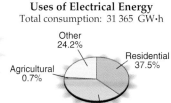

- Other 24.2%
- Residential 37.5%
- Agricultural 0.7%
- Mining and Manufacturing 37.6%

Halifax is one of Canada's busiest cargo ports. Unlike most other eastern ports in Canada, it usually is free of ice and open to shipping all winter long.

GREENLAND
(KALAALLIT NUNAAT) (Denmark)

Davis Strait

Baffin Bay

Baffin Island

QUEBEC

Ungava Peninsula

Hudson Strait

Akpatok I.

Kuujjuaq

Salluit

Belcher Is.

Mansel I.

Nottingham I.

Coats I.

Southampton I.

Hudson Bay

Churchill

Wapusk National Park

Caribou River P.W.P.

MANITOBA

Numaykoos Lakes P.W.P.

Sand Lakes P.W.P.

SASKATCHEWAN

Clearwater River P.P.

Athabasca Sand Dunes P.W.P.

Wollaston L.

L. Athabasca

ALBERTA

Fort McMurray

Peace River

Grande Prairie

Dawson Creek

BRITISH COLUMBIA

Fort Nelson

Northern Rocky Mts. P.P.

Rocky Mountains

Kwadacha Wilderness P.P.

Spatsizi Plateau Wilderness P.P.

Williston Lake

Prince Rupert

Kitimat

Hecate Str.

Watson Lake

Fort Liard

Fort Providence

Hay River

Fort Resolution

Fort Smith

Wood Buffalo National Park

Great Slave Lake

Yellowknife

NORTHWEST TERRITORIES

Great Bear Lake

Fort Simpson

Fort Norman

Norman Wells

Franklin Mts.

Mackenzie Mts.

Nahanni National Park 2773m

Selwyn Mts.

Horn Plateau

Mackenzie R.

Inuvik

Tuktoyaktuk

Beaufort Sea

ARCTIC OCEAN

Sachs Harbour

Banks I.

Aulavik N.P.

Prince Patrick I.

M'Clure Strait

Melville I.

Mackenzie King I.

Queen Elizabeth Islands

Ellef Ringnes I.

Amund Ringnes I.

Axel Heiberg I.

Ellesmere Island

Qttinirpaaq National Park

Barbeau Peak 2616m

Kane Basin

Bathurst I.

Cornwallis I.

Resolute

Devon I.

Jones Sound

Lancaster Sound

Somerset I.

Prince of Wales I.

Peel Sound

Victoria Island

Holman

Cambridge Bay

Kugluktuk

Coronation Gulf

Dolphin and Union Str.

Amundsen Gulf

Tuktut Nogait N.P.

Boothia Pen.

Gulf of Boothia

King William I.

Kugaaruk

NUNAVUT

Baker Lake

Rankin Inlet

Arviat

Chesterfield Inlet

Roes Welcome Sound

Melville Peninsula

Igloolik

Prince Charles I.

Foxe Channel

Foxe Basin

Foxe Peninsula

Southampton I.

Borden Pen.

Brodeur Pen.

Bylot I.

Pond Inlet

Sirmilik National Park

Clyde River

Auyuittuq National Park

Iqaluit

Hall Pen.

Pangnirtung

Cumberland Pen.

Cumberland Sd.

Frobisher Bay

Meta Incognita Pen.

YUKON TERRITORY

Dawson

Pelly Crossing

Whitehorse

Old Crow

Vuntut N.P.

Ivvavik N.P.

ALASKA (U.S.)

Fairbanks

Haines Junction

Kluane N.P.

Mt. Logan 5959m

Tatshenshini-Alsek Wilderness P.P.

Fairweather Mt. 4663m

Juneau

ARCTIC CIRCLE

N

NORTHERN CANADA
Political

BOUNDARIES

—·—·— International boundary

———— Internal boundary (province or territory)

CITIES

• Dawson   Small city

★ Whitehorse   Provincial, territorial, or state capital

1 cm represents 160 km

0 100 200 300 400 500 Kilometres

Complete legend on page 7

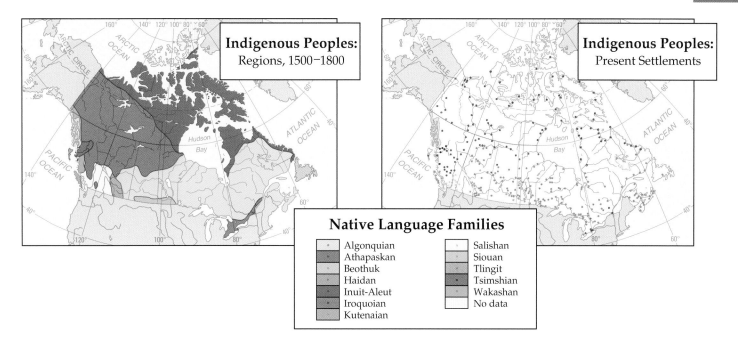

Indigenous Peoples:
Regions, 1500−1800

Indigenous Peoples:
Present Settlements

Native Language Families

- Algonquian
- Athapaskan
- Beothuk
- Haidan
- Inuit-Aleut
- Iroquoian
- Kutenaian
- Salishan
- Siouan
- Tlingit
- Tsimshian
- Wakashan
- No data

Tungsten and copper come from this mine in the western Northwest Territories. Other mines in Northern Canada yield gold, silver, uranium, lead, zinc, and cadmium.

In 1999 the eastern portion of the Northwest Territories was established as the territory of Nunavut. The Inuit, about 85% of the new territory's population, have maintained their traditional way of life while adapting to modern advances in transportation, housing, and communication.

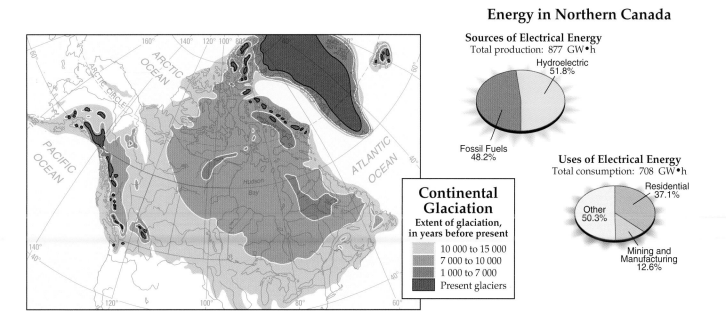

Continental Glaciation
Extent of glaciation, in years before present

- 10 000 to 15 000
- 7 000 to 10 000
- 1 000 to 7 000
- Present glaciers

Energy in Northern Canada

Sources of Electrical Energy
Total production: 877 GW•h

- Hydroelectric 51.8%
- Fossil Fuels 48.2%

Uses of Electrical Energy
Total consumption: 708 GW•h

- Residential 37.1%
- Other 50.3%
- Mining and Manufacturing 12.6%

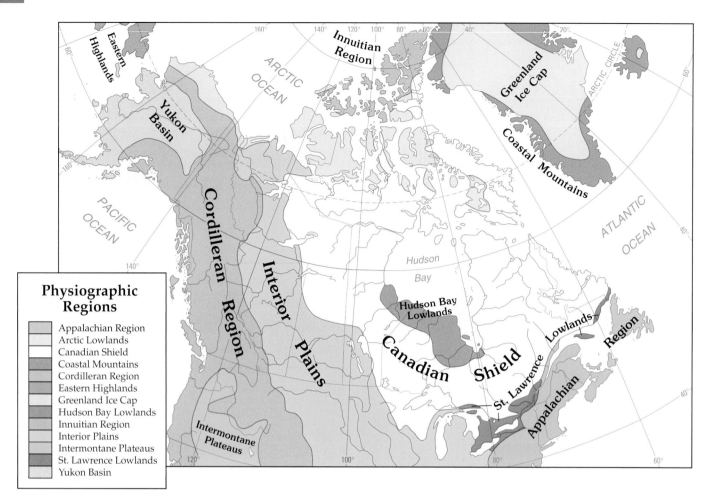

Physiographic Regions

- Appalachian Region
- Arctic Lowlands
- Canadian Shield
- Coastal Mountains
- Cordilleran Region
- Eastern Highlands
- Greenland Ice Cap
- Hudson Bay Lowlands
- Innuitian Region
- Interior Plains
- Intermontane Plateaus
- St. Lawrence Lowlands
- Yukon Basin

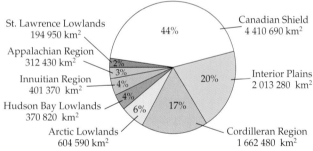

St. Lawrence Lowlands
194 950 km²

Appalachian Region
312 430 km²

Innuitian Region
401 370 km²

Hudson Bay Lowlands
370 820 km²

Arctic Lowlands
604 590 km²

Canadian Shield
4 410 690 km² — 44%

Interior Plains
2 013 280 km² — 20%

Cordilleran Region
1 662 480 km² — 17%

6%, 4%, 4%, 3%, 2%

Total Area of Canada: 9 970 610 km²

One of Canada's most level regions is the Hudson Bay Lowlands. It was part of the floor of Hudson Bay until the continent rose after being freed from the weight of glacial ice.

Cross Section of Canada

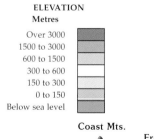

ELEVATION
Metres

Over 3000	
1500 to 3000	
600 to 1500	
300 to 600	
150 to 300	
0 to 150	
Below sea level	

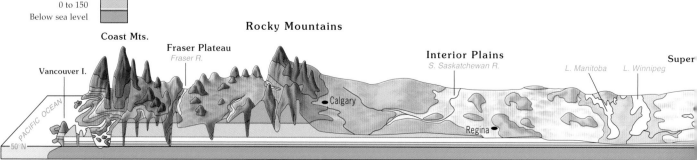

Rocky Mountains

Coast Mts.

Fraser Plateau
Fraser R.

Interior Plains
S. Saskatchewan R.

L. Manitoba   *L. Winnipeg*

Super

Vancouver I.

PACIFIC OCEAN

Calgary

Regina

50° N

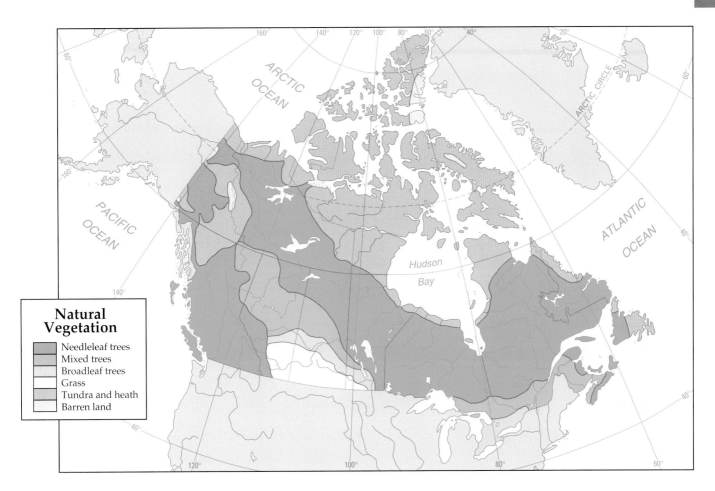

Natural Vegetation

- Needleleaf trees
- Mixed trees
- Broadleaf trees
- Grass
- Tundra and heath
- Barren land

Lake Superior, one of the Great Lakes, is located on the Canadian Shield. It is the world's largest body of fresh water.

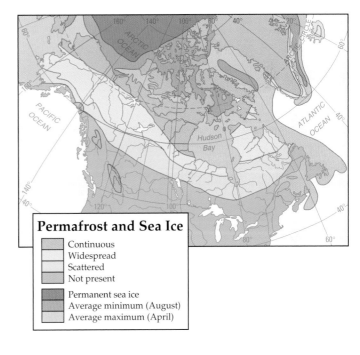

Permafrost and Sea Ice

- Continuous
- Widespread
- Scattered
- Not present

- Permanent sea ice
- Average minimum (August)
- Average maximum (April)

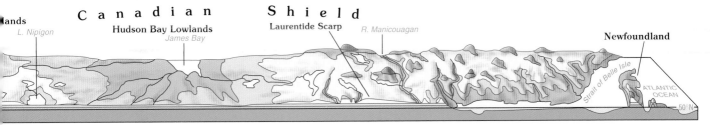

C a n a d i a n   S h i e l d

lands
L. Nipigon

Hudson Bay Lowlands
James Bay

Laurentide Scarp
R. Manicouagan

Newfoundland

Strait of Belle Isle

ATLANTIC OCEAN

50°N

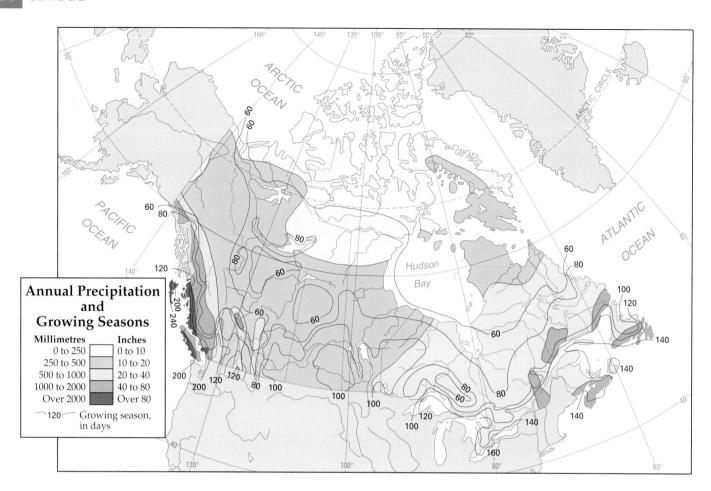

Annual Precipitation and Growing Seasons

Millimetres
- 0 to 250
- 250 to 500
- 500 to 1000
- 1000 to 2000
- Over 2000

Inches
- 0 to 10
- 10 to 20
- 20 to 40
- 40 to 80
- Over 80

~120~ Growing season, in days

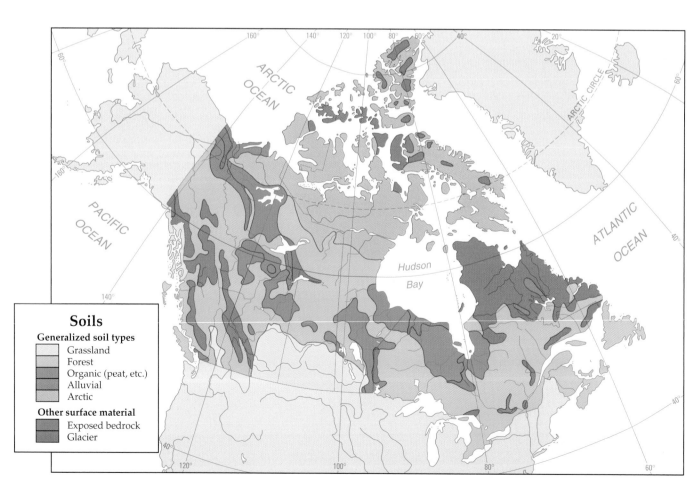

Soils

Generalized soil types
- Grassland
- Forest
- Organic (peat, etc.)
- Alluvial
- Arctic

Other surface material
- Exposed bedrock
- Glacier

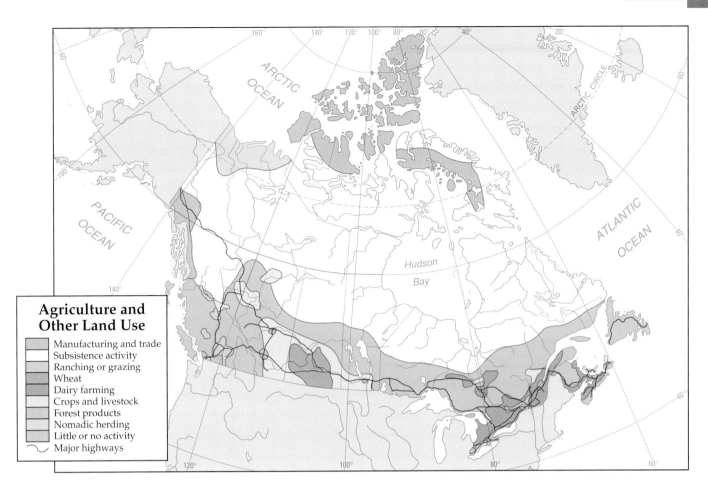

Agriculture and Other Land Use

- Manufacturing and trade
- Subsistence activity
- Ranching or grazing
- Wheat
- Dairy farming
- Crops and livestock
- Forest products
- Nomadic herding
- Little or no activity
- ～ Major highways

Productivity by Province

British Columbia 12.0%
Alberta 13.9%
Saskatchewan 3.0%
Manitoba 3.2%
Ontario 40.6%
Quebec 21.1%
Newfoundland and Labrador 1.3%
P.E.I. 0.3%
Nova Scotia 2.3%
New Brunswick 1.9%

Northwest Territories 0.3%
Nunavut 0.1%
Yukon Territory 0.1%

Total gross domestic product: $1 084.8 million

Value of Agriculture by Province

Other provinces 9.3%
Manitoba 9.6%
Quebec 14.3%
Saskatchewan 17.5%
Ontario 23.7%
Alberta 25.6%

Total annual value:
$34.3 billion

Change in Canadian Farms

		1931	1951	1971	1991
Number of people engaged in farming (= 100 000)		3.3 million	2.9 million	1.5 million	0.9 million
Farmers, as a percentage of Canadian population (= percentage)		31.7%	20.8%	6.9%	3.2%
Number of farms (= 100 000 farms)		730 000	620 000	370 000	280 000
Average farm size (= 100 hectares)		91 hectares	113 hectares	188 hectares	242 hectares

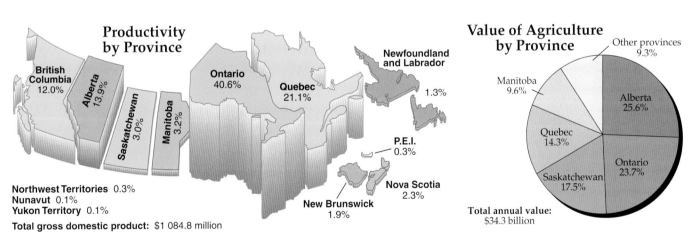

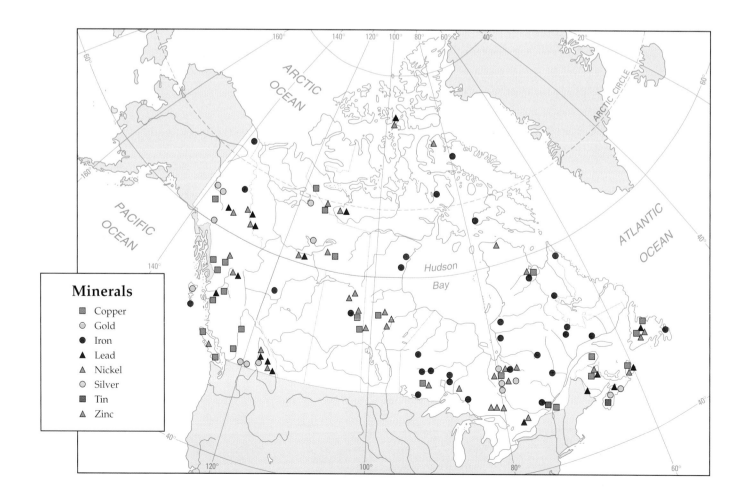

Energy Resources

Known reserves

- ▪ Uranium
- Coal
- Oil (petroleum)
- Natural gas
- Oil pipeline
- Natural gas pipeline

ARCTIC OCEAN

PACIFIC OCEAN

ATLANTIC OCEAN

Hudson Bay

ARCTIC CIRCLE

Minerals

- ▪ Copper
- ● Gold
- ● Iron
- ▲ Lead
- ▲ Nickel
- ○ Silver
- ▪ Tin
- ▲ Zinc

ARCTIC OCEAN

PACIFIC OCEAN

ATLANTIC OCEAN

Hudson Bay

ARCTIC CIRCLE

Economic Comparisons

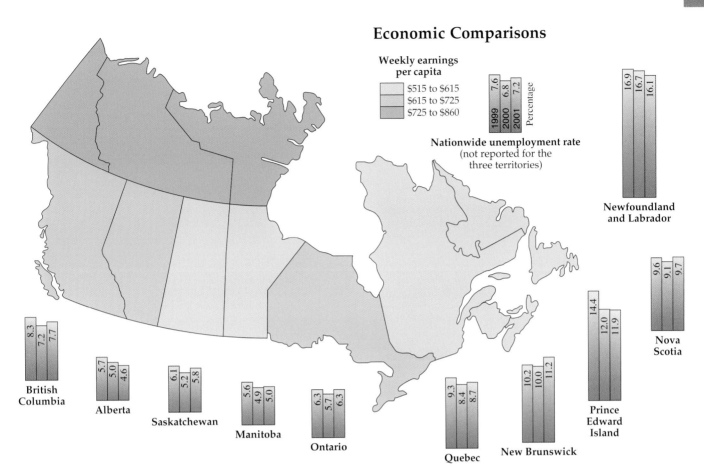

Weekly earnings per capita

$515 to $615
$615 to $725
$725 to $860

Nationwide unemployment rate
(not reported for the three territories)

1999 7.6
2000 6.8
2001 7.2
Percentage

British Columbia
8.3 7.2 7.7

Alberta
5.7 5.0 4.6

Saskatchewan
6.1 5.2 5.8

Manitoba
5.6 4.9 5.0

Ontario
6.3 5.7 6.3

Quebec
9.3 8.4 8.7

New Brunswick
10.2 10.0 11.2

Prince Edward Island
14.4 12.0 11.9

Newfoundland and Labrador
16.9 16.7 16.1

Nova Scotia
9.6 9.1 9.7

Forestry Exports

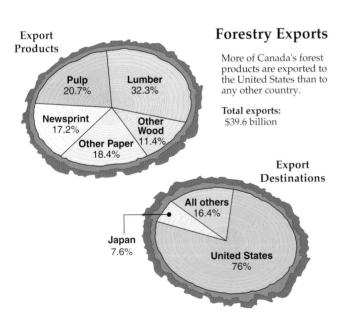

Export Products

Pulp 20.7%
Lumber 32.3%
Newsprint 17.2%
Other Wood 11.4%
Other Paper 18.4%

More of Canada's forest products are exported to the United States than to any other country.

Total exports: $39.6 billion

Export Destinations

All others 16.4%
Japan 7.6%
United States 76%

CANADA Balance of Trade

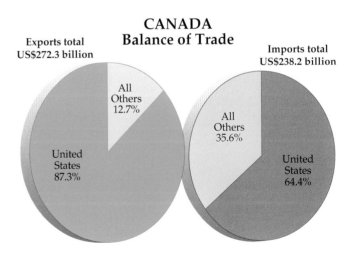

Exports total US$272.3 billion

All Others 12.7%
United States 87.3%

Imports total US$238.2 billion

All Others 35.6%
United States 64.4%

Value of Mining by Region

Annual value: $17.8 billion

Ontario 30.9%
Prairie Provinces 21.2%
Quebec 19.6%
British Columbia 10.8%
Others 17.5%

Export Destinations	
United States	87.3%
European Union	4.6%
Japan	2.2%
China	1.2%
South Korea	0.5%
Mexico	0.5%
Australia	0.3%
All others	3.4%

Import Sources	
United States	64.4%
European Union	10.3%
Japan	4.7%
China	3.6%
Mexico	3.4%
South Korea	1.4%
Taiwan	1.4%
All others	10.8%

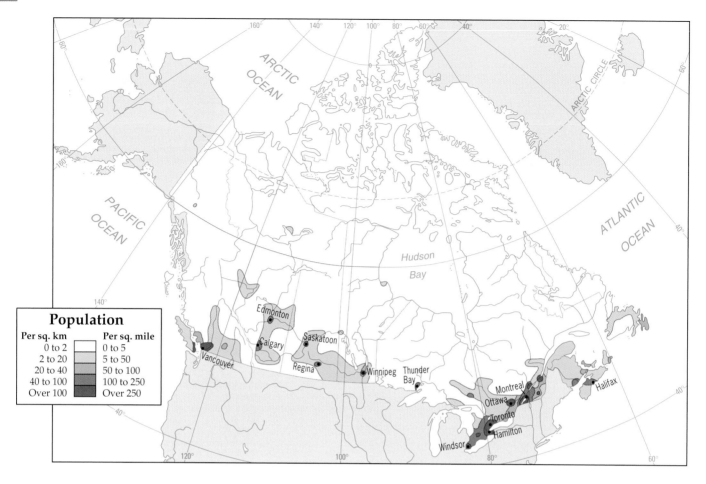

Population

Per sq. km	Per sq. mile
0 to 2	0 to 5
2 to 20	5 to 50
20 to 40	50 to 100
40 to 100	100 to 250
Over 100	Over 250

CANADA Urban Population

Canadian cities continue to grow, but the proportion of Canadians living in or near cities hardly changed between 1976 and 2001.

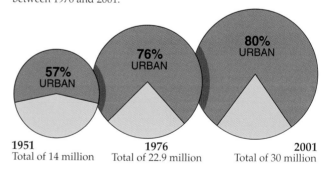

1951	1976	2001
57% URBAN	76% URBAN	80% URBAN
Total of 14 million	Total of 22.9 million	Total of 30 million

CANADA
Natural Population Growth

Canada's natural population growth: 0.4%

World's average natural population growth: 1.2%

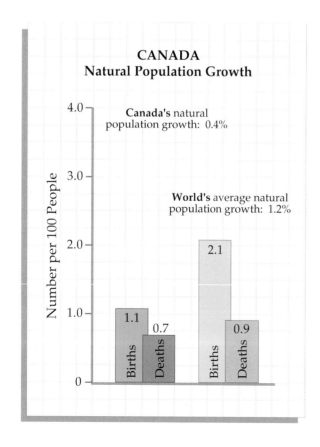

Number per 100 People

4.0

3.0

2.0

1.0

0

Births 1.1 Deaths 0.7 Births 2.1 Deaths 0.9

Toronto dominates the cultural and economic life of Canada. Its growing metropolitan area now extends to the horizon and beyond.

Growth of Metropolitan Areas
1951-1971 and 1981-2001

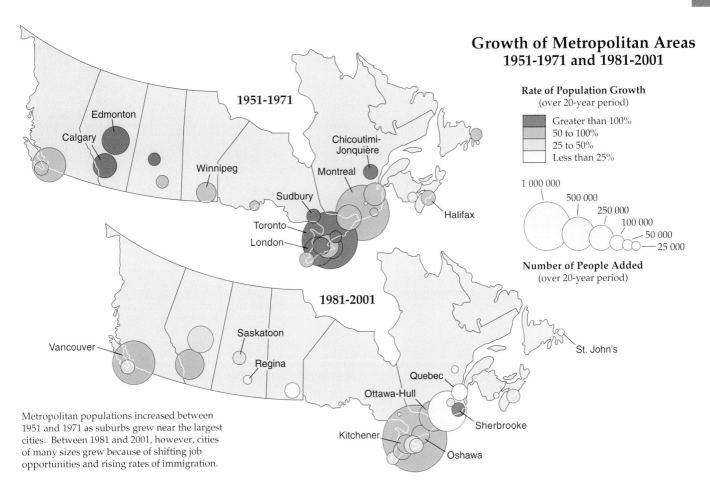

1951-1971

Edmonton
Calgary
Winnipeg
Chicoutimi-Jonquière
Montreal
Sudbury
Toronto
London
Halifax

Rate of Population Growth
(over 20-year period)

Greater than 100%
50 to 100%
25 to 50%
Less than 25%

1 000 000
500 000
250 000
100 000
50 000
25 000

Number of People Added
(over 20-year period)

1981-2001

Vancouver
Saskatoon
Regina
St. John's
Quebec
Ottawa-Hull
Sherbrooke
Kitchener
Oshawa

Metropolitan populations increased between 1951 and 1971 as suburbs grew near the largest cities. Between 1981 and 2001, however, cities of many sizes grew because of shifting job opportunities and rising rates of immigration.

Metropolitan Toronto in 1931

Brampton
Toronto
Lake Ontario

1 cm represents 11 km

0   10   20   30 km

Metropolitan Toronto in 1951

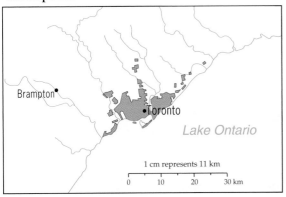

Brampton
Toronto
Lake Ontario

1 cm represents 11 km

0   10   20   30 km

Metropolitan Toronto in 1971

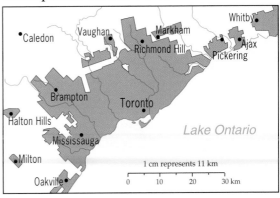

Richmond Hill   Markham
North York   Scarborough
York   East York
Brampton   Etobicoke   Toronto
Mississauga
Lake Ontario
Oakville

1 cm represents 11 km

0   10   20   30 km

Metropolitan Toronto in 2001

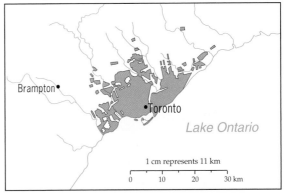

Caledon   Vaughan   Markham   Whitby
Richmond Hill   Ajax   Pickering
Brampton   Toronto
Halton Hills   Mississauga   Lake Ontario
Milton
Oakville

1 cm represents 11 km

0   10   20   30 km

Urbanization

• Cities and towns with 30 000 residents or more

▨ Extent of Toronto's built-up area

Since 1945, metropolitan areas have grown outside central cities. Outlying towns and farms have become busy suburbs. Toronto's consolidation in 1998 was another form of metropolitan growth.

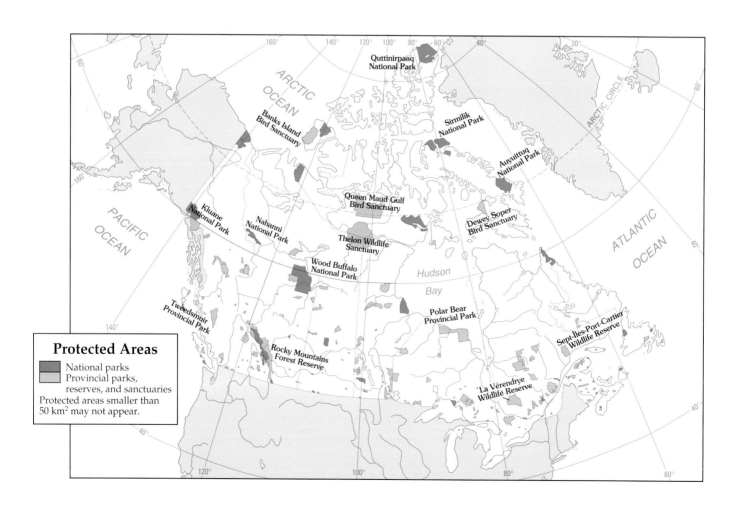

Threats to Water Quality by Manufacturing

Estimated threat by drainage basin

- High
- Medium
- Low
- No manufacturing threat
- • Contaminated sites
- — Drainage basin boundary

ARCTIC OCEAN

PACIFIC OCEAN

ATLANTIC OCEAN

Hudson Bay

Protected Areas

- National parks
- Provincial parks, reserves, and sanctuaries

Protected areas smaller than 50 km² may not appear.

Quttinirpaaq National Park

Banks Island Bird Sanctuary

Sirmilik National Park

Auyuittuq National Park

Kluane National Park

Nahanni National Park

Queen Maud Gulf Bird Sanctuary

Dewey Soper Bird Sanctuary

Thelon Wildlife Sanctuary

Wood Buffalo National Park

Tweedsmuir Provincial Park

Polar Bear Provincial Park

Sept-Îles-Port-Cartier Wildlife Reserve

Rocky Mountains Forest Reserve

La Vérendrye Wildlife Reserve

ARCTIC OCEAN

PACIFIC OCEAN

ATLANTIC OCEAN

Hudson Bay

ARCTIC CIRCLE

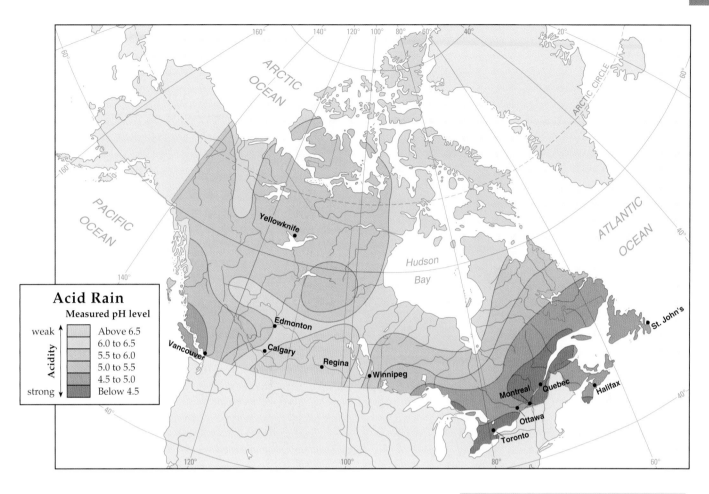

Acid Rain

Measured pH level

weak

Acidity

strong

	Above 6.5
	6.0 to 6.5
	5.5 to 6.0
	5.0 to 5.5
	4.5 to 5.0
	Below 4.5

Domestic Water Use

In Canada, a family of four uses 1372 litres of water indoors each day. Only 206 litres, or 15 percent, are used for preparing food or drinking.

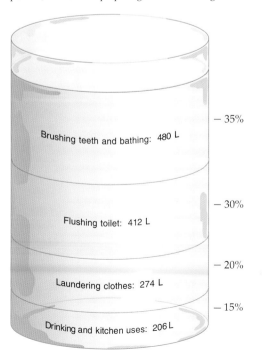

Brushing teeth and bathing: 480 L — 35%

Flushing toilet: 412 L — 30%

Laundering clothes: 274 L — 20%

Drinking and kitchen uses: 206 L — 15%

Sulphur Dioxide Emissions

Emissions of sulphur dioxide (SO_2), a major source of acid rain in Canada, come mostly from the United States. Both countries have successfully reduced emissions since 1970.

Thousands of metric tonnes of SO_2 per year

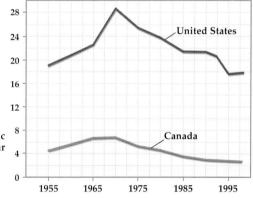

United States

Canada

The future of the Beaufort Sea beluga whale is uncertain, and the St. Lawrence beluga is endangered. Many other marine mammals have been threatened and even made extinct by hunting and by degradation of habitat.

Success in convincing consumers to recycle aluminum beverage cans has helped establish public awareness of the need to use resources responsibly.

C A N A D A

Vancouver
Cape Flattery
Strait of Juan de Fuca
Mt. Olympus 2428m
Seattle
WASHINGTON
Puget Sound
Grand Coulee Dam
Franklin D. Roosevelt Lake
Lake Pend Oreille
Coeur d'Alene Lake
Flathead Lake
Milk R.
Missouri R.
Lake Manitoba
Cape Blanco
Portland
Columbia R.
Cascade Range
Coast Ranges
Blue Mts.
Snake R.
OREGON
Columbia Plateau
Bitterroot Range
Mts.
Salmon River
IDAHO
M O N T A N A
Yellowstone R.
Fort Peck Lake
Powder R.
G r e a t
N O R T H
D A K O T A
Lake Sakakawea
Cape Mendocino
Shasta Lake
Goose Lake
American Falls Res.
Yellowstone Lake
Bighorn Mts.
Bighorn R.
Lake Oahe
S O U T H
D A K O T A
Lake F
Pyramid Lake
Humboldt R.
Ruby Mts.
Great Salt Lake Desert
Great Salt Lake
R O C K Y
W Y O M I N G
Great Divide Basin
Pathfinder Res.
Seminoe Res.
Platte R.
Niobrara R.
N E B R A S K A
Republican R.
Platte
Sacramento Valley
Sacramento R.
Lake Tahoe
Carson Sink
Sierra Nevada
NEVADA
Great Basin
Utah Lake
Sevier Lake
UTAH
Uinta Mts.
Wasatch Range
Green R.
Colorado R.
Front Range
Park Range
Mt. Elbert 4399m
Denver
Pikes Peak 4301m
S. Platte R.
Arkansas R.
Smoky Hill R.
K A
San Francisco
Monterey Bay
PACIFIC
OCEAN
San Joaquin R.
San Joaquin Valley
Coast Ranges
C A L I F O R N I A
Mt. Whitney 4418m
Death Valley 86m
Lake Mead
Colorado Plateau
Glen Canyon Dam
Grand Canyon
Lake Powell
Little Colorado R.
San Juan Mts.
C O L O R A D O
M o u n t a i n s
Sangre de Cristo Mts.
Canadian R.
P l a i n s
O K
Pt. Conception
Los Angeles
Channel Islands
Mojave Desert
Salton Sea
Hoover Dam
Parker Dam
A R I Z O N A
Gila R.
Phoenix
Salt R.
N E W   M E X I C O
Sacramento Mts.
Elephant Butte Res.
Llano Estacado
T E
San Diego
Tijuana
Imperial Valley
Colorado R.
R.
El Paso
Rio Grande
Pecos R.
Edwards Plateau
M E X I C O
Monterrey

125°W 120°W 115°W 110°W 105°W 100°W 130°W
45°N 40°N 35°N 30°N

HAWAII
PACIFIC OCEAN
Kauai
Niihau
Oahu
Pearl Harbor
Molokai
Lanai
Maui
Kahoolawe
Hawaii
Mauna Loa 4169m
160°W 158°W 156°W
22°N 20°N
0 100 200 Miles
0 100 200 Kilometres

Point Barrow
Chukchi Sea
Beaufort Sea
RUSSIA
Bering Strait
Brooks Range
ARCTIC CIRCLE
Seward Peninsula
Norton Sound
ALASKA
Yukon R.
CANADA
St. Lawrence I.
Mt. McKinley 6194m
Anchorage
Kuskokwim R.
Tanana R.
Alaska Range
Nunivak I.
Kenai Peninsula
Aleutian Islands
Alaska Peninsula
Kodiak I.
Gulf of Alaska
Alexander Archipelago
Bering Sea
180° 175°W 170°W 165°W 160°W 155°W 150°W 145°W
70°N 65°N 60°N 55°N
0 200 400 Miles
0 200 400 Kilometres

MINNESOTA

WISCONSIN

MICHIGAN

Upper Peninsula

Lower Peninsula

C A N A D A

Lake Winnipeg

Lake of the Woods

Red Lake

Lake Nipigon

Lake Superior

Lake Huron

Lake Michigan

Georgian Bay

St. Paul
Minneapolis

Mississippi R.
Des Moines R.
Rock R.

IOWA

C e n t r a l   L o w l a n d

ILLINOIS   INDIANA   OHIO

Chicago

Detroit

Cleveland

Lake Erie

Toronto

Montreal

St. Lawrence R.

Lake Ontario

Niagara Falls

MAINE

Moosehead Lake

Gulf of St. Lawrence

Bay of Fundy

NEW YORK

Lake Champlain

Adirondack Mts.

VERMONT
NEW HAMPSHIRE
Green Mts.
White Mts.

Boston
MASSACHUSETTS
Cape Cod
RHODE ISLAND
CONNECTICUT

New York City
Long Island

NEW JERSEY

PENNSYLVANIA

Allegheny Plateau

Hudson R.

M o u n t a i n s

A p p a l a c h i a n

WEST VIRGINIA

MARYLAND
Washington, D.C.
DELAWARE
Delaware Bay

VIRGINIA

P i e d m o n t

Potomac R.
James R.
Chesapeake Bay

Albemarle Sound

Cape Hatteras

Pamlico Sound

NORTH CAROLINA

A t l a n t i c   C o a s t a l   P l a i n

Roanoke R.

KANSAS

Kansas City
Kansas R.
Missouri R.
Lake of the Ozarks

MISSOURI

Ozark Plateau

Table Rock Lake

Boston Mts.

OKLAHOMA

ARKANSAS

Ouachita Mts.

Lake O' the Cherokees

Arkansas R.

KENTUCKY

Ohio R.
Cumberland R.

TENNESSEE

Memphis

Tennessee R.

Cumberland Plateau

Atlanta
Clark Hill Lake

SOUTH CAROLINA

Charleston

Saluda R.
Santee R.
Pee Dee R.

TEXAS

Dallas

Houston

Brazos R.
Red R.
Toledo Bend Res.
Sam Rayburn Res.

Padre I.

LOUISIANA

New Orleans

Galveston Bay
Atchafalaya R.

G u l f   C o a s t a l   P l a i n

MISSISSIPPI

ALABAMA

GEORGIA

Tombigbee R.
Alabama R.
Chattahoochee R.
Altamaha R.

Mobile Bay

Apalachee Bay

Mississippi River Delta

FLORIDA

Tampa Bay

Lake Okeechobee

The Everglades

Miami

Cape Canaveral

Cape Sable

Florida Keys

Dry Tortugas

Straits of Florida

A T L A N T I C

O C E A N

G u l f   o f   M e x i c o

TROPIC OF CANCER

C U B A

N

UNITED STATES
Physical

⊛ Washington, D.C.	International boundary
★ Atlanta	State boundary
● Detroit	National capital
	State capital
	Major city

ELEVATION

Metres	Feet
Over 3000	Over 10,000
1500 to 3000	5,000 to 10,000
600 to 1500	2,000 to 5,000
300 to 600	1,000 to 2,000
150 to 300	500 to 1,000
0 to 150	0 to 500
Below sea level	Below sea level

WATER DEPTH

Less than 200	Less than 600
Greater than 200	Greater than 600

0   100   200   300 Miles

0   100   200   300 Kilometres

Complete legend on page 7

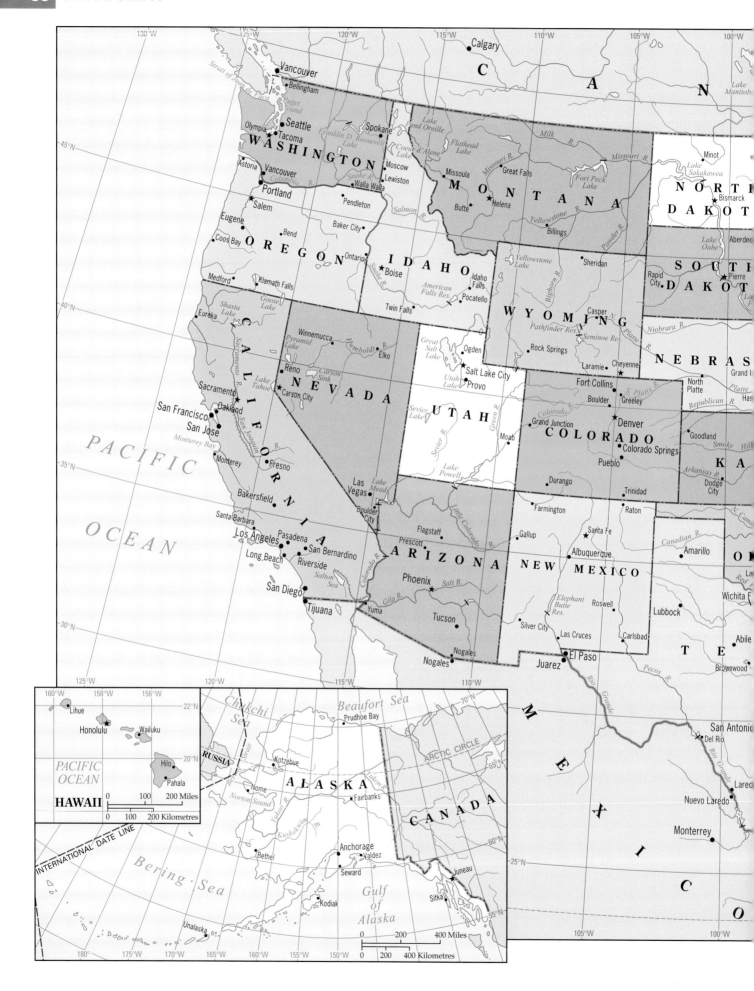

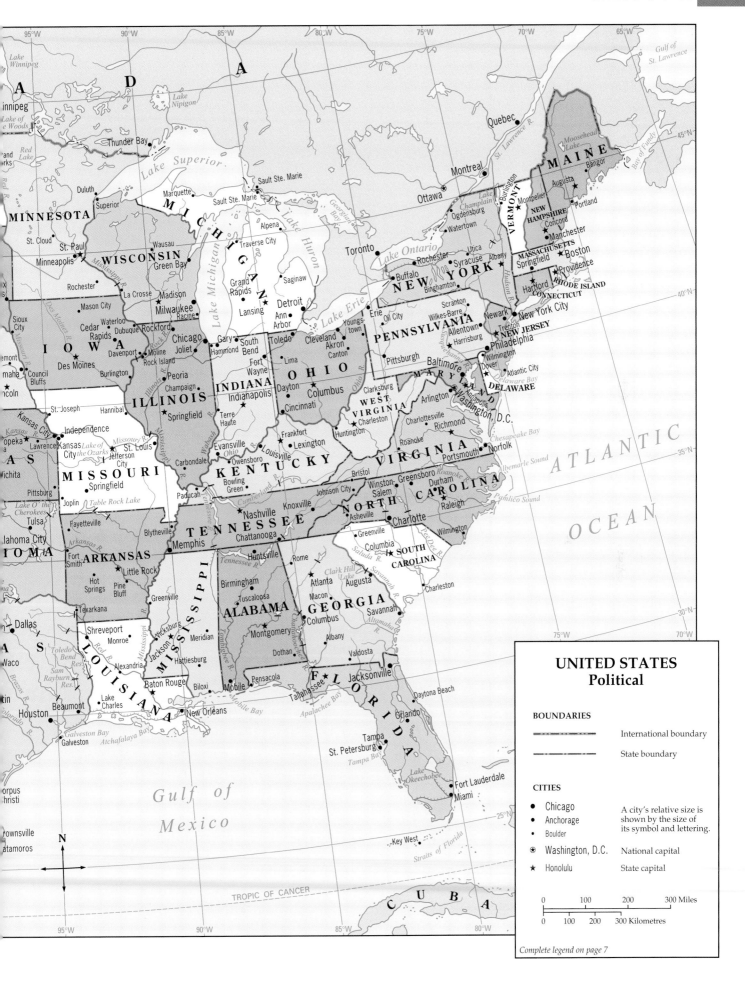

UNITED STATES
Political

BOUNDARIES

International boundary

State boundary

CITIES

● Chicago

● Anchorage

• Boulder

A city's relative size is shown by the size of its symbol and lettering.

⊛ Washington, D.C.   National capital

★ Honolulu   State capital

| 0 | 100 | 200 | 300 Miles |
| 0 | 100 | 200 | 300 Kilometres |

Complete legend on page 7

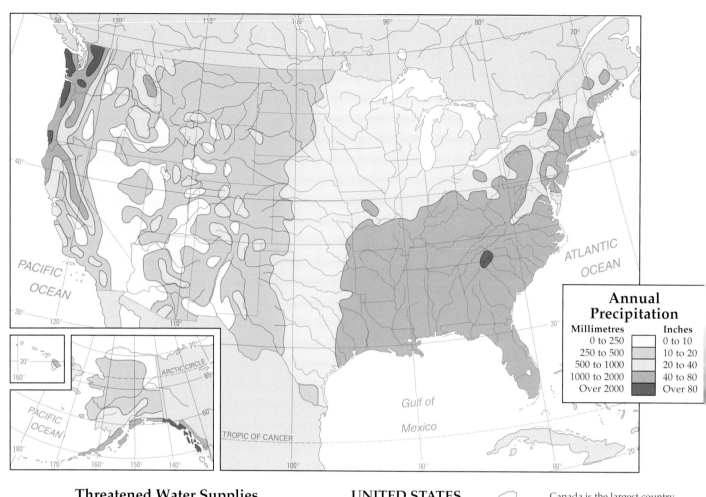

Annual Precipitation

Millimetres	Inches
0 to 250	0 to 10
250 to 500	10 to 20
500 to 1000	20 to 40
1000 to 2000	40 to 80
Over 2000	Over 80

Threatened Water Supplies

Rivers and aquifers in the arid regions of the West and Great Plains are being drained to supply water for farm and ranch irrigation, hydroelectric plants, flood-control dams, and industrial and residential needs.

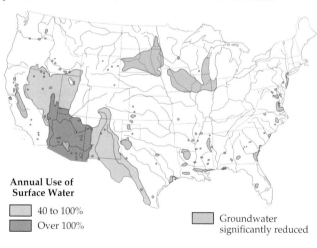

Annual Use of Surface Water

	40 to 100%
	Over 100%
	Groundwater significantly reduced

UNITED STATES Area Comparison

Canada is the largest country in the Western Hemisphere. It extends farther from east to west and from north to south than the 48 contiguous states of the United States.

Contiguous U.S.	7 989 737 km²
Canada	9 970 610 km²

Cross Section of the United States

ELEVATION

Metres		Feet
Over 3000		Over 10,000
1500 to 3000		5,000 to 10,000
600 to 1500		2,000 to 5,000
300 to 600		1,000 to 2,000
150 to 300		500 to 1,000
0 to 150		0 to 500
Below sea level		Below sea level

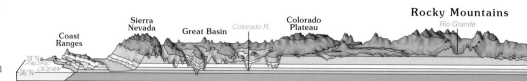

Coast Ranges · Sierra Nevada · Great Basin · Colorado R. · Colorado Plateau · Rocky Mountains · Rio Grande

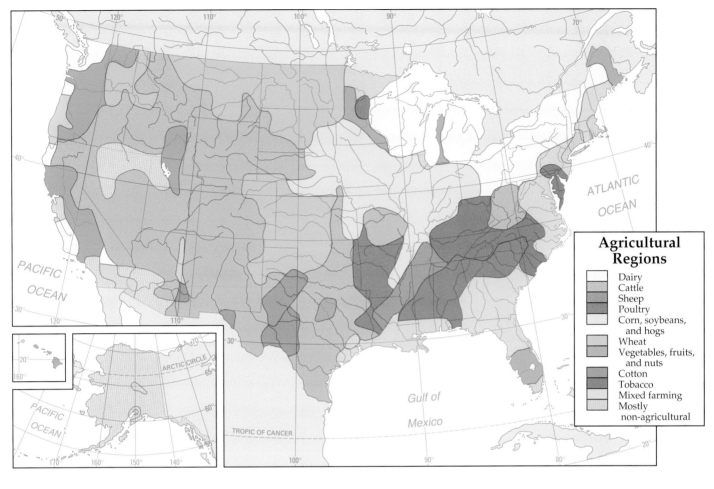

Agricultural Regions

- Dairy
- Cattle
- Sheep
- Poultry
- Corn, soybeans, and hogs
- Wheat
- Vegetables, fruits, and nuts
- Cotton
- Tobacco
- Mixed farming
- Mostly non-agricultural

PACIFIC OCEAN

ATLANTIC OCEAN

ARCTIC CIRCLE

PACIFIC OCEAN

TROPIC OF CANCER

Gulf of Mexico

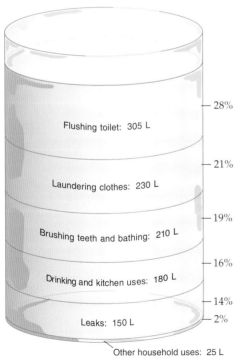

- 28% — Flushing toilet: 305 L
- 21% — Laundering clothes: 230 L
- 19% — Brushing teeth and bathing: 210 L
- 16% — Drinking and kitchen uses: 180 L
- 14%
- 2% — Leaks: 150 L

Other household uses: 25 L

The United States is the world's largest producer and exporter of corn.

Domestic Water Use

In the United States, a family of four uses 1100 litres of water indoors each day. Only 180 litres, or 16 percent, are used for preparing food or drinking.

Great Plains   Ozark Plateau   Central Lowland   Appalachian Mountains   Atlantic Coastal Plain

Mississippi R.   Tennessee R.

ATLANTIC OCEAN

38°N

36°N

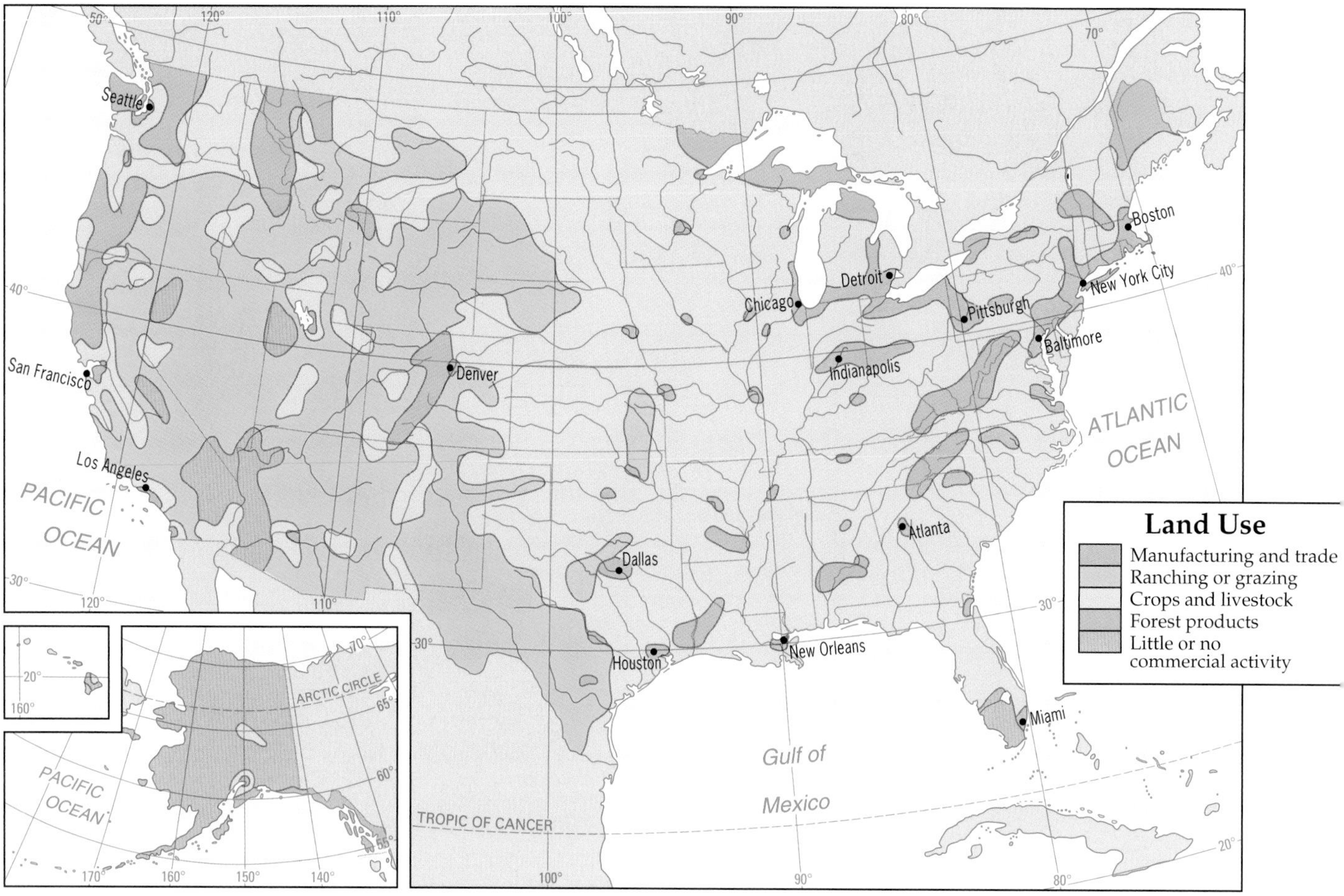

Seattle

San Francisco

Los Angeles

PACIFIC OCEAN

Denver

Dallas

Houston

New Orleans

Chicago

Detroit

Indianapolis

Pittsburgh

Baltimore

New York City

Boston

Atlanta

Miami

ATLANTIC OCEAN

Gulf of Mexico

TROPIC OF CANCER

ARCTIC CIRCLE

PACIFIC OCEAN

Land Use

- Manufacturing and trade
- Ranching or grazing
- Crops and livestock
- Forest products
- Little or no commercial activity

PACIFIC OCEAN

ATLANTIC OCEAN

Gulf of Mexico

TROPIC OF CANCER

ARCTIC CIRCLE

PACIFIC OCEAN

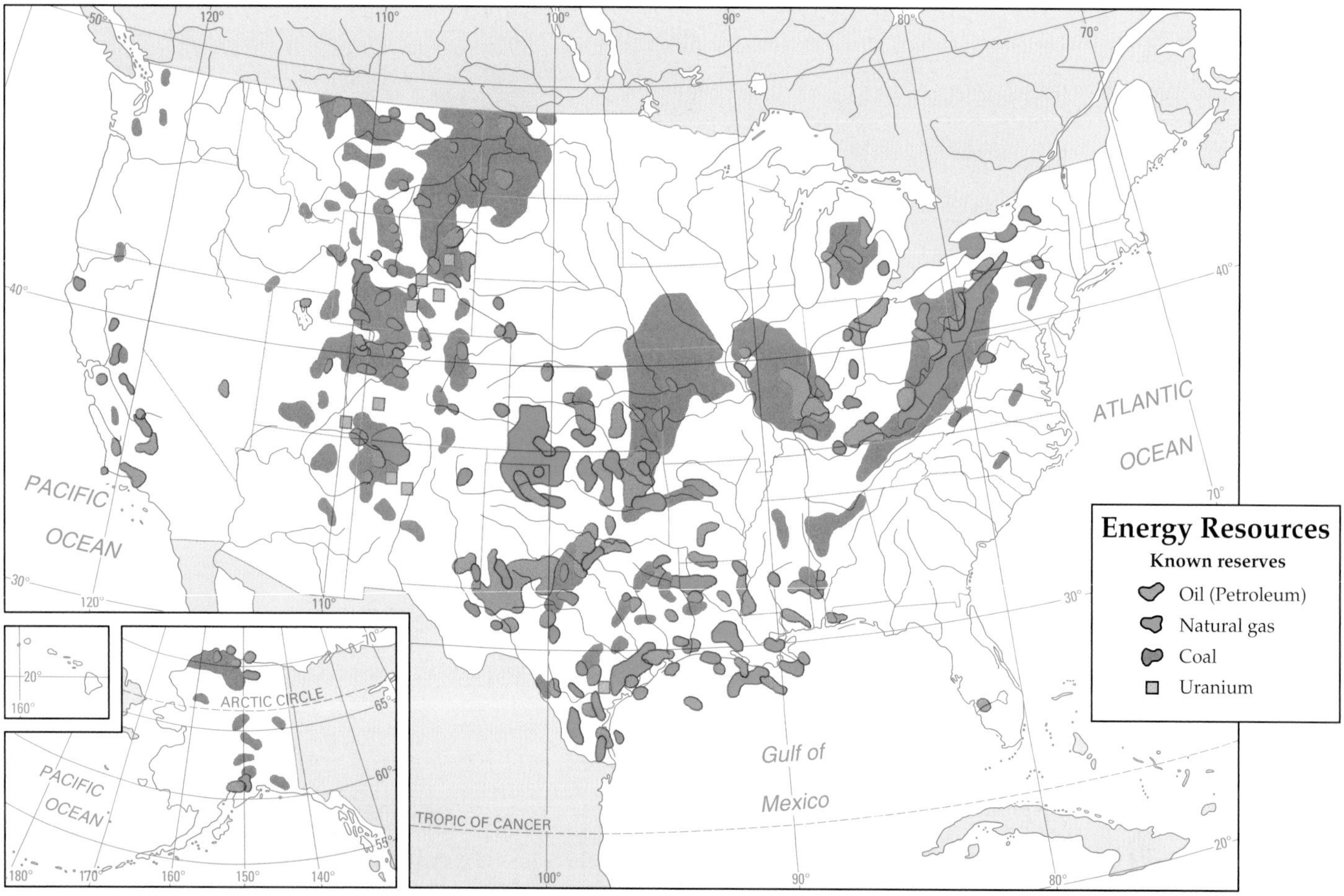

Energy Resources

Known reserves

- Oil (Petroleum)
- Natural gas
- Coal
- Uranium

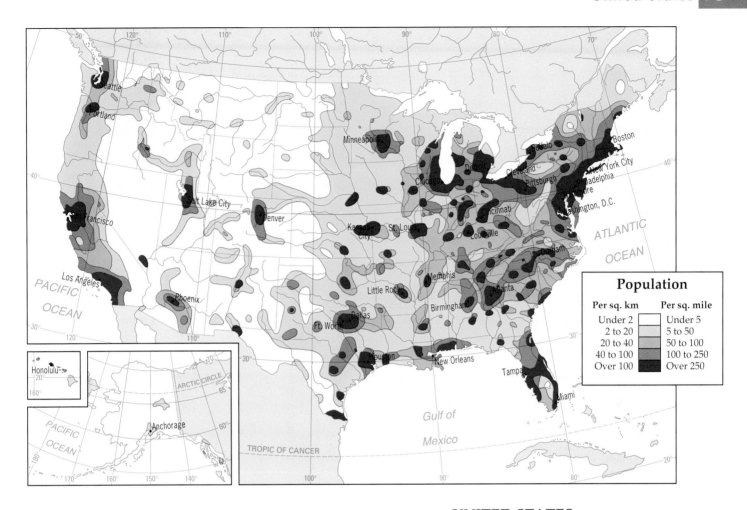

UNITED STATES
Natural Population Growth

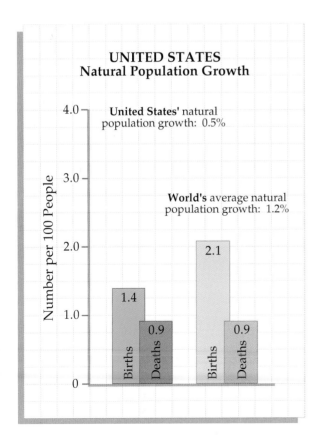

United States' natural population growth: 0.5%

World's average natural population growth: 1.2%

Number per 100 People

4.0

3.0

2.0 — 2.1

1.4

1.0 — 0.9 — 0.9

0

Births Deaths Births Deaths

UNITED STATES
Balance of Trade

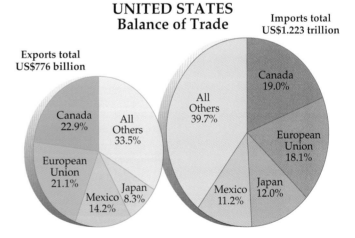

Exports total US$776 billion

Imports total US$1.223 trillion

Canada 22.9%
European Union 21.1%
Mexico 14.2%
Japan 8.3%
All Others 33.5%

All Others 39.7%
Canada 19.0%
European Union 18.1%
Japan 12.0%
Mexico 11.2%

Population

Per sq. km	Per sq. mile
Under 2	Under 5
2 to 20	5 to 50
20 to 40	50 to 100
40 to 100	100 to 250
Over 100	Over 250

New York City, with a metropolitan population of more than 16 million people, is the largest city in the United States. It is the country's leading centre of finance, trade, telecommunications, and the arts.

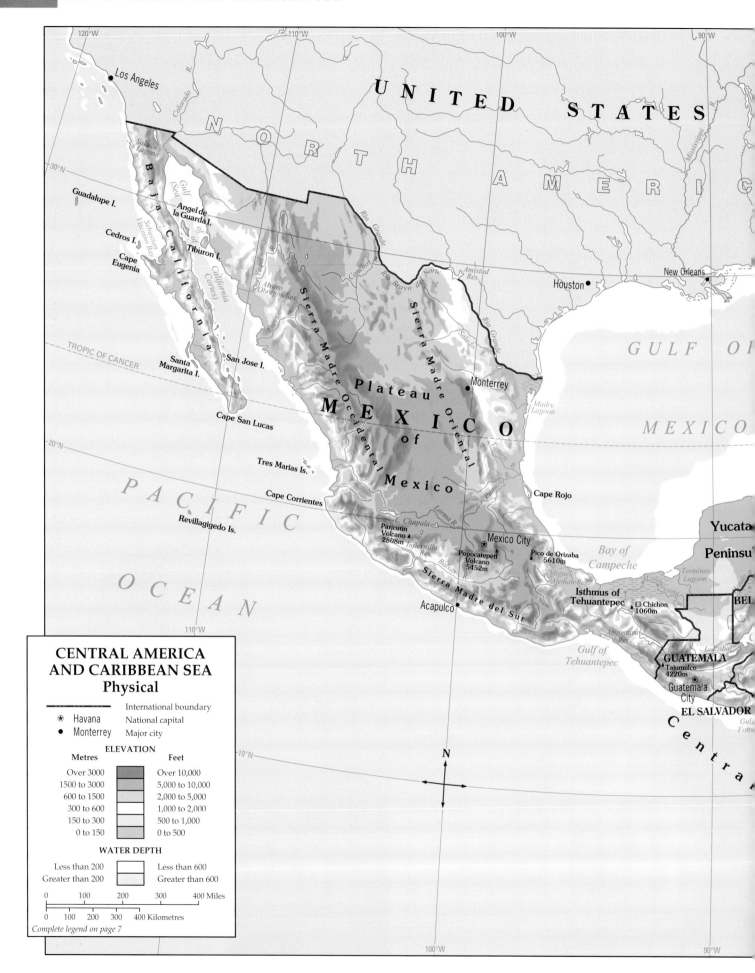

UNITED STATES

Los Angeles

120°W

110°W

100°W

90°W

NORTH AMERICA

New Orleans

Houston

30°N

Guadalupe I.

Angel de
la Guarda I.

Cedros I.

Tiburon I.

Cape
Eugenia

Salada
Lagoon

Gulf
(Sea)
of

Sebastian
Vizcaino Bay

California
(Cortes)

Colorado R.

Yaqui R.

Alvaro
Obregon Res.

Conchos R.

Rio Grande

Rio Bravo del Norte

Amistad
Res.

Saludo R.

Rio Grande

GULF OF

MEXICO

TROPIC OF CANCER

Santa
Margarita I.

San Jose I.

Baja California

Fuerte R.

Sierra Madre Occidental

Plateau
of

Monterrey

Madre
Lagoon

Cape San Lucas

Sierra Madre Oriental

MEXICO
of
Mexico

Tamesi R.

Tampico R.

Cape Rojo

20°N

Tres Marias Is.

Cape Corrientes

Paricutin
Volcano
2808m

L. Chapala

Infiernillo
Res.

Lerma R.

Mexico City

Popocatepetl
Volcano
5452m

Pico de Orizaba
5610m

Bay of
Campeche

Yucata

Peninsu

PACIFIC

Revillagigedo Is.

Balsas R.

Miguel
Aleman Res.

Terminos
Lagoon

OCEAN

Acapulco

Sierra Madre del Sur

Isthmus of
Tehuantepec

El Chichon
1060m

BEL

110°W

Gulf of
Tehuantepec

Angostura Res.

GUATEMALA
Tajumulco
4220m

Guatemala
City

Central

EL SALVADOR

Gul
Fons

10°N

N

100°W

90°W

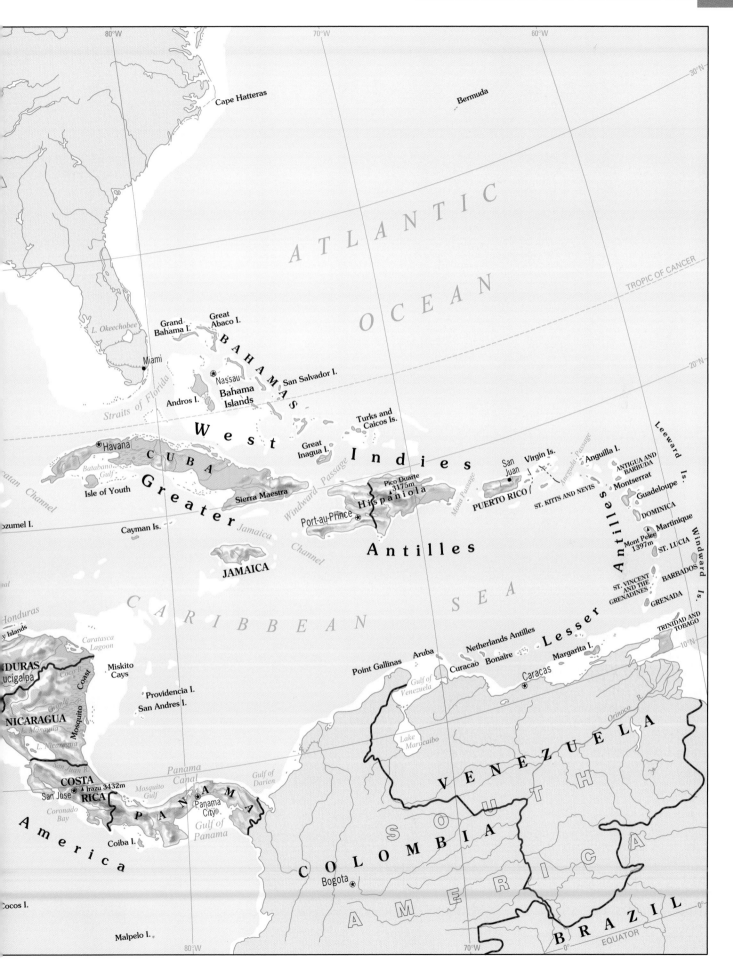

ATLANTIC

OCEAN

TROPIC OF CANCER

Cape Hatteras

Bermuda

80°W

70°W

60°W

30°N

20°N

L. Okeechobee

Grand
Bahama I.

Great
Abaco I.

Miami

B A H A M A S

Nassau

Bahama
Islands

San Salvador I.

Andros I.

Straits of Florida

West

Indies

Turks and
Caicos Is.

Great
Inagua I.

Havana

CUBA

Batabano
Gulf

Yucatan Channel

Isle of Youth

Greater

Sierra Maestra

Cozumel I.

Cayman Is.

Jamaica
Channel

Windward Passage

Hispaniola

Pico Duarte
3175m

Port-au-Prince

Antilles

JAMAICA

Mona Passage

San
Juan

PUERTO RICO

Virgin Is.

Anegada Passage

Anguilla I.

ST. KITTS AND NEVIS

Leeward Is.

ANTIGUA AND
BARBUDA

Montserrat

Guadeloupe

DOMINICA

Martinique

Mont Pelée
1397m

ST. LUCIA

Lesser

Antilles

Windward Is.

ST. VINCENT
AND THE
GRENADINES

BARBADOS

GRENADA

TRINIDAD AND
TOBAGO

C A R I B B E A N

SEA

Honduras

Bay Islands

Caratasca
Lagoon

DURAS

ucigalpa

Coco R.

Mosquito
Coast

Miskito
Cays

Providencia I.

San Andres I.

NICARAGUA

L. Managua

L. Nicaragua

San Juan R.

COSTA

Irazu 3432m

San Jose

RICA

Coronado
Bay

Grande

Mosquito
Gulf

Coiba I.

America

Malpelo I.

Cocos I.

Point Gallinas

Aruba

Netherlands Antilles

Curacao Bonaire

Margarita I.

Caracas

Gulf of
Venezuela

Lake
Maracaibo

Panama
Canal

Gulf of
Darien

PANAMA

Panama
City

Gulf of
Panama

VENEZUELA

Orinoco R.

COLOMBIA

Bogota

SOUTH

AMERICA

BRAZIL

EQUATOR

80°W

70°W

0°

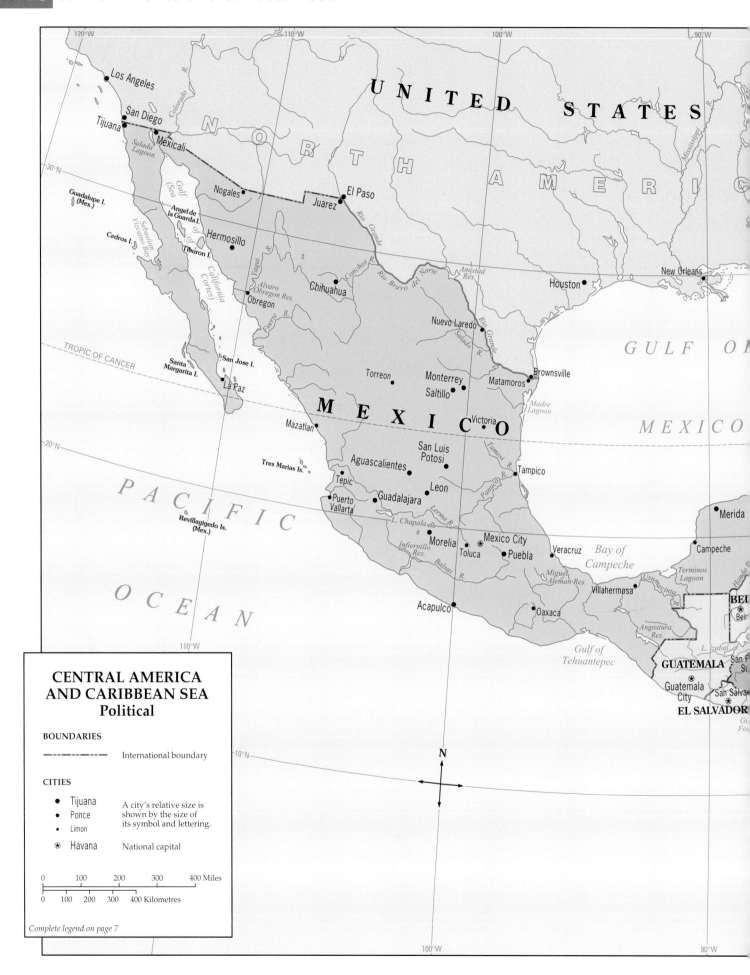

120°W   110°W   100°W   90°W

UNITED STATES

NORTH AMERICA

Los Angeles
San Diego
Tijuana
Mexicali
Salada Lagoon
Nogales
El Paso
Juarez
Rio Grande

30°N

Guadalupe I.
(Mex.)

Angel de
la Guarda I.
Hermosillo

Cedros I.

Sebastian Vizcaino Bay

Tiburon I.

Alvaro Obregon Res.
Obregon

Chihuahua
Conchos R.
Rio Bravo del Norte
Amistad Res.

Houston

New Orleans

Mississippi

Nuevo Laredo
Rio Grande
Salado R.

GULF O

TROPIC OF CANCER

Santa Margarita I.

San Jose I.

La Paz

Gulf (Sea)
Gulf of California (Cortes)

Torreon
Monterrey
Saltillo
Matamoros
Brownsville
Madre Lagoon

MEXICO

MEXICO

20°N

Mazatlan

Tres Marias Is.

MEXICO

Victoria

San Luis Potosi

Aguascalientes
Leon
Tepic
Puerto Vallarta
Guadalajara
L. Chapala
Lerma R.

Tamesi R.
Tampico
Panuco R.

Merida

PACIFIC

Revillagigedo Is.
(Mex.)

Infiernillo Res.
Morelia
Toluca
Mexico City
Puebla
Balsas R.
Veracruz

Bay of Campeche

Campeche

Terminos Lagoon

Miguel Aleman Res.
Villahermosa
Usumacinta R.

BEL
Belr

OCEAN

110°W

Acapulco

Oaxaca

Gulf of Tehuantepec

Angostura Res.

L. Izabal

GUATEMALA San F
St

Guatemala City

San Salva

EL SALVADOR

Gu
Fo

10°N

N

100°W   90°W

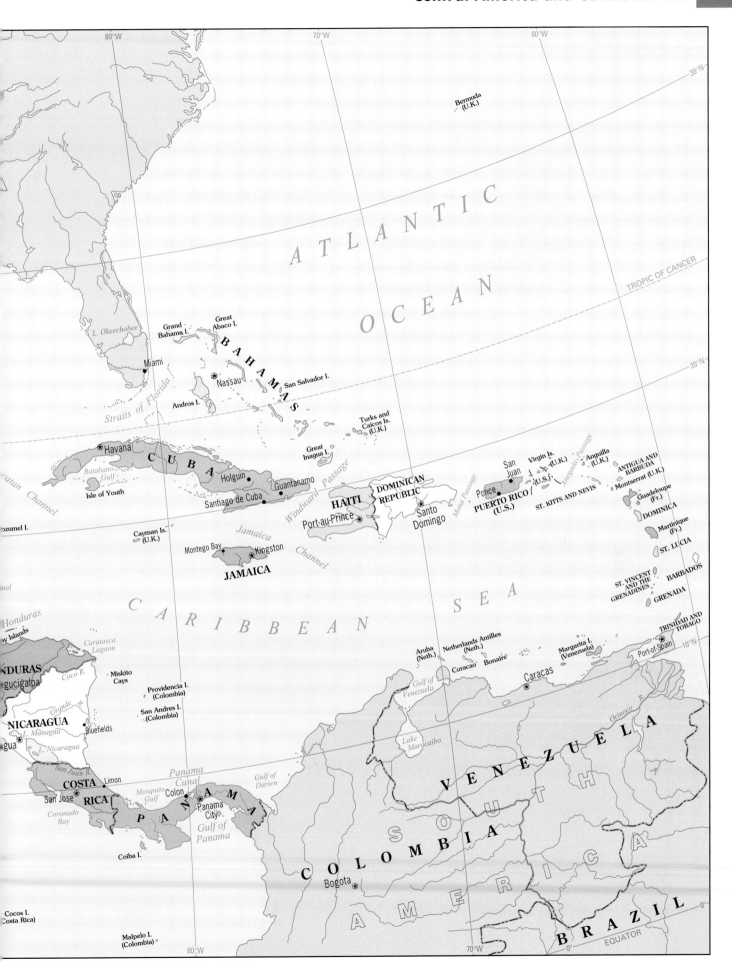

ATLANTIC

OCEAN

TROPIC OF CANCER

Bermuda (U.K.)

L. Okeechobee

Grand Bahama I.
Great Abaco I.

Miami

B A H A M A S

Nassau
San Salvador I.

Straits of Florida

Andros I.

Turks and Caicos Is. (U.K.)

Great Inagua I.

Havana

C U B A

Holguin

Guantanamo

Batabano Gulf

Isle of Youth

Santiago de Cuba

Windward Passage

DOMINICAN REPUBLIC

Virgin Is. (U.K.)
Anguilla (U.K.)

San Juan

Ponce

PUERTO RICO (U.S.)

ANTIGUA AND BARBUDA

Montserrat (U.K.)

ST. KITTS AND NEVIS

Guadeloupe (Fr.)

DOMINICA

HAITI

Port-au-Prince

Santo Domingo

Mona Passage

Anegada Passage

Cayman Is. (U.K.)

Jamaica Channel

Montego Bay
Kingston

JAMAICA

Martinique (Fr.)

ST. LUCIA

ST. VINCENT AND THE GRENADINES

BARBADOS

GRENADA

C A R I B B E A N   S E A

TRINIDAD AND TOBAGO

Honduras

Bay Islands

Caratasca Lagoon

Aruba (Neth.)
Netherlands Antilles (Neth.)

Margarita I. (Venezuela)

Port-of-Spain

NDURAS

ucigalpa

Coco R.

Miskito Cays

Curacao
Bonaire

Caracas

Gulf of Venezuela

Grande R.

Providencia I. (Colombia)

NICARAGUA

L. Managua

Bluefields

San Andres I. (Colombia)

Lake Maracaibo

V E N E Z U E L A

Orinoco R.

gua

L. Nicaragua

San Juan R.

COSTA
Limon

Panama Canal

Colon

Gulf of Darien

San Jose
RICA

Mosquito Gulf

P A N A M A

Panama City

Coronado Bay

Gulf of Panama

C O L O M B I A

S O U T H

A M E R I C A

Coiba I.

Cocos I. (Costa Rica)

Bogota

Malpelo I. (Colombia)

B R A Z I L

EQUATOR

Yucatan Channel

Cozumel I.

80°W

70°W

60°W

30°N

20°N

10°N

80°W

70°W

0°

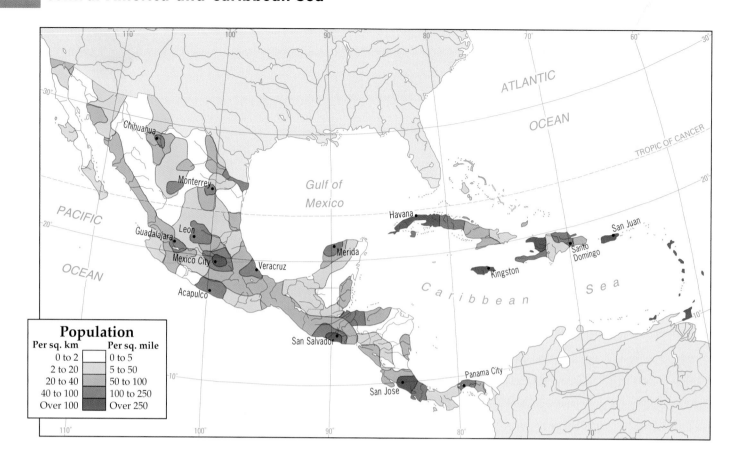

Population

Per sq. km	Per sq. mile
0 to 2	0 to 5
2 to 20	5 to 50
20 to 40	50 to 100
40 to 100	100 to 250
Over 100	Over 250

HAITI
Natural Population Growth

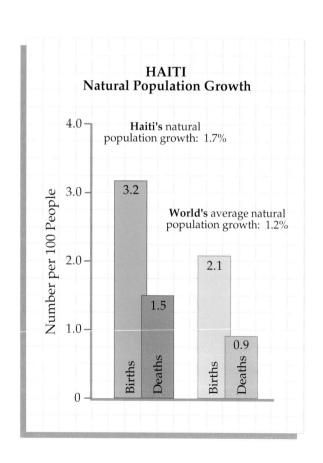

Haiti's natural population growth: 1.7%

World's average natural population growth: 1.2%

Number per 100 People

3.2 Births
1.5 Deaths
2.1 Births
0.9 Deaths

MEXICO
Balance of Trade

Exports total US$168 billion

Imports total US$176 billion

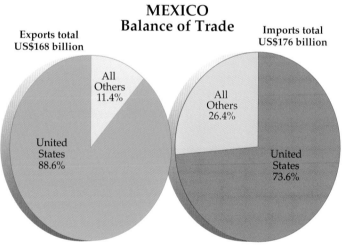

All Others 11.4%
United States 88.6%

All Others 26.4%
United States 73.6%

Mexico City's Population Growth

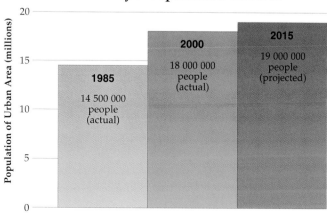

Population of Urban Area (millions)

1985
14 500 000 people (actual)

2000
18 000 000 people (actual)

2015
19 000 000 people (projected)

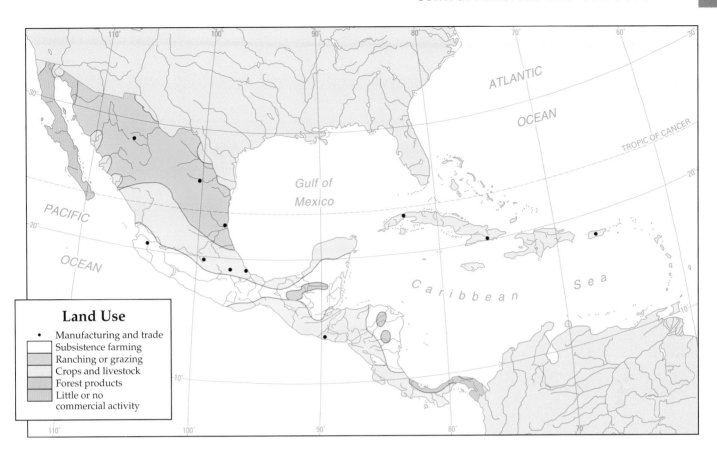

Land Use

- • Manufacturing and trade
- Subsistence farming
- Ranching or grazing
- Crops and livestock
- Forest products
- Little or no commercial activity

JAMAICA
Balance of Trade

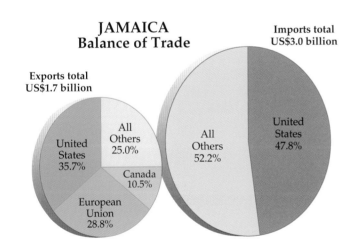

Exports total
US$1.7 billion

United States 35.7%

All Others 25.0%

Canada 10.5%

European Union 28.8%

Imports total
US$3.0 billion

All Others 52.2%

United States 47.8%

Latin America

- Spanish
- Portuguese
- French
- Other (non-Latin)

Central America is part of a larger culture region called Latin America, which includes 33 countries. Most of the people in this region speak one of the Latin-based languages of Spanish, Portuguese, or French.

Caribbean people enjoy daily visits to open-air markets that offer a variety of fresh tropical produce.

SOUTH AMERICA
Physical

⊛ Lima	International boundary
⊛ Lima	National capital
● Recife	Major city

ELEVATION

Metres		Feet
Over 6000		Over 20,000
3000 to 6000		10,000 to 20,000
1500 to 3000		5,000 to 10,000
600 to 1500		2,000 to 5,000
300 to 600		1,000 to 2,000
150 to 300		500 to 1,000
0 to 150		0 to 500

WATER DEPTH

Less than 200	Less than 600
Greater than 200	Greater than 600

0   250   500   750   1000 Miles

0   250   500   750   1000 Kilometres

Complete legend on page 7

SOUTH AMERICA
Political

BOUNDARIES

------------- International boundary

CITIES

● Sao Paulo   A city's relative size is
● Barquisimeto   shown by the size of
• Cuzco   its symbol and lettering.

⊛ Lima   National capital

0   250   500   750   1000 Miles

0   250   500   750   1000 Kilometres

Complete legend on page 7

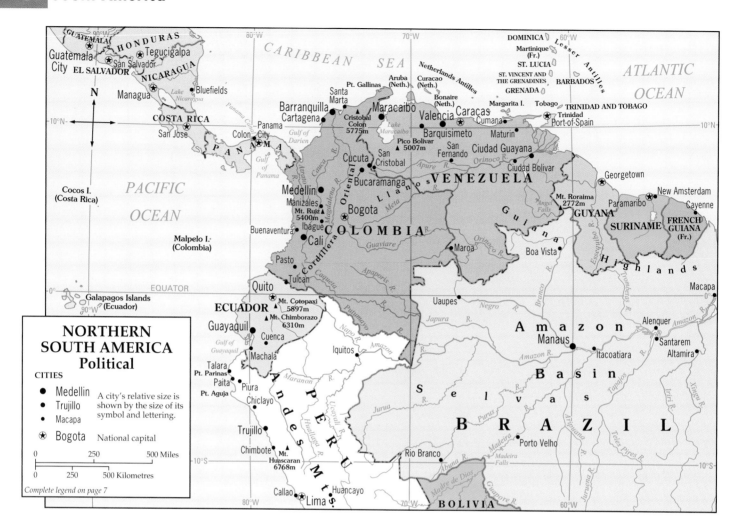

NORTHERN SOUTH AMERICA Political

CITIES

● **Medellin**   A city's relative size is
● Trujillo   shown by the size of its
• Macapa   symbol and lettering.

⊛ **Bogota**   National capital

| 0 | 250 | 500 Miles |

| 0 | 250 | 500 Kilometres |

Complete legend on page 7

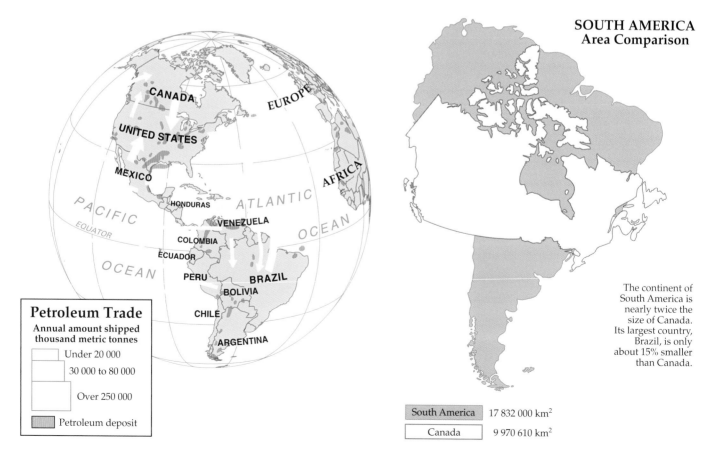

Petroleum Trade
**Annual amount shipped
thousand metric tonnes**

Under 20 000

30 000 to 80 000

Over 250 000

Petroleum deposit

SOUTH AMERICA Area Comparison

The continent of
South America is
nearly twice the
size of Canada.
Its largest country,
Brazil, is only
about 15% smaller
than Canada.

| South America | 17 832 000 km² |
| Canada | 9 970 610 km² |

Tropical Rain Forests

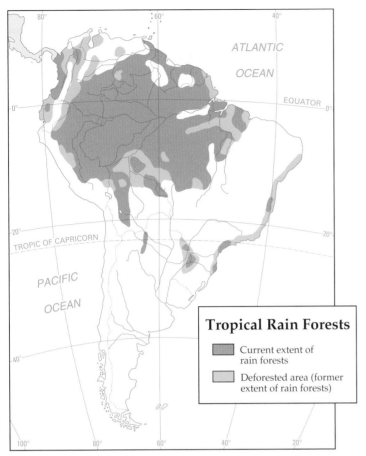

Current extent of rain forests

Deforested area (former extent of rain forests)

Brazil's economic development often comes at the expense of the Amazon rain forest. Deforestation increases annually as trees are cut down to make way for farms and highways.

Minerals and Energy Resources

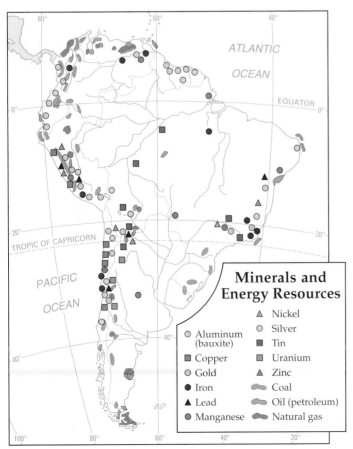

- Aluminum (bauxite)
- Copper
- Gold
- Iron
- Lead
- Manganese
- Nickel
- Silver
- Tin
- Uranium
- Zinc
- Coal
- Oil (petroleum)
- Natural gas

Indigenous Peoples

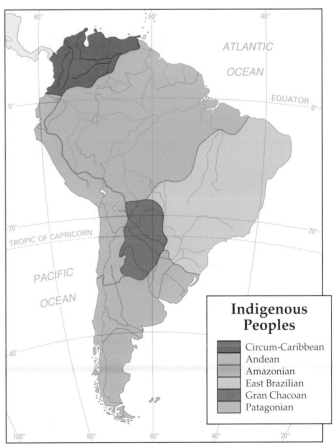

- Circum-Caribbean
- Andean
- Amazonian
- East Brazilian
- Gran Chacoan
- Patagonian

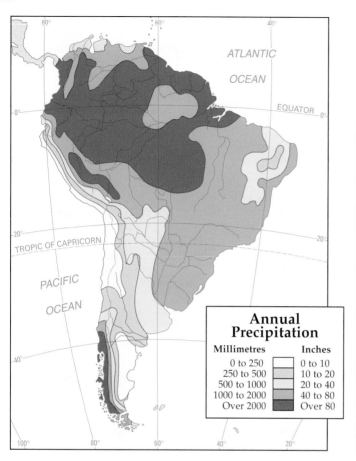

Annual Precipitation

Millimetres		Inches
0 to 250		0 to 10
250 to 500		10 to 20
500 to 1000		20 to 40
1000 to 2000		40 to 80
Over 2000		Over 80

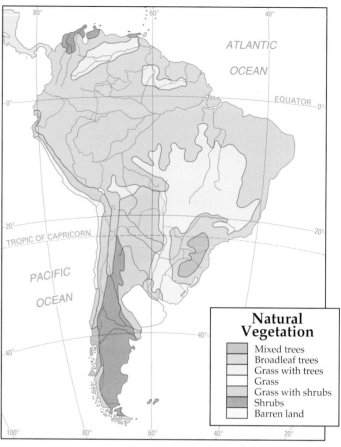

Natural Vegetation

- Mixed trees
- Broadleaf trees
- Grass with trees
- Grass
- Grass with shrubs
- Shrubs
- Barren land

Brazil's urban population is a diverse mixture of European, African, and Indian ancestry.

VENEZUELA Balance of Trade

Exports total US$32.8 billion

United States and Puerto Rico 57.0%

All Others 43.0%

Imports total US$14.7 billion

All Others 47.0%

United States 53.0%

Cross Section of South America

ELEVATION

Metres		Feet
Over 6000		Over 20,000
3000 to 6000		10,000 to 20,000
1500 to 3000		5,000 to 10,000
600 to 1500		2,000 to 5,000
300 to 600		1,000 to 2,000
150 to 300		500 to 1,000
0 to 150		0 to 500
Below sea level		Below sea level

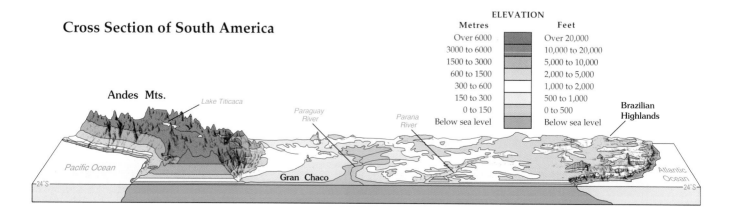

Andes Mts.

Lake Titicaca

Paraguay River

Parana River

Brazilian Highlands

Pacific Ocean

Gran Chaco

Atlantic Ocean

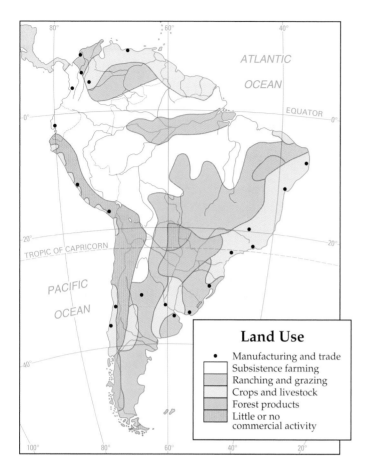

Land Use

- Manufacturing and trade
- Subsistence farming
- Ranching and grazing
- Crops and livestock
- Forest products
- Little or no commercial activity

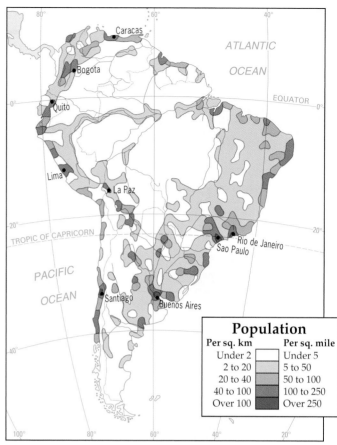

Population

Per sq. km	Per sq. mile
Under 2	Under 5
2 to 20	5 to 50
20 to 40	50 to 100
40 to 100	100 to 250
Over 100	Over 250

BRAZIL
Natural Population Growth

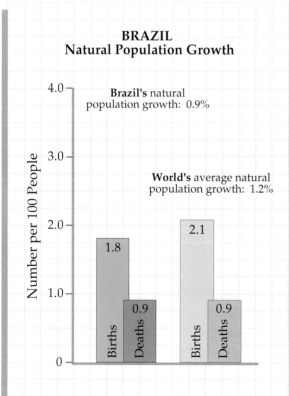

Brazil's natural population growth: 0.9%

World's average natural population growth: 1.2%

Number per 100 People

4.0
3.0
2.0
1.0
0

1.8 Births
0.9 Deaths
2.1 Births
0.9 Deaths

CHILE
Balance of Trade

Exports total US$18 billion

European Union 27.0%
All Others 43.0%
United States 16.0%
Japan 14.0%

Imports total US$17 billion

All Others 42.0%
United States 24.0%
European Union 23.0%
Argentina 11.0%

More Indians live in Peru than in any other South American country. Many still farm and bring goods to market in the highlands where their ancestors, the Incas, once reigned.

ATLANTIC

OCEAN

ARCTIC

ARCTIC CIRCLE

PRIME MERIDIAN

N O R W E G I A N

S E A

Lofoten
Is.

ICELAND

Reykjavik

Surtsey I.

Hekla
1491m

Trondheims Fjord

Sogne Fjord

Hardanger Fjord

Bokna Fjord

Oslo

S
c
a
n
d
i
n
a
v
i
a

S
W
E
D
E
N

N
O
R
W
A
Y

L. Mälaren

Faeroe
Islands

Rockall

Shetland
Islands

Hebrides

Orkney Is.

Grampian Mts.

N O R T H

S E A

Gotland

Gotaland

Jutland

DENMARK

Copenhagen

Bornholm

Kattegat

Skagerrak

Vättern

TO
RUSS

IRELAND

UNITED
KINGDOM

Great Britain

Irish Sea

Cambrian Mts.

British Isles

London

Frisian Is.

NETHERLANDS

N o r t h e r n

GERMANY

P O L A

Wars

Celtic

Sea

English Channel

Strait of Dover

Channel Is.

Seine R.

BELGIUM

LUXEMBOURG

Ore

Mts.

Elbe R.

CZECH REPUBLIC

Vis

Car

SLOVA

Cape Finisterre

Bay of
Biscay

F R A N C E

Paris Basin

Paris

Loire

Aquitaine
Basin

Massif
Central

Mt. Blanc
4807m

SWITZERLAND

LIECH.

A l p s

Munich

Danube R.

AUSTRIA

HUNGARY

Great Hung.

Cantabrian Mts.

Douro R.

Duero R.

PORTUGAL

S P A I N

Pyrenees

Ebro R.

ANDORRA

MONACO

Ligurian
Sea

Po R.

SLOVENIA

CROATIA

Adriatic

Lisbon

Tagus R.

Madrid

Iberian

Peninsula

Guadiana

Cape St. Vincent

Guadalquivir R.

Balearic Sea

Corsica

VATICAN CITY

SAN
MARINO

Apennines

Sea

BOSNIA

D i n a r i c

SER

Rome

ITALY

A

Strait of
Gibraltar

GIBRALTAR (U.K.)

Balearic Islands

Sardinia

Vesuvius
1277m

Tyrrhenian
Sea

Gulf of
Taranto

Ionian
Sea

MACEDO

ALBANIA

Pindus

M O R O C C O

Algiers

A
F
R
I
C
A

A L G E R I A

T U N I S I A

M E D I T E R R A N E A N

Tunis

Sicily

MALTA
Maltese Islands

Peloponnes

WESTERN
SAHARA
(adm. Morocco)

Gulf of
Lion

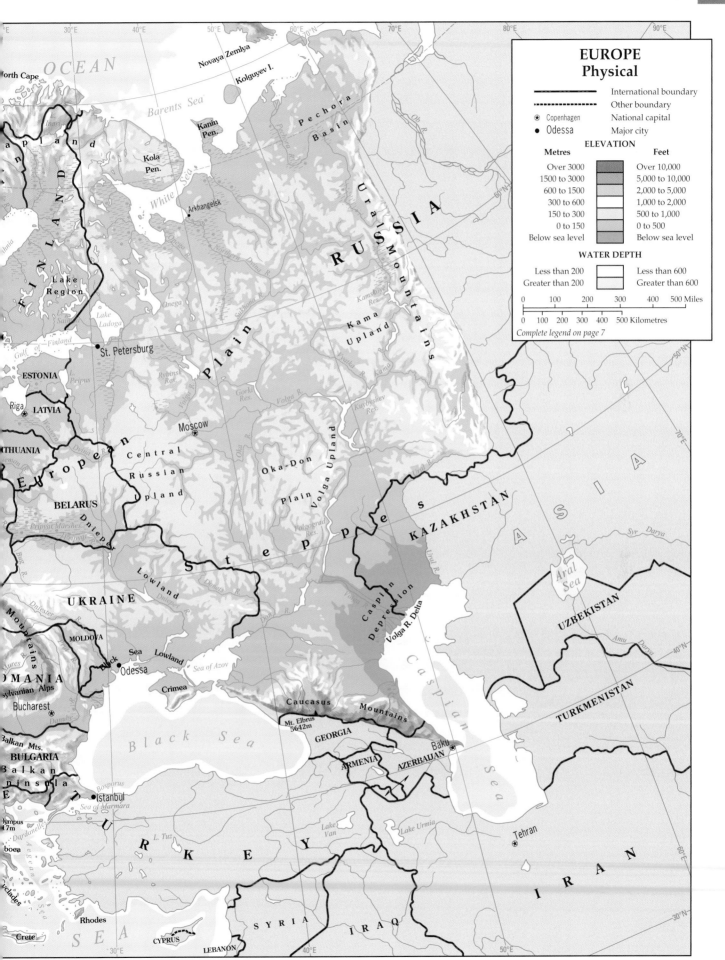

OCEAN

North Cape

Novaya Zemlya

Barents Sea

Kolguyev I.

Kanin
Pen.

Kola
Pen.

Pechora
Basin

Arkhangelsk

FINLAND

Lake
Region

Lake
Ladoga

L. Onega

Kamskoye
Res.

RUSSIA

Ural Mountains

White Sea

Gulf of Finland

St. Petersburg

ESTONIA

L. Peipus

Riga

LATVIA

LITHUANIA

Rybinsk
Res.

Gorky
Res.

Kuybyshev
Res.

Kama
Upland

Moscow

Central

Russian

Upland

BELARUS

Pripyat Marshes

Dnieper

Oka-Don

Plain

Volga Upland

Lowland

UKRAINE

Dniester

MOLDOVA

ROMANIA

Black Sea

Odessa

Crimea

Sea of Azov

Lowland

Volgograd
Res.

Caspian
Depression

Volga R. Delta

KAZAKHSTAN

Aral
Sea

Syr Darya

UZBEKISTAN

Amu Darya

TURKMENISTAN

Transylvanian Alps

Bucharest

Balkan Mts.

BULGARIA

Balkan

Peninsula

Caucasus Mountains

Mt. Elbrus
5642m

GEORGIA

ARMENIA

AZERBAIJAN

Baku

Caspian Sea

TURKEY

Bosporus

Istanbul

Sea of Marmara

Olympus

Dardanelles

boea

L. Tuz

Lake
Van

Lake Urmia

Tehran

IRAN

Rhodes

Crete

SEA

CYPRUS

LEBANON

SYRIA

IRAQ

EUROPE
Physical

————————		International boundary
- - - - - - - - - - -		Other boundary
✸ Copenhagen		National capital
● Odessa		Major city

ELEVATION

Metres		Feet
Over 3000		Over 10,000
1500 to 3000		5,000 to 10,000
600 to 1500		2,000 to 5,000
300 to 600		1,000 to 2,000
150 to 300		500 to 1,000
0 to 150		0 to 500
Below sea level		Below sea level

WATER DEPTH

Less than 200		Less than 600
Greater than 200		Greater than 600

0	100	200	300	400	500 Miles

0	100	200	300	400	500 Kilometres

Complete legend on page 7

ICELAND

Reykjavik

Sursey I. (Iceland)

ARCTIC CIRCLE

PRIME MERIDIAN

ARCTIC

Lofoten Is.

NORWEGIAN SEA

Faeroe Is. (Den.)

Trondheims Fiord

Trondheim

N

Rockall (U.K.)

Shetland Is. (U.K.)

Sogne Fiord

Bergen

Hardanger Fiord

Lillehammer

Bokna Fiord

Oslo

NORWAY

SWEDEN

L. Malaren

Stock

Orkney Is. (U.K.)

Stavanger

L. Vattern

L. Vanern

Norrkoping

Goteborg

SCOTLAND

Glasgow

Edinburgh

NORTH SEA

Skagerrak

Kattegat

Arhus

DENMARK

Copenhagen

Malmo

Bornholm (Den.)

Baltic

NORTHERN IRELAND

Belfast

IRELAND

Dublin

Cork

UNITED KINGDOM

Leeds

ENGLAND

Liverpool

Irish Sea

WALES

Cardiff

Birmingham

Bristol

London

Southampton

Thames R.

Gdansk

RUS

Amsterdam

Ijsselmeer

The Hague

Rotterdam

NETHERLANDS

Hamburg

Rhine R.

Essen

Cologne

Berlin

GERMANY

Poznan

War

POLA

ATLANTIC OCEAN

Celtic Sea

English Channel

Strait of Dover

Le Havre

Channel Is. (U.K.)

Lille

Brussels

BELGIUM

Bonn

LUXEMBOURG

Luxembourg

Frankfurt

Leipzig

Wroclaw

Prague

CZECH REPUBLIC

Krakow

Nantes

Seine R.

Paris

Orleans

Loire R.

FRANCE

Stuttgart

Munich

Danube R.

SLOVA

Bay of Biscay

Limoges

Bordeaux

Bern

SWITZERLAND

Geneva

Lyon

Rhone R.

LIECH

Vaduz

AUSTRIA

Vienna

Bratislava

Graz

HUNGARY

Buda

La Coruna

Porto

Douro R.

Bilbao

Toulouse

Turin

Milan

Po R.

Venice

SLOVENIA

Ljubljana

Szeged

PORTUGAL

Lisbon

Duero R.

Zaragoza

SPAIN

Tagus R.

Madrid

ANDORRA

Barcelona

Marseille

Gulf of Lion

MONACO

Genoa

Ligurian Sea

SAN MARINO

Florence

Tiber R.

CROATIA

Zagreb

BOSNIA

Sarajevo

Belg

SER

Guadiana

Ebro R.

Seville

Guadalquivir R.

Valencia

Balearic Sea

Palma

Balearic Islands (Spain)

Bastia

Corsica (Fr.)

Sardinia (Italy)

Adriatic Sea

Malaga

GIBRALTAR (U.K.)

Strait of Gibraltar

Cagliari

VATICAN CITY

Rome

ITALY

Naples

Bari

Tyrrhenian Sea

Gulf of Taranto

Tirana

S

MACED

ALBANIA

Rabat

Algiers

MEDITERRANEAN

Palermo

Messina

Sicily

Ionian Sea

MOROCCO

AFRICA

ALGERIA

TUNISIA

Tunis

MALTA

Valletta

WESTERN SAHARA (adm. Morocco)

40°W

30°W

20°W

10°W

70°N

0°

10°E

60°N

50°N

40°N

30°N

30°W

20°W

10°W

0°

10°E

20°E

EUROPE
Political

BOUNDARIES

—··—··—··	International boundary
—·—·—·—	Internal boundary
-------------	Other boundary (disputed or undefined)

CITIES

● Barcelona

● Glasgow

• Constanta

⊛ Moscow   National capital

A city's relative size is shown by the size of its symbol and lettering.

0	100	200	300	400	500 Miles

0	100	200	300	400	500 Kilometres

Complete legend on page 7

OCEAN

merfest

Vardo

Barents Sea

Novaya Zemlya

Kolguyev I.

L. Inari

Murmansk

runa

RUSSIA

Oulu

White Sea

Arkhangelsk

Ob R.

Vaasa

FINLAND

Syktyvkar

Onega R.

Northern Dvina R.

Pechora R.

Tampere

L. Saimaa

Lake Ladoga

Sukhona R.

L. Onega

Kamskoye Res.

Perm

Turku

Helsinki

Gulf of Finland

St. Petersburg

Tallin

ESTONIA

L. Peipus

Rybinsk Res.

Vyatka R.

Kama R.

Ufa

Riga

LATVIA

Pskov

Yaroslavl

Gorki Res.

Volga R.

Kazan

Kuybyshev Res.

ITHUANIA

Moscow

Nizhniy Novgorod

Oka R.

Samara

Orenburg

Vilnius

Western Dvina R.

Tula

Volga R.

Ural R.

Minsk

Bryansk

Orel

Oral

A S I A

BELARUS

Voronezh

Saratov

KAZAKHSTAN

Pripyat Marshes

Pripyat R.

Volgograd Res.

Ural R.

Syr Darya

Chernobyl

Bug R.

Kiev

Kharkiv

Donets R.

Volgograd

Volga R.

Aral Sea

Lviv

UKRAINE

Dnieper R.

Donetsk

Don R.

Astrakhan

UZBEKISTAN

Dniester R.

Dnipropetrovsk

Rostov-na-Donu

Amu Darya

MOLDOVA

Chisinau

Odessa

Sea of Azov

Novorossiysk

Groznyy

Caspian Sea

TURKMENISTAN

Cluj-Napoca

Prut R.

Kerch

Krasnodar

OMANIA

Sevastopol

Danube R.

Constanta

Black Sea

GEORGIA

Tbilisi

Ashgabat

Bucharest

Varna

Baku

Sofia

BULGARIA

ARMENIA

Yerevan

AZERBAIJAN

Plovdiv

Bosporus

E

Sea of Marmara

Istanbul

Dardanelles

T U R K E Y

Lake Van

Lake Urmia

Tehran

essaloniki

Aegean Sea

boea

Ankara

L. Tuz

I R A N

Athens

S E A

Nicosia

SYRIA

IRAQ

CYPRUS

Crete (Greece)

LEBANON

ATLANTIC OCEAN

Norwegian Sea

Shetland Is. (U.K.)

Bergen

NORWAY **SWEDEN**

Oslo

Stavanger

Kristiansand

Cape Lindesnes

Hardanger Fjord

Sogne Fiord

Bohin Fjord

Lake Vanern

Goteborg

Orkney Is.

Stornoway

Wick

The Minch

Outer Hebrides

Inner Hebrides

Inverness

Moray Firth

Loch Ness

H i g h l a n d s

Ben Nevis 1343m

Grampian Mts.

Aberdeen

SCOTLAND

Dundee

Firth of Forth

Edinburgh

Glasgow

Ayr

North Sea

Skagerrak

DENMARK

Alborg

Arhus

Helsingborg

Kattegat

Copenhagen

Malmo

Esbjerg

Odense

Fyn

Sjaelland

Jutland

55°N

N

Londonderry

NORTHERN IRELAND

Belfast

U N I T E D K I N G D O M

Great Britain

Donegal Bay

North Channel

Sligo

Dundalk

IRELAND

Galway

Dublin

Irish Sea

Newcastle upon Tyne

Pennines

Isle of Man

ENGLAND

Bradford

York

Leeds

Hull

Liverpool

Manchester

Sheffield

Nottingham

Kiel

Lubeck

Hamburg

Bremen

Elbe R.

Magdeburg

Hannover

W. Frisian Is. E. Frisian Is.

Groningen

NETHERLANDS

IJsselmeer

Amsterdam

The Hague

Utrecht

Arnhem

Rotterdam

Essen

Dortmund

Dusseldorf

Cologne

GERMANY

Erfurt

Galway Bay

Shannon R.

St. George's Channel

Limerick

Tralee

Waterford

Cork

Cobh

Barrow R.

Wicklow Mts.

Celtic Sea

Colwyn Bay

Cambrian Mts.

Aberystwyth

WALES

Cardiff

Stoke-on-Trent

Leicester

Birmingham

Coventry

Stratford-upon-Avon

Oxford

Norwich

The Wash

Cambridge

Ipswich

London

Thames R.

Bristol

Bath

Bristol Channel

Dover

Canterbury

Strait of Dover

Flanders

Ghent

Antwerp

Lille

BELGIUM

Brussels

Liege

Bonn

Rhine R.

Frankfurt

Mannheim

Stuttgart

50°N

Exeter

Southampton

Portsmouth

Plymouth

Isle of Wight

Land's End

Calais

English Channel

Amiens

Oise R.

Reims

Meuse R.

LUXEMBOURG

Luxembourg

Ardennes

Verdun

Metz

Nancy

Alsace

Black Forest

Strasbourg

Danube R.

Bavarian Plateau

Channel Islands (U.K.)

Cherbourg

Le Havre

Rouen

Paris Basin

Seine R.

Marne R.

Bavarian

Caen

Normandy

Gulf of St. Malo

Paris

Versailles

Chartres

Paris Basin

Champagne

Brest

St. Malo

Brittany

Rennes

Le Mans

Le Mans

Orleans

Loire R.

Burgundy

Dijon

Mulhouse

Basel

Zurich

LIECHTENSTEIN

AUSTRIA

Angers

Tours

Vienne R.

Cher R.

Saone R.

Besancon

Doubs R.

Bern

SWITZERLAND

Rhine R.

Nantes

FRANCE

La Rochelle

Bay of Biscay

Limoges

Clermont-Ferrand

St. Etienne

Vichy

Allier R.

Lyon

Geneva

L. Geneva

Mt.Blanc 4807m

Rhone R.

Milan

Grenoble

Turin

Po R.

45°N

Bordeaux

Gironde R.

Dordogne R.

Lot R.

Massif Central

Aquitaine Basin

Garonne R.

Toulouse

Nimes

Montpellier

Avignon

Aix-en-Provence

Rhone R.

Durance R.

Marseille

Riviera

MONACO

Nice

Toulon

Ligurian Sea

ITALY

Genoa

Santander

San Sebastian

Bilbao

Pyrenees

Pau

Narbonne

Perpignan

Gulf of Lions

Corsica

Bastia

Ebro R.

Andorra la Vella

ANDORRA

Mediterranean Sea

Ajaccio

SPAIN

Zaragoza

Duero R.

Barcelona

Strait of Bonifacio

WESTERN EUROPE
Political

BOUNDARIES

—·—·—·—	International boundary
—·—·—·—	Internal boundary

CITIES

● **London**   A city's relative size is
● Cologne   shown by the size of
· Limerick   its symbol and lettering.

✪ **Paris**   National capital

0	50	100	150	200 Miles

0	50	100	150	200 Kilometres

Complete legend on page 7

CENTRAL EUROPE
Political

BOUNDARIES

—··—··— International boundary

———— Internal boundary (republic or territory)

CITIES

● Milan

● Bremen

· Salzburg

☆ Warsaw — National capital

A city's relative size is shown by the size of its symbol and lettering.

0 50 100 150 200 Miles

0 50 100 150 200 Kilometres

Complete legend on page 7

North Sea

SWEDEN
Goteborg · Jonkoping · Visby · Gotland (Sweden) · Oland

DENMARK
Alborg · Arhus · Esbjerg · Copenhagen · Helsingborg · Malmo · Schleswig · Kiel · Fyn · Odense · Sjaelland · Jutland

Skagerrak · Kattegat · Bornholm (Den.) · Rugen

LATVIA · Riga · Gulf of Riga
LITHUANIA · Kaunas · Vilnius · Neman R.
ESTONIA
BELARUS · Hrodna

Baltic Sea · Gulf of Gdansk · Kaliningrad TO RUSSIA

POLAND
Gdynia · Gdansk · Elblag · Bialystok · Szczecin · Bydgoszcz · Poznan · Wloclawek · ☆ Warsaw · Kalisz · Lodz · Radom · Lublin · Wroclaw · Czestochowa · Ostrowiec · Katowice · Krakow · Przemysl
Pomerania · Northern European Plain · Warta R. · Vistula R. · Bug R. · Odra R.

GERMANY
Bremerhaven · Bremen · Hamburg · Lubeck · Rostock · Hannover · Berlin · Brandenburg · Potsdam · Magdeburg · Braunschweig · Bielefeld · Munster · Dortmund · Essen · Kassel · Halle · Leipzig · Dresden · Erfurt · Chemnitz · Aachen · Bonn · Cologne · Dusseldorf · Wiesbaden · Frankfurt · Mannheim · Bayreuth · Nuremberg · Regensberg · Stuttgart · Ulm · Augsburg · Munich
Mittelland Canal · Elbe R. · Spree R. · Weser R. · Main R. · Danube · Ore Mts. · Black Forest

NETHERLANDS · Amsterdam · The Hague · Rotterdam
W. Frisian Is. · E. Frisian Is.
BELGIUM · Liege
LUXEMBOURG · Luxembourg
FRANCE · Basel · Alsace · Rhine R.

CZECH REPUBLIC · Prague · Plzen · Bohemia · Ostrava · Brno · Moravia · Moravia R.

SLOVAKIA · Bratislava · Kosice · Carpathian Mountains

SWITZERLAND · Zurich · Bern · Vaduz · Geneva · Mt. Blanc 4807m
LIECHTENSTEIN
L. Constance · L. Como · L. Geneva · Rhone R. · Adige R. · Po R.

AUSTRIA · Linz · Salzburg · Vienna · Innsbruck · Graz · Klagenfurt · Bolzano

HUNGARY · Budapest · Miskolc · Debrecen · Szeged · Pecs · Subotica · Great Hungarian Plain · L. Balaton · Danube R. · Tisza R. · Drava R. · Mures R.

SLOVENIA · Ljubljana · Maribor
CROATIA · Zagreb · Rijeka · Osijek · Banja Luka · Zadar · Split · Sava R.
BOSNIA-HERZEGOVINA · Sarajevo · Mostar · Dinaric Alps · Dalmatia · Dubrovnik
SERBIA-MONTENEGRO · Belgrade · Novi Sad · Cacak · Krusevac · Nis · Pec · Pristina · Podgorica · Morava R.

ROMANIA · Satu Mare · Oradea · Cluj-Napoca · Timisoara · Brasov · Braila · Galati · Ploiesti · Bucharest · Craiova · Constanta · Transylvanian Alps · Danube Delta · Olt R. · Danube R.

UKRAINE · Lviv · Chernivtsi · Zhytomyr · Dniester R. · Dnieper Lowland · Dnieper R.
MOLDOVA · Iasi · Chisinau · Odessa · Prut R. · Black Sea Lowland

Black Sea

BULGARIA · Sofia · Varna · Burgas · Ruse · Plovdiv · Balkan Mountains · Rhodope Mts. · Maritsa R.

MACEDONIA · Skopje · Bitola
ALBANIA · Tirana · Korce
TURKEY · Istanbul · Edirne · Bursa · Izmir · Bosporus · Sea of Marmara · Dardanelles

GREECE · Thessaloniki · Serrai · Xanthi · Florina · Larisa · Volos · Lamia · Agrinion · Patras · Piraeus · Athens · Mt. Olympus 2917m · Pindus Mts. · Vardar R. · Aegean Sea · Thasos · Samothrace · Lemnos · Lesbos · Chios · Samos · Euboea · Sporades · Cyclades · Dodecanese · Rhodes · Corfu · Ionian Islands · Peloponnesus · Sea of Crete · Khania · Iraklion · Crete

ITALY · Turin · Milan · Genoa · Brescia · Verona · Padua · Venice · Trieste · Parma · Modena · Bologna · Ferrara · Carrara · Pisa · Florence · Rimini · Ancona · Livorno · Perugia · Rome · VATICAN CITY · Naples · Foggia · Bari · Brindisi · Taranto · Salerno · Cosenza · Catanzaro · Reggio di Calabria · Messina · Catania · Palermo · Mt. Vesuvius 1277m · Mt. Etna 3323m
SAN MARINO · MONACO · Nice · Riviera · Apennines · Ligurian Sea · Adriatic Sea · Tyrrhenian Sea · Ionian Sea · Tiber R. · Strait of Messina · Gulf of Taranto
Corsica (Fr.) · Bastia · Ajaccio · Elba · Sardinia · Sassari · Cagliari · Sicily · Lipari Is. · Pantelleria (It.) · Lampedusa (It.)
MALTA · Valletta · Maltese Is. · Strait of Bonifacio

Mediterranean Sea

ALGERIA · Annaba · Tunis · Carthage
TUNISIA · Sfax

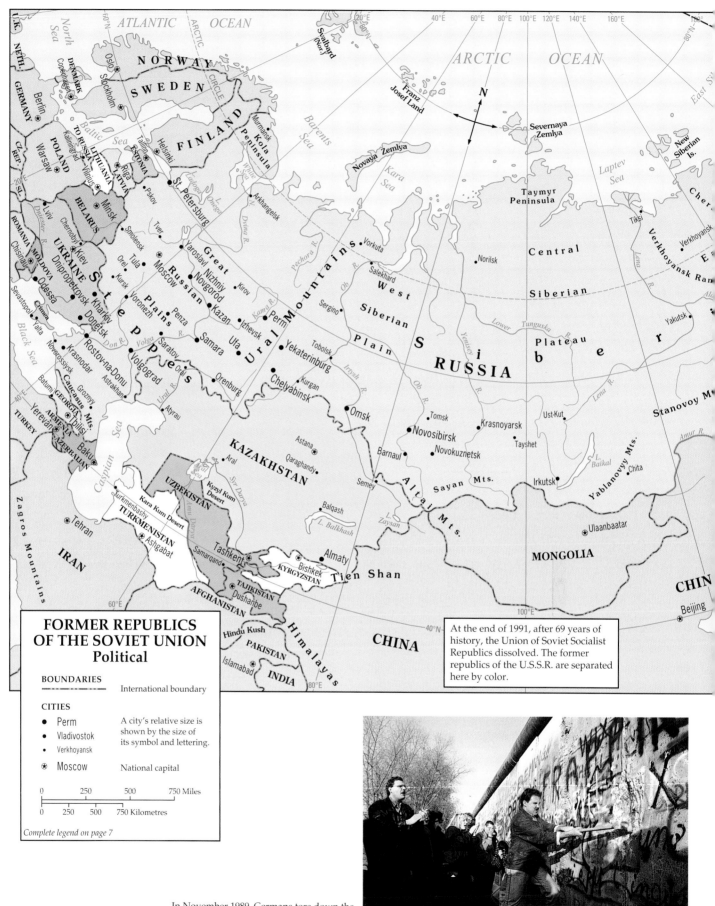

ATLANTIC OCEAN

ARCTIC OCEAN

U.K.
NETH.
GERMANY
Berlin
CZECH REP.
SL.
POLAND
Warsaw
TO RUSSIA
Kaliningrad
LITHUANIA
Vilnius
ROMANIA
Chisinau
MOLDOVA
UKRAINE
Lviv
Dniester
BELARUS
Minsk
Chernobyl
Kiev
Dnipropetrovsk
Kharkiv
Donetsk
Odessa
Sevastopol
Crimea
Yalta
Black Sea
Novorossiysk
Krasnodar
Rostov-na-Donu
Batumi
GEORGIA
Tbilisi
Caucasus Mts.
ARMENIA
Yerevan
AZERBAIJAN
Baku
TURKEY
Zagros Mountains
Tehran
IRAN

DENMARK
Copenhagen
NORWAY
Oslo
Stockholm
SWEDEN
Baltic Sea
ESTONIA
Tallinn
Riga
LATVIA
Pskov
FINLAND
Helsinki
St. Petersburg
L. Onega
Murmansk
Kola Peninsula
White Sea
Arkhangelsk
N. Dvina R.
Tver
Smolensk
Yaroslavl
Moscow
Nizhniy Novgorod
Orel
Tula
Kursk
Voronezh
Penza
Great Russian Plains
Kazan
Izhevsk
Samara
Volga R.
Saratov
Don R.
Volgograd
Astrakhan
Ural R.
Atyrau
Caspian Sea

Svalbard (Nor.)
ARCTIC CIRCLE
Barents Sea
Franz Josef Land
Novaya Zemlya
Kara Sea
Severnaya Zemlya
N
Pechora R.
Vorkuta
Salekhard
Ural Mountains
Perm
Yekaterinburg
Kama R.
Ufa
Orenburg
Chelyabinsk
Kurgan
Omsk
Ob R.
Tobolsk
Irtysh R.
Sergino
West Siberian Plain
Astana
Qaraghandy
KAZAKHSTAN
Semey
Aral
Aral Sea
Kyzyl Kum Desert
Syr Darya
Balqash
L. Balkhash
Altai Mts.
L. Zaysan

Taymyr Peninsula
Laptev Sea
New Siberian Is.
Tiksi
Verkhoyansk
Verkhoyansk Range
E
Central Siberian Plateau
Siberia
RUSSIA
Norilsk
Yenisey R.
Lower Tunguska
Yakutsk
Lena R.
Tomsk
Novosibirsk
Krasnoyarsk
Tayshet
Novokuznetsk
Barnaul
Sayan Mts.
Ust-Kut
Irkutsk
L. Baikal
Yablonovyy Mts.
Chita
Stanovoy Mts.
Amur R.
MONGOLIA
Ulaanbaatar
East Si
Cher
Ala

Turkmenbashy
Kara Kum Desert
TURKMENISTAN
Ashgabat
Amu Darya
UZBEKISTAN
Samarqand
Tashkent
KYRGYZSTAN
Bishkek
TAJIKISTAN
Dushanbe
Almaty
Tien Shan
AFGHANISTAN
Hindu Kush
PAKISTAN
Islamabad
Himalayas
INDIA
CHINA
Beijing
CHIN

FORMER REPUBLICS OF THE SOVIET UNION
Political

BOUNDARIES

International boundary

CITIES

● **Perm**

● Vladivostok

• Verkhoyansk

⊛ Moscow   National capital

A city's relative size is shown by the size of its symbol and lettering.

0   250   500   750 Miles

0   250   500   750 Kilometres

Complete legend on page 7

At the end of 1991, after 69 years of history, the Union of Soviet Socialist Republics dissolved. The former republics of the U.S.S.R. are separated here by color.

In November 1989, Germans tore down the Berlin Wall. It was an event that symbolized the collapse of over 40 years of Communist rule in Eastern Europe.

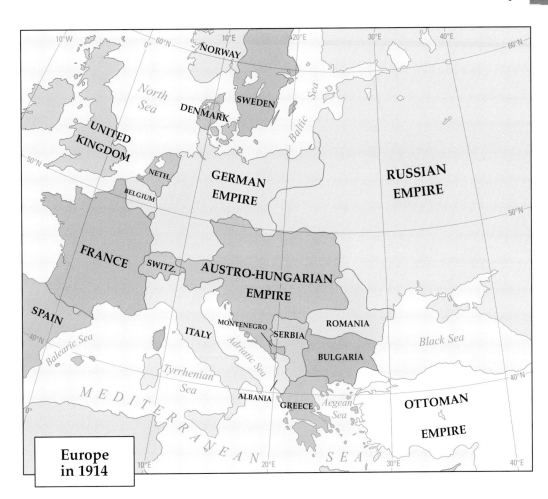

Europe in 1914

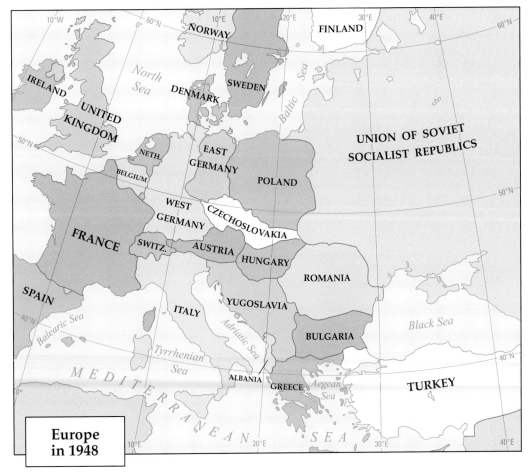

Twentieth-century Europe saw radical changes in governments and boundaries. World War I brought the break-up of imperialistic monarchies and the formation of new, smaller states. Some of these, like Czechoslovakia, acquired democratic governments only to fall to Communism after World War II. Then, between 1989 and 1992, all the Communist governments of Europe were overthrown, and again new nations were formed.

Europe in 1948

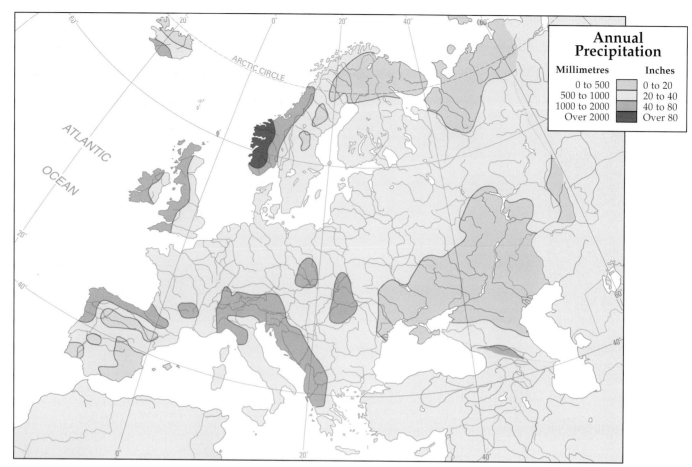

Annual Precipitation

Millimetres		Inches
0 to 500		0 to 20
500 to 1000		20 to 40
1000 to 2000		40 to 80
Over 2000		Over 80

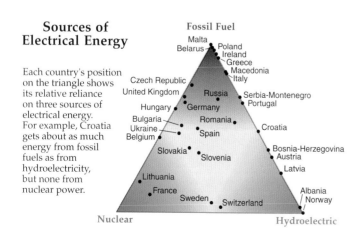

Vienna, Austria's capital, is the most prosperous city in Central Europe. Austria stands at the crossroads between former Communist states and democratically governed countries.

UNITED KINGDOM Area Comparison

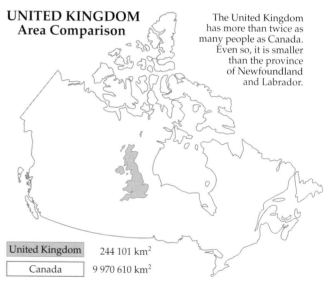

The United Kingdom has more than twice as many people as Canada. Even so, it is smaller than the province of Newfoundland and Labrador.

United Kingdom	244 101 km²
Canada	9 970 610 km²

Sources of Electrical Energy

Each country's position on the triangle shows its relative reliance on three sources of electrical energy. For example, Croatia gets about as much energy from fossil fuels as from hydroelectricity, but none from nuclear power.

Fossil Fuel

Malta
Belarus
Poland
Ireland
Greece
Macedonia
Italy
Czech Republic
United Kingdom
Serbia-Montenegro
Portugal
Russia
Hungary
Germany
Bulgaria
Romania
Ukraine
Spain
Croatia
Belgium
Slovakia
Bosnia-Herzegovina
Slovenia
Austria
Lithuania
Latvia
France
Sweden
Switzerland
Albania
Norway

Nuclear

Hydroelectric

The Alps are an important region for farming and industry as well as a major tourist attraction. Railways crisscross the mountains that were a barrier to travel for centuries.

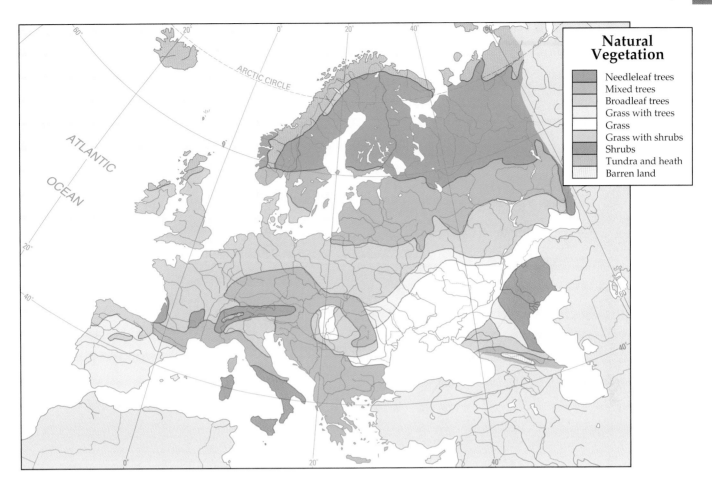

Natural Vegetation

- Needleleaf trees
- Mixed trees
- Broadleaf trees
- Grass with trees
- Grass
- Grass with shrubs
- Shrubs
- Tundra and heath
- Barren land

ARCTIC CIRCLE

ATLANTIC OCEAN

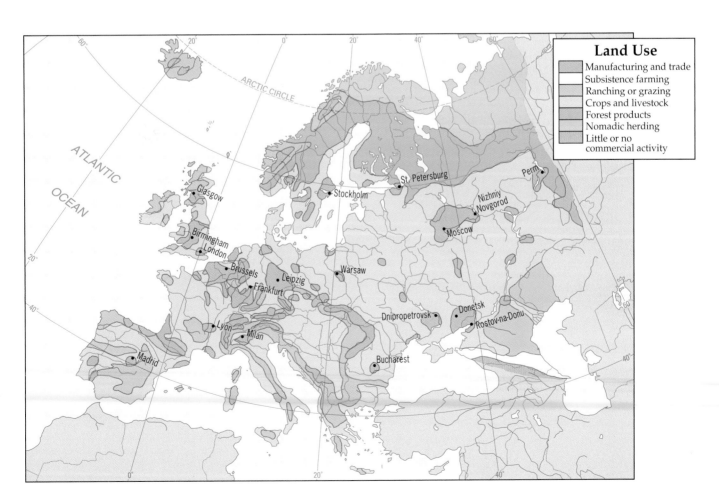

Land Use

- Manufacturing and trade
- Subsistence farming
- Ranching or grazing
- Crops and livestock
- Forest products
- Nomadic herding
- Little or no commercial activity

ARCTIC CIRCLE

ATLANTIC OCEAN

Glasgow

Stockholm

St. Petersburg

Perm

Nizhniy Novgorod

Birmingham
London

Brussels

Moscow

Leipzig

Warsaw

Frankfurt

Lyon

Dnipropetrovsk

Donetsk

Milan

Rostov-na-Donu

Madrid

Bucharest

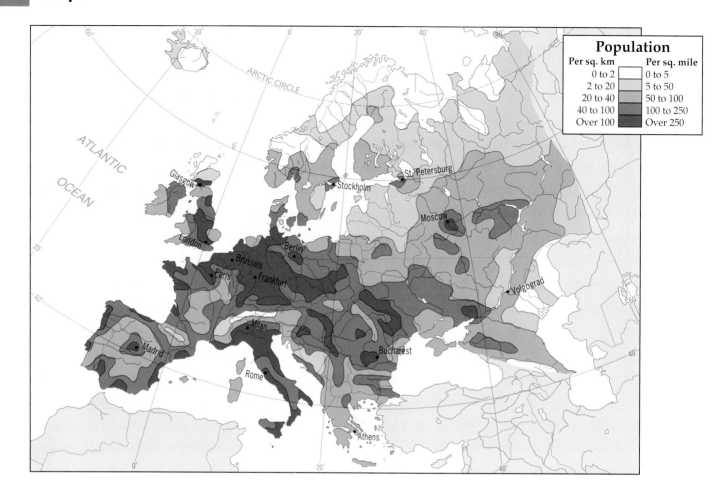

Population

Per sq. km		Per sq. mile
	0 to 2	0 to 5
	2 to 20	5 to 50
	20 to 40	50 to 100
	40 to 100	100 to 250
	Over 100	Over 250

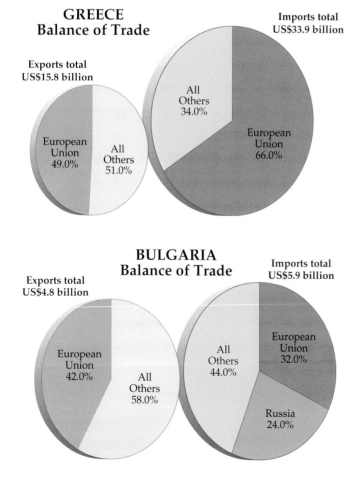

GREECE
Balance of Trade

Exports total
US$15.8 billion

Imports total
US$33.9 billion

European Union 49.0%
All Others 51.0%

All Others 34.0%
European Union 66.0%

BULGARIA
Balance of Trade

Exports total
US$4.8 billion

Imports total
US$5.9 billion

European Union 42.0%
All Others 58.0%

All Others 44.0%
European Union 32.0%
Russia 24.0%

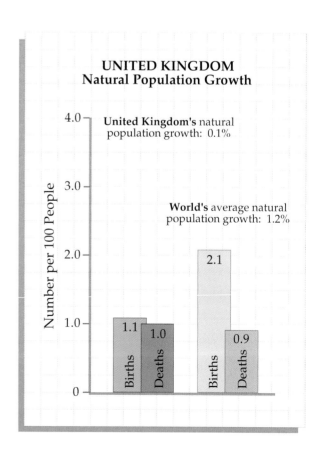

UNITED KINGDOM
Natural Population Growth

United Kingdom's natural population growth: 0.1%

World's average natural population growth: 1.2%

Number per 100 People

4.0

3.0

2.0

1.0

0

1.1 Births
1.0 Deaths

2.1 Births
0.9 Deaths

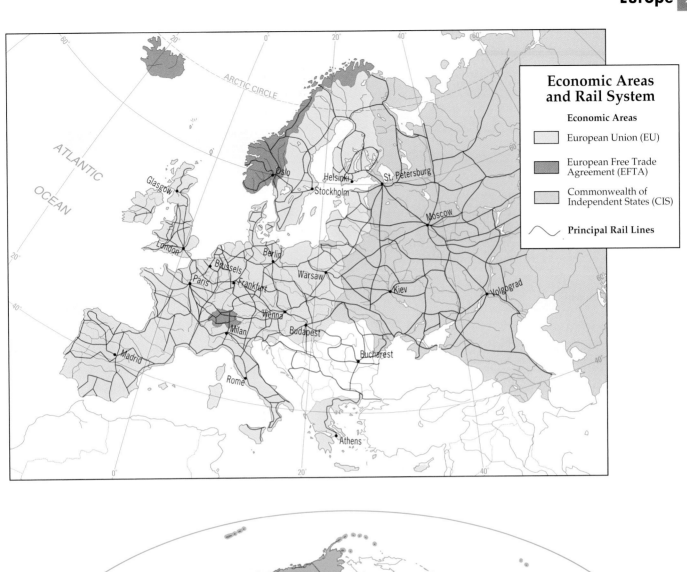

Economic Areas and Rail System

Economic Areas

- European Union (EU)
- European Free Trade Agreement (EFTA)
- Commonwealth of Independent States (CIS)
- ‍Principal Rail Lines

Western European Imperialism

- Colonizing countries of Western Europe
- Past and present colonies and other territories of Western European countries

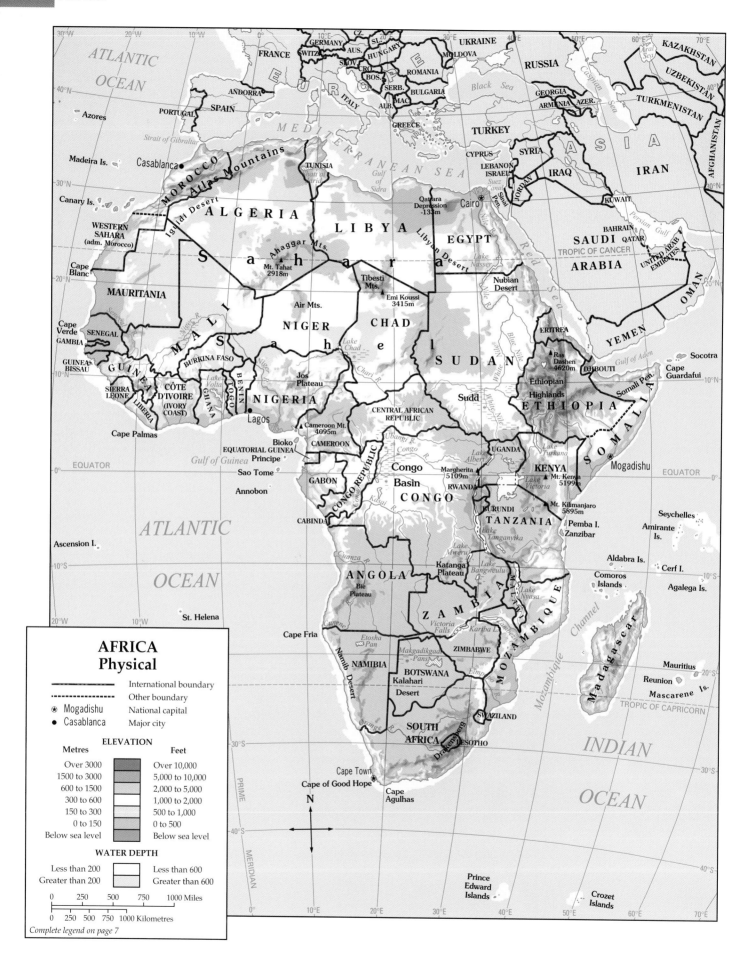

**AFRICA
Physical**

International boundary
Other boundary
⊛ Mogadishu   National capital
● Casablanca   Major city

ELEVATION

Metres	Feet
Over 3000	Over 10,000
1500 to 3000	5,000 to 10,000
600 to 1500	2,000 to 5,000
300 to 600	1,000 to 2,000
150 to 300	500 to 1,000
0 to 150	0 to 500
Below sea level	Below sea level

WATER DEPTH

Less than 200	Less than 600
Greater than 200	Greater than 600

0   250   500   750   1000 Miles

0   250 500 750 1000 Kilometres

Complete legend on page 7

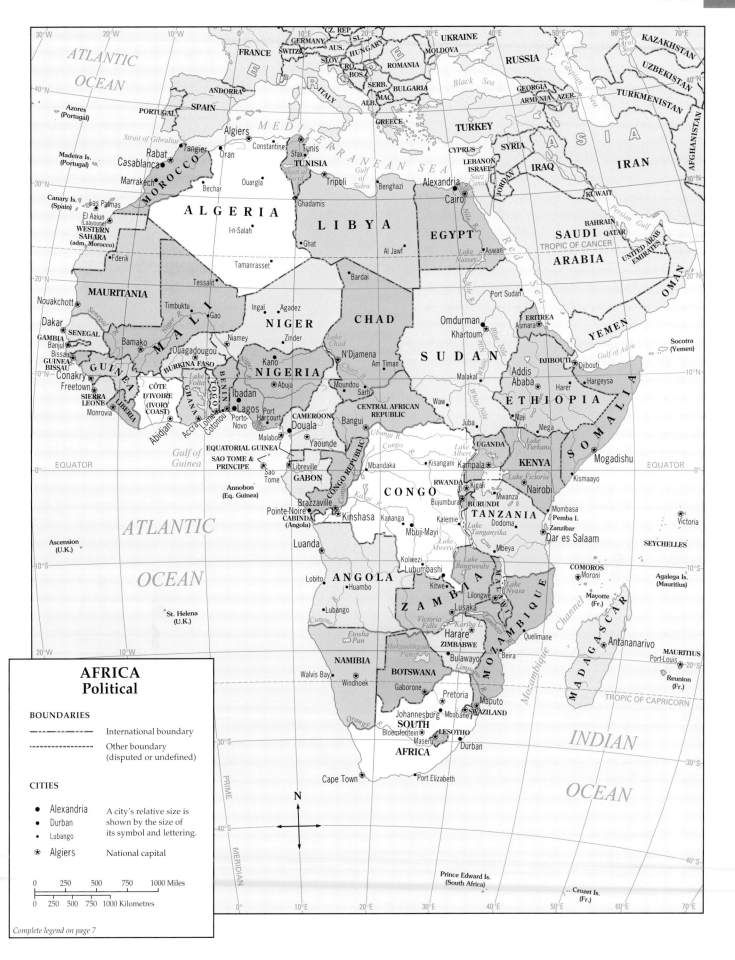

AFRICA
Political

BOUNDARIES

— ·· — ·· — International boundary

------------- Other boundary
(disputed or undefined)

CITIES

● **Alexandria**   A city's relative size is
● **Durban**   shown by the size of
· Lubango   its symbol and lettering.

⊛ **Algiers**   National capital

0	250	500	750	1000 Miles
0	250	500	750	1000 Kilometres

Complete legend on page 7

N

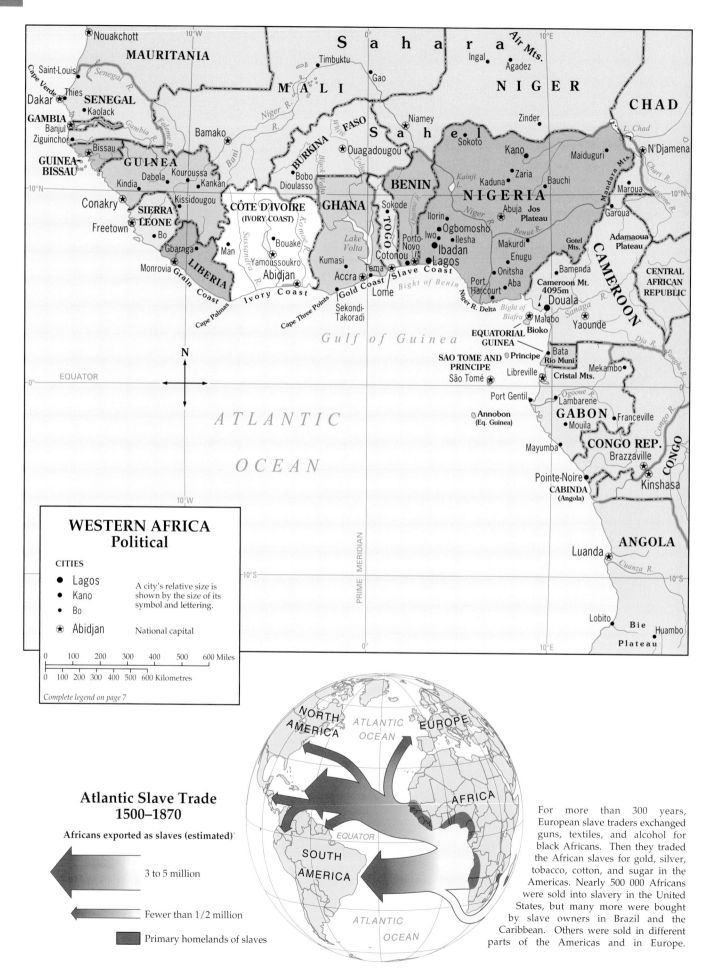

WESTERN AFRICA
Political

CITIES

● **Lagos**

● **Kano**

• **Bo**

A city's relative size is shown by the size of its symbol and lettering.

✪ **Abidjan** National capital

0 100 200 300 400 500 600 Miles

0 100 200 300 400 500 600 Kilometres

Complete legend on page 7

Atlantic Slave Trade
1500–1870

Africans exported as slaves (estimated)

3 to 5 million

Fewer than 1/2 million

■ Primary homelands of slaves

For more than 300 years, European slave traders exchanged guns, textiles, and alcohol for black Africans. Then they traded the African slaves for gold, silver, tobacco, cotton, and sugar in the Americas. Nearly 500 000 Africans were sold into slavery in the United States, but many more were bought by slave owners in Brazil and the Caribbean. Others were sold in different parts of the Americas and in Europe.

SOUTH AFRICA
Political

CITIES

● Soweto   A city's relative size is shown by the size of its symbol and lettering.

• Bisho

✪ Pretoria   National capital

| 0 | 100 | 200 | 300 Miles |
| 0 | 100 | 200 | 300 Kilometres |

Complete legend on page 7

SOUTH AFRICA
Balance of Trade

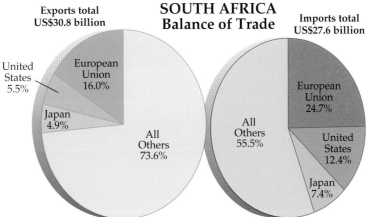

Exports total US$30.8 billion

- United States 5.5%
- European Union 16.0%
- Japan 4.9%
- All Others 73.6%

Imports total US$27.6 billion

- European Union 24.7%
- United States 12.4%
- Japan 7.4%
- All Others 55.5%

Ethnic Composition of South Africa

Many new groups have entered South Africa since 1994 while many former residents have left. Migration and population growth continue to alter the country's ethnic composition.

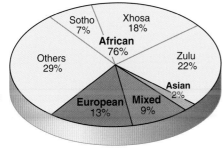

African 76%
- Sotho 7%
- Xhosa 18%
- Zulu 22%
- Asian 2%
- Mixed 9%
- European 13%
- Others 29%

South Africa's total population: 41.5 million

The end of legal apartheid in 1994 gave the children of South Africa a new future with majority rule.

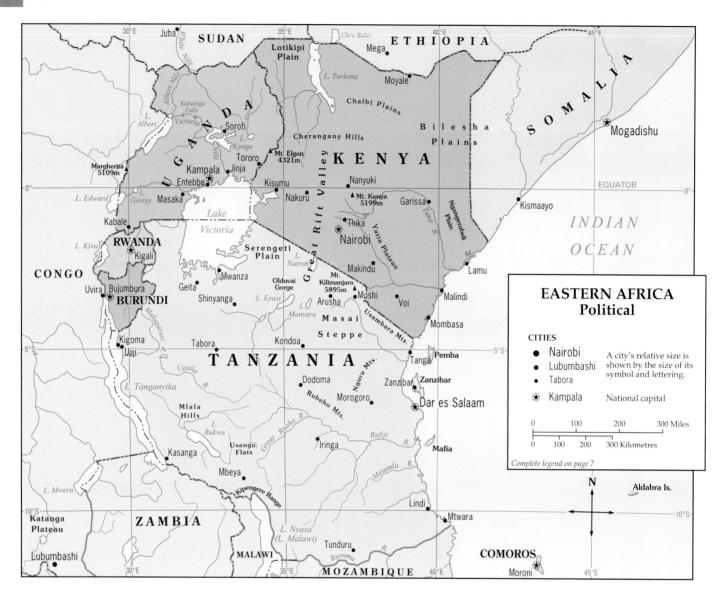

EASTERN AFRICA
Political

CITIES

● Nairobi	A city's relative size is shown by the size of its symbol and lettering.
● Lubumbashi	
● Tabora	
✪ Kampala	National capital

0   100   200   300 Miles

0 100 200 300 Kilometres

Complete legend on page 7

N

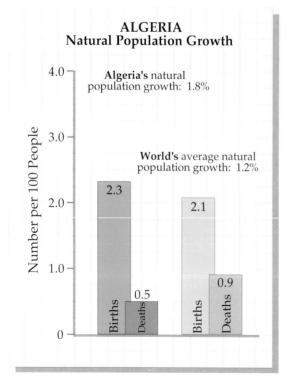

ALGERIA
Natural Population Growth

Algeria's natural population growth: 1.8%

World's average natural population growth: 1.2%

Number per 100 People

4.0

3.0

2.0 — 2.3 (Births) — 0.5 (Deaths)

2.0 — 2.1 (Births) — 0.9 (Deaths)

1.0

0

Rise to Independence 1940 to Today

☐ Independent

▨ Nonindependent

Today

1940

At the beginning of 1940, almost all of Africa was ruled by European colonial powers. But in the following years, a move toward independence swept the continent. Today, the only nonindependent area left is Western Sahara, which is controlled by Morocco.

The cheetah, a hunter of incredible speed, is losing both its habitat and prey to human encroachment into its territory.

Endangered Species

Present range of species

- ☐ Cheetah
- ▨ Black Rhinoceros
- ▩ Mountain Gorilla
- ▧ North African Ostrich

The cheetah, black rhino, ostrich, and gorilla are only four of the many endangered species that once freely roamed Africa.

The black rhinoceros lives on grassland and brush vegetation. Its distinctive horn makes it a target for poachers.

The mountain gorilla leads a quiet life, living off forest vegetation. It has no real enemies except human beings.

The flightless ostrich can roam the plains for long periods without water. Demand for its skin and plumes threaten its survival in the wild.

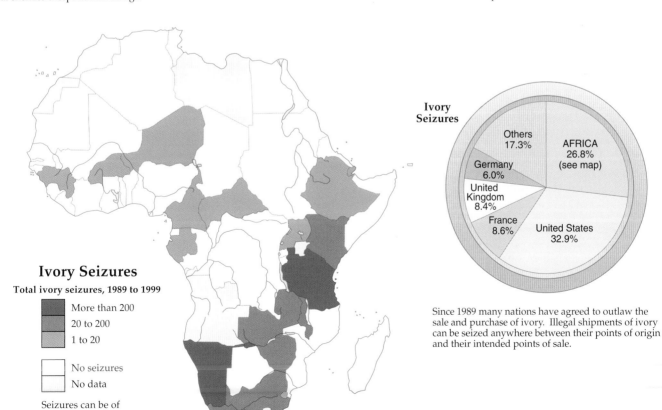

Ivory Seizures

Total ivory seizures, 1989 to 1999

- ▪ More than 200
- ▨ 20 to 200
- ▧ 1 to 20

- ☐ No seizures
- ☐ No data

Seizures can be of any amount of ivory.

Ivory Seizures

Others 17.3%
AFRICA 26.8% (see map)
Germany 6.0%
United Kingdom 8.4%
France 8.6%
United States 32.9%

Since 1989 many nations have agreed to outlaw the sale and purchase of ivory. Illegal shipments of ivory can be seized anywhere between their points of origin and their intended points of sale.

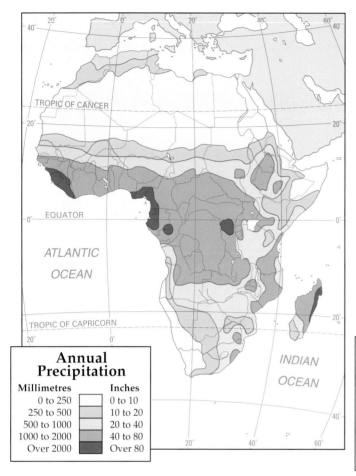

Annual Precipitation

Millimetres	Inches
0 to 250	0 to 10
250 to 500	10 to 20
500 to 1000	20 to 40
1000 to 2000	40 to 80
Over 2000	Over 80

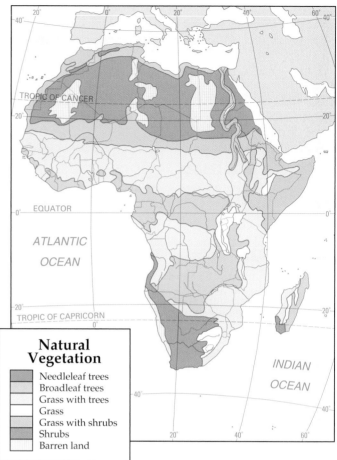

Natural Vegetation

- Needleleaf trees
- Broadleaf trees
- Grass with trees
- Grass
- Grass with shrubs
- Shrubs
- Barren land

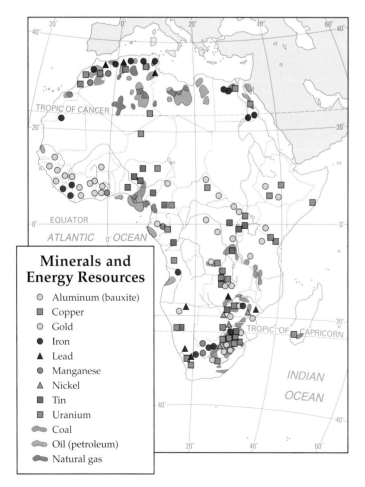

Minerals and Energy Resources

- ◯ Aluminum (bauxite)
- ▢ Copper
- ◯ Gold
- ● Iron
- ▲ Lead
- ● Manganese
- △ Nickel
- ▪ Tin
- ▪ Uranium
- ▬ Coal
- ▬ Oil (petroleum)
- ▬ Natural gas

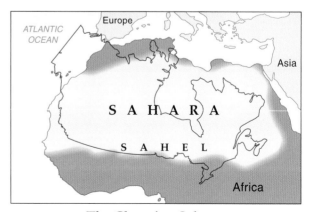

A Moroccan market displays locally grown produce and handwoven carpets. Many Moroccans and other North Africans dress in traditional Islamic style.

The Changing Sahara

The Sahara stretches across a greater area than mainland Canada. During droughts it expands southward and in wet periods it shrinks back. Most recent years have been dry.

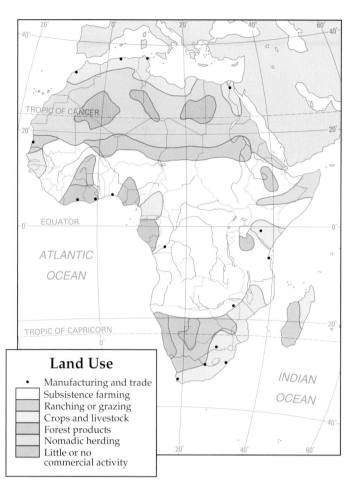

Land Use

- • Manufacturing and trade
- Subsistence farming
- Ranching or grazing
- Crops and livestock
- Forest products
- Nomadic herding
- Little or no commercial activity

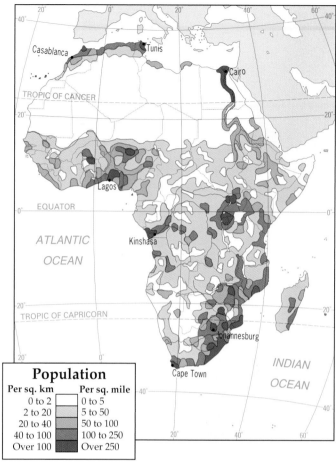

Population

Per sq. km	Per sq. mile
0 to 2	0 to 5
2 to 20	5 to 50
20 to 40	50 to 100
40 to 100	100 to 250
Over 100	Over 250

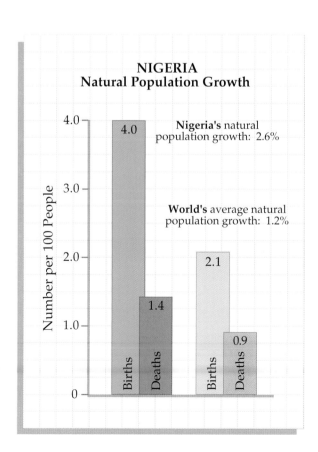

NIGERIA
Natural Population Growth

Nigeria's natural population growth: 2.6%

World's average natural population growth: 1.2%

Number per 100 People

Births 4.0
Deaths 1.4
Births 2.1
Deaths 0.9

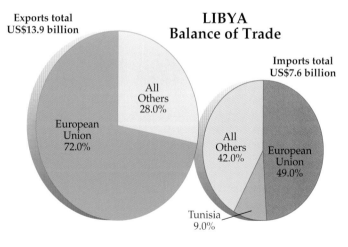

Exports total US$13.9 billion

LIBYA
Balance of Trade

All Others 28.0%

European Union 72.0%

Imports total US$7.6 billion

All Others 42.0%

European Union 49.0%

Tunisia 9.0%

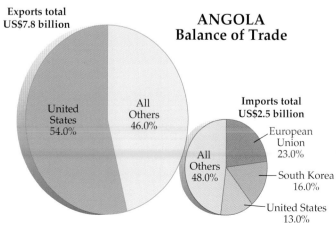

Exports total US$7.8 billion

ANGOLA
Balance of Trade

United States 54.0%

All Others 46.0%

Imports total US$2.5 billion

All Others 48.0%

European Union 23.0%

South Korea 16.0%

United States 13.0%

MEDITERRANEAN BASIN AND PERSIAN GULF
Political

BOUNDARIES

——·——·—— International boundary

------------ Other boundary (disputed or undefined)

CITIES

● Giza

● Seville

· Rasht

✪ Algiers   National capital

A city's relative size is shown by the size of its symbol and lettering.

National capital

| 0 | 100 | 200 | 300 | 400 | 500 Miles |

| 0 | 100 | 200 | 300 | 400 | 500 Kilometres |

Complete legend on page 7

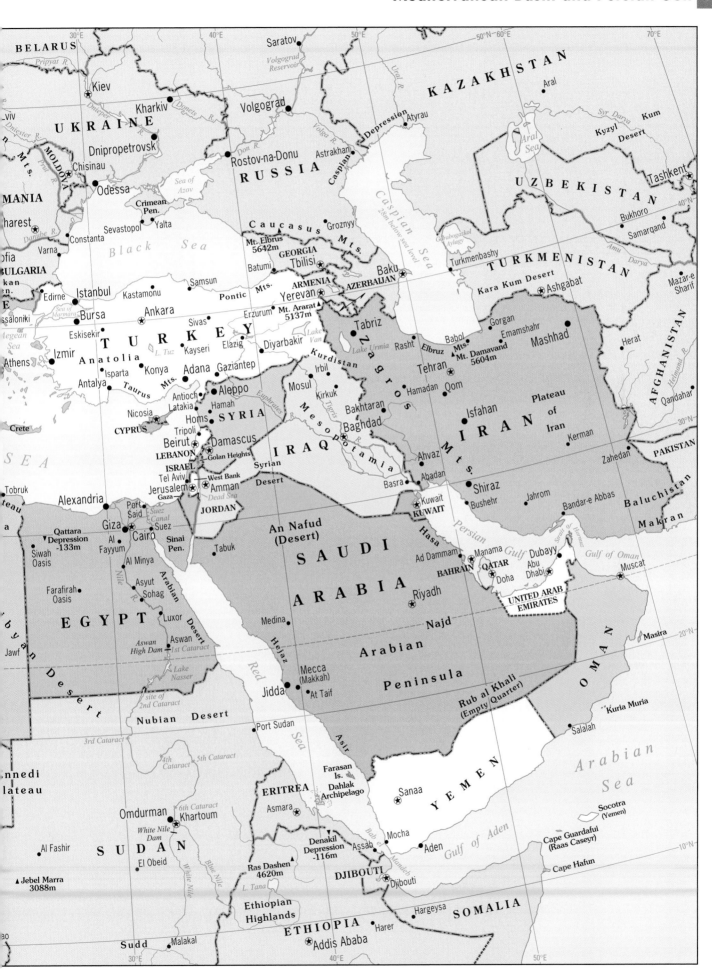

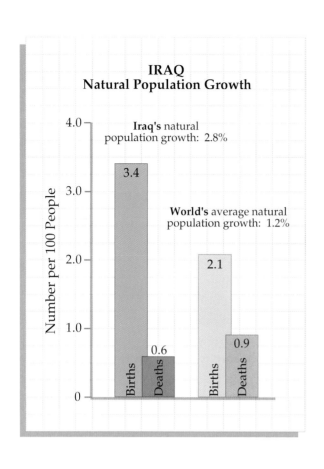

IRAQ
Natural Population Growth

Iraq's natural population growth: 2.8%

World's average natural population growth: 1.2%

Number per 100 People

- Births 3.4
- Deaths 0.6
- Births 2.1
- Deaths 0.9

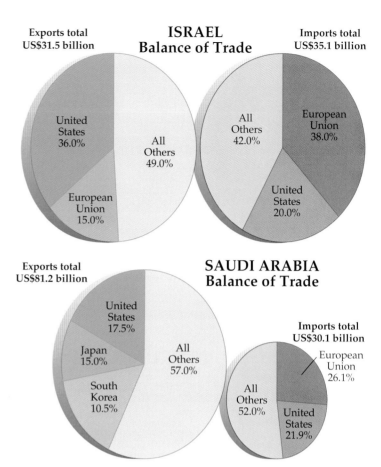

ISRAEL
Balance of Trade

Exports total US$31.5 billion
- United States 36.0%
- All Others 49.0%
- European Union 15.0%

Imports total US$35.1 billion
- All Others 42.0%
- European Union 38.0%
- United States 20.0%

SAUDI ARABIA
Balance of Trade

Exports total US$81.2 billion
- United States 17.5%
- Japan 15.0%
- South Korea 10.5%
- All Others 57.0%

Imports total US$30.1 billion
- European Union 26.1%
- All Others 52.0%
- United States 21.9%

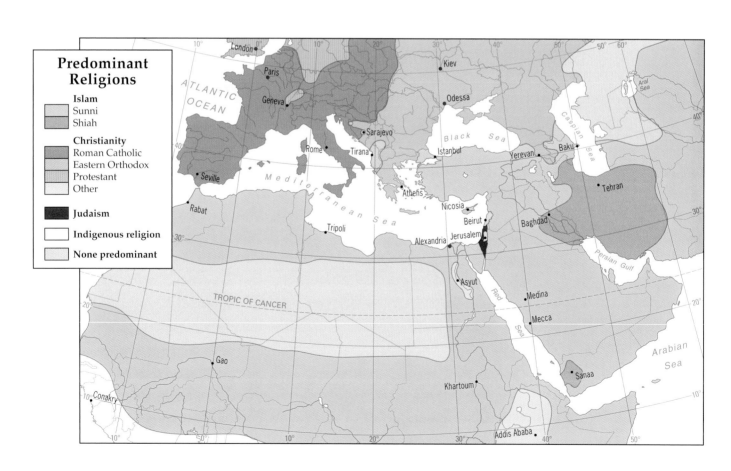

Predominant Religions

Islam
- Sunni
- Shiah

Christianity
- Roman Catholic
- Eastern Orthodox
- Protestant
- Other

- Judaism
- Indigenous religion
- None predominant

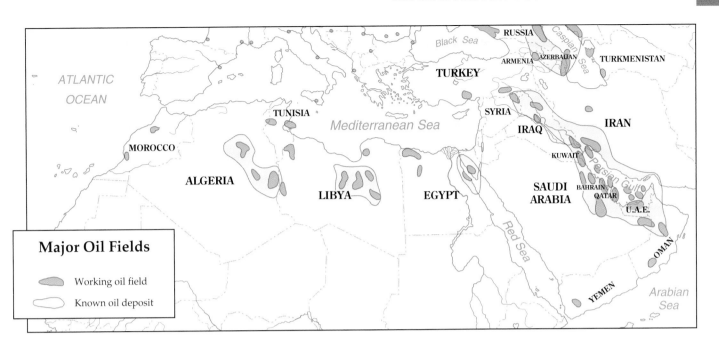

Major Oil Fields

- Working oil field
- Known oil deposit

Dependence on OPEC Oil

Annual OPEC exports (number of barrels)

3 978 500 000	All other countries	44.1%
343 100 000	France	3.8%
478 150 000	Italy	5.3%
777 450 000	South Korea	8.6%
1 620 600 000	Japan	18.0%
1 825 000 000	United States	20.2%

Percentage of total OPEC exports

Canada both imports and exports petroleum. About 31% of its imports come from OPEC countries, accounting for about 1.2% of total OPEC exports.

OPEC: Organization of Petroleum Exporting Countries

Changing Boundaries

Israel occupied the area shown in dark orange until 1967. After the Six Day War of that year, it also controlled the parts of Egypt, Jordan, and Syria shown in light orange.

In stages during 1975, 1979, and 1982, Israel returned the Sinai Peninsula to Egypt. But Israel remained in control of the Gaza Strip, West Bank, and Golan Heights.

In 1994 Israel withdrew from the Gaza Strip and turned it over to its Palestinian occupants. But negotiations to have Israel similarly pull out of the West Bank failed in 2000.

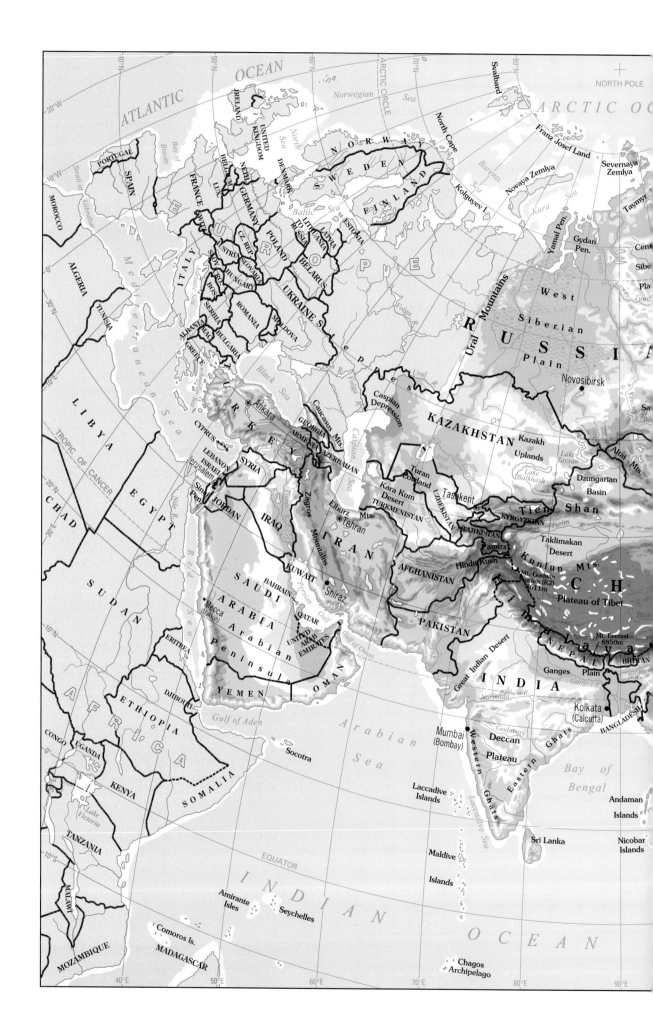

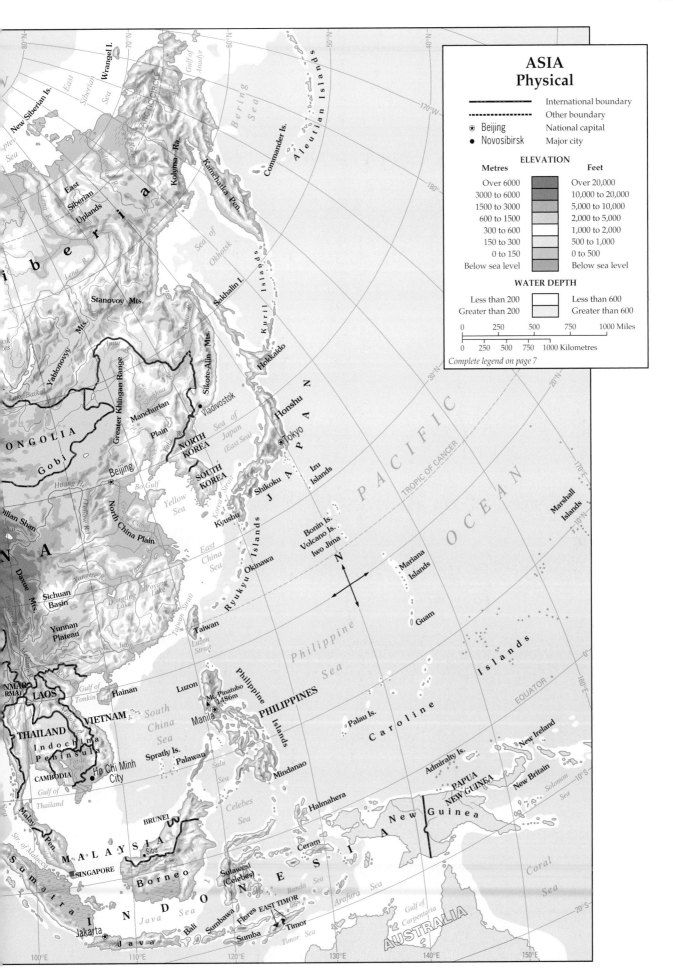

ASIA
Physical

——————— International boundary

- - - - - - - - Other boundary

⊛ Beijing   National capital

● Novosibirsk   Major city

ELEVATION

Metres		Feet
Over 6000		Over 20,000
3000 to 6000		10,000 to 20,000
1500 to 3000		5,000 to 10,000
600 to 1500		2,000 to 5,000
300 to 600		1,000 to 2,000
150 to 300		500 to 1,000
0 to 150		0 to 500
Below sea level		Below sea level

WATER DEPTH

Less than 200		Less than 600
Greater than 200		Greater than 600

0   250   500   750   1000 Miles

0   250   500   750   1000 Kilometres

Complete legend on page 7

ASIA
Political

BOUNDARIES

International boundary

Other boundary
(disputed or undefined)

CITIES

● Karachi

● Vladivostok

• Macao

⊛ Tokyo

A city's relative size is
shown by the size of
its symbol and lettering.

National capital

| 0 | 250 | 500 | 750 | 1000 Miles |

| 0 | 250 | 500 | 750 | 1000 Kilometres |

Complete legend on page 7

INTL. DATE LINE

ARCTIC CIRCLE

Wrangel I.

New Siberian Is.

East
Siberian
Sea

Kolyma R.

Gulf of Anadyr

Bering Sea

Commander Is.

Aleutian Islands (U.S.)

Indigirka R.

Ptev Sea

Tiksi

Lena R.

Yana R.

Magadan

Sea of Okhotsk

Petropavlovsk-Kamchatskiy

Yakutsk

Amur R.

Khabarovsk

Sakhalin I.

Kuril Islands (Russia)

Chita

Lake Baikal

Ulaanbaatar

MONGOLIA

Qiqihar

Songhua

Harbin

Jilin

Changchun

Fushun

Shenyang

NORTH KOREA

⊛ Pyongyang

Vladivostok

Sea of Japan (East Sea)

Sapporo

Sendai

Tokyo

J A P A N

Yokohama

Beijing

Dalian

Tianjin

Yellow R.

SOUTH KOREA

⊛ Seoul

Pusan

Kyoto

Osaka

Hiroshima

Nagasaki

Taiyuan

Qingdao

Yellow Sea

Huang He

Qinghai Lake

Lanzhou

Nanjing

Shanghai

East China Sea

Xian

Wuhan

Yangtze R.

Hangzhou

Dongting Lake

Poyang Lake

Chengdu

Chongqing

Fuzhou

Ryukyu Islands (Japan)

Kunming

Guangzhou

Taipei

TAIWAN

Taiwan Strait

Macao

Hong Kong

Luzon Strait

Mekong R.

Hanoi

Mandalay

MYANMAR (BURMA)

LAOS

Vientiane

VIETNAM

Da Nang

Yangon (Rangoon)

THAILAND

Bangkok

Gulf of Tonkin

South China Sea

Quezon City

Manila

PHILIPPINES

Cebu

Davao

Sulu Sea

Spratly Is. (disputed)

Phnom Penh

CAMBODIA

Ho Chi Minh City

Gulf of Thailand

Songkhla

Celebes Sea

Manado

Bandar Seri Begawan

BRUNEI

Sibu

Kuala Lumpur

M A L A Y S I A

Str. of Malacca

Medan

SINGAPORE

Pontianak

Banjarmasin

Padang

Palembang

I N D O N E S I A

Makassar

Java Sea

Jakarta

Semarang

Surabaya

Bandung

Kupang

Timor

Timor Sea

EAST TIMOR

Dili

Banda Sea

Arafura Sea

Gulf of Carpentaria

Jayapura

PAPUA NEW GUINEA

AUSTRALIA

Coral Sea

Solomon Sea

P A C I F I C   O C E A N

Philippine Sea

TROPIC OF CANCER

Bonin Is. (Japan)

Volcano Is. (Japan)

Northern Mariana Islands (U.S.)

Guam (U.S.)

PALAU

FEDERATED STATES OF MICRONESIA

MARSHALL ISLANDS

EQUATOR

N

C H I N A

Nanjing

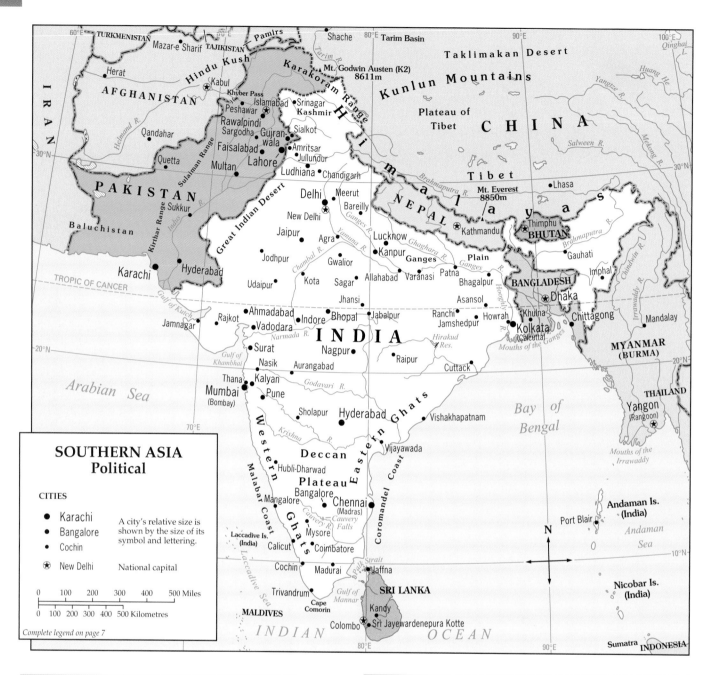

SOUTHERN ASIA
Political

CITIES

● **Karachi** — A city's relative size is shown by the size of its symbol and lettering.

● **Bangalore**

• Cochin

⊛ **New Delhi** — National capital

```
0    100   200   300   400   500 Miles
0  100 200 300 400 500 Kilometres
```

Complete legend on page 7

India's Ganges River is considered sacred by Hindus, who bathe in its waters to purify themselves.

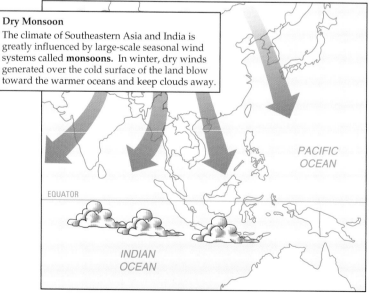

Dry Monsoon
The climate of Southeastern Asia and India is greatly influenced by large-scale seasonal wind systems called **monsoons**. In winter, dry winds generated over the cold surface of the land blow toward the warmer oceans and keep clouds away.

SOUTHEASTERN ASIA
Political

CITIES

● **Guangzhou**

● **Medan**

· Ipoh

A city's relative size is shown by the size of its symbol and lettering.

✪ **Bangkok** National capital

0   100   200   300   400 Miles

0 100 200 300 400 Kilometres

Complete legend on page 7

Himalayas
Thimphu ✪
BHUTAN

INDIA

BANGLADESH
Dhaka

Kolkata
(Calcutta)

Myitkyina

Yunnan Plateau

Kunming

CHINA

Chongqing

Zunyi

Changsha

Wuzhou

TROPIC OF CANCER

Guangzhou

Macao

Hong Kong

Namtu

Mandalay

MYANMAR
(BURMA)

N

Bay
of
Bengal

Thayetmyo

Myanaung

Pegu

Bassein

Moulmein

Yangon
(Rangoon)

*Mouths of
the Irrawaddy*

Chiang Rai

Chiang Mai

THAILAND

Khon Kaen

Dien Bien Phu

LAOS

Vientiane
(Viangchan)

Louangphrabang

Hanoi ✪

Haiphong

Nam Dinh

Vinh

*Gulf of
Tonkin*

Haikou

Hainan

Savannakhet

Hue

Da Nang

Nakhon
Ratchasima

Mun R.

Chi R.

*Khone
Falls*

VIETNAM

Plateau
of
Kontum

Qui Nhon

Andaman Is.
(India)

Port Blair

Andaman

Sea

Mergui

Archipelago

Isthmus
of Kra

Thon Buri

Bangkok ✪

CAMBODIA

*Tonle
Sap*

Phnom Penh

Kratie

Bien Hoa

Nha Trang

Ho Chi Minh City (Saigon)

Paracel Is.
(disputed)

*South
China
Sea*

Mt. Pinatubo
1486m

Manila ✪

Quezon
City

Luzon

*Luzon
Strait*

Mindoro

PHILIPPINES

Nicobar Is.
(India)

**INDIAN
OCEAN**

Surat Thani

Songkhla

Malay

Pinang
(George Town)

Medan

Pematangsiantar

Simeulue

Nias

Sumatra

Long
Xuyen

Can
Tho

*Mouths of
the Mekong*

Con Son Is.

Spratly Is.
(disputed)

Palawan

*Sulu
Sea*

Balabac Strait

Kota Kinabalu

Bandar Seri Begawan

BRUNEI ✪

Sabah

Sandakan

Tarakan

*Celebes
Sea*

Natuna I.
(Indonesia)

M

Peninsula

Ipoh

Kelang

Kuala Lumpur

Johor Baharu

SINGAPORE

Pontianak

A

L

A

Y

S

I

A

Sarawak

Sibu

Kuching

Kapuas R.

Rajang R.

Kayan R.

Serasan Strait

Strait of Malacca

Borneo

Sulawesi

Makassar Strait

EQUATOR

I   N   D   O   N   E   S   I   A

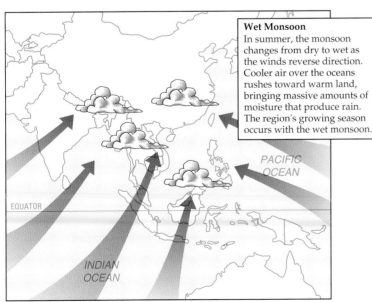

Wet Monsoon
In summer, the monsoon changes from dry to wet as the winds reverse direction. Cooler air over the oceans rushes toward warm land, bringing massive amounts of moisture that produce rain. The region's growing season occurs with the wet monsoon.

PACIFIC
OCEAN

EQUATOR

INDIAN
OCEAN

Terraces maximize the growing space for rice in hilly terrain.
Rice is the most important food crop in southeastern Asia.

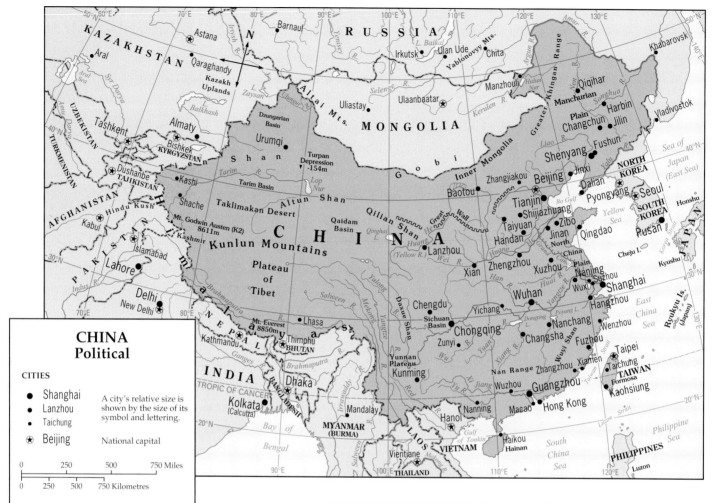

CHINA
Political

CITIES

● Shanghai   A city's relative size is
● Lanzhou   shown by the size of its
• Taichung   symbol and lettering.

⊛ Beijing   National capital

```
0        250       500        750 Miles
0    250   500   750 Kilometres
```

Complete legend on page 7

CHINA
Natural Population Growth

China's natural
population growth: 0.9%

World's average natural
population growth: 1.2%

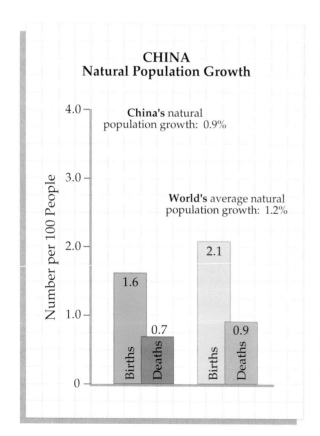

Number per 100 People

4.0
3.0
2.0
2.1
1.6
1.0
0.9
0.7
0

Births Deaths Births Deaths

Bicycles in China

Number of bicycles in use: 369.2 million

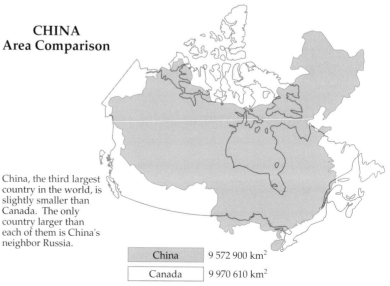

Number of automobiles in use: 6.6 million

Nearly half of the people who work in
urban China commute by bicycle.

CHINA
Area Comparison

China, the third largest
country in the world, is
slightly smaller than
Canada. The only
country larger than
each of them is China's
neighbor Russia.

| China | 9 572 900 km² |
| Canada | 9 970 610 km² |

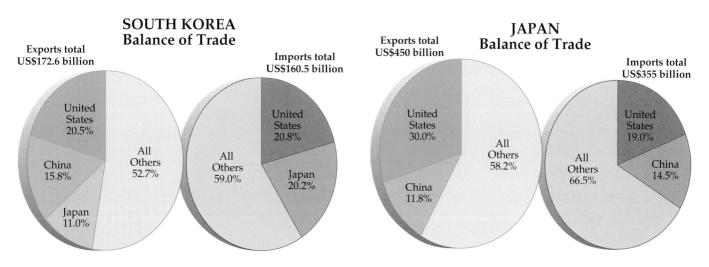

EASTERN ASIA
Political

CITIES

● Pusan

● Sapporo

• Akita

A city's relative size is shown by the size of its symbol and lettering.

✪ Tokyo   National capital

| 0 | 100 | 200 | 300 Miles |
| 0 | 100 | 200 | 300 Kilometres |

Complete legend on page 7

SOUTH KOREA
Balance of Trade

Exports total US$172.6 billion

United States 20.5%
China 15.8%
Japan 11.0%
All Others 52.7%

Imports total US$160.5 billion

United States 20.8%
Japan 20.2%
All Others 59.0%

JAPAN
Balance of Trade

Exports total US$450 billion

United States 30.0%
China 11.8%
All Others 58.2%

Imports total US$355 billion

United States 19.0%
China 14.5%
All Others 66.5%

Leading Automobile Manufacturers

	Automobiles manufactured per year	Percentage of world production
Japan	8 137 000	21.6%
United States	5 855 000	15.5%
Germany	4 855 000	12.9%
France	2 670 000	7.1%
Spain	2 257 000	6.0%
Other countries	13 919 000	36.9%

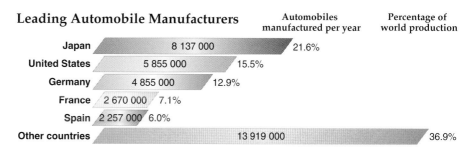

Japan's automakers have assembly plants in a number of locations in the United States.

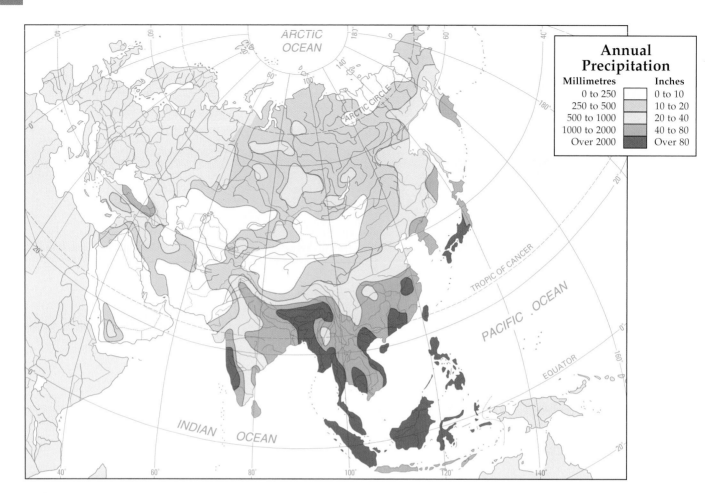

Annual Precipitation

Millimetres	Inches
0 to 250	0 to 10
250 to 500	10 to 20
500 to 1000	20 to 40
1000 to 2000	40 to 80
Over 2000	Over 80

The Himalayas, located in southern Asia, are the world's highest mountain system.

INDONESIA
Area Comparison

The combined land area of Indonesia's 17 000 islands is about one-fifth the size of Canada. Three islands located partly or entirely in Indonesia—Sumatra, Borneo and New Guinea—are each larger than all five Great Lakes combined.

Indonesia	1 907 961 km²
Canada	9 970 610 km²

Cross Section of Asia

ELEVATION

Metres		Feet
Over 6000		Over 20,000
3000 to 6000		10,000 to 20,000
1500 to 3000		5,000 to 10,000
600 to 1500		2,000 to 5,000
300 to 600		1,000 to 2,000
150 to 300		500 to 1,000
0 to 150		0 to 500
Below sea level		Below sea level

Plate:

Mediterranean Sea

CYPRUS **SYRIA** **IRAQ** Persian Gulf **IRAN** **AFGHANISTAN**

PAKISTAN **INDIA**

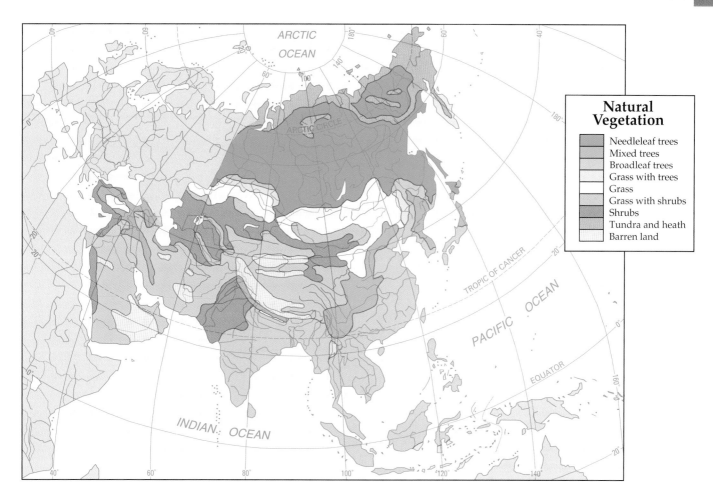

Natural Vegetation

- Needleleaf trees
- Mixed trees
- Broadleaf trees
- Grass with trees
- Grass
- Grass with shrubs
- Shrubs
- Tundra and heath
- Barren land

PAKISTAN
Balance of Trade

Exports total
US$8.6 billion

- United States 24.0%
- All Others 76.0%

Imports total
US$9.6 billion

- United Arab Emirates 8.0%
- Saudi Arabia 8.0%
- United States 6.0%
- All Others 78.0%

CHINA
Balance of Trade

Exports total
US$329.1 billion

- United States 30.1%
- All Others 43.4%
- Japan 15.1%
- European Union 11.4%

Imports total
US$307.4 billion

- Japan 20.0%
- United States 11.3%
- All Others 59.3%
- South Korea 9.4%

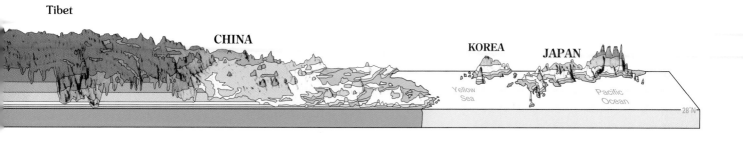

Tibet

CHINA

KOREA

JAPAN

Yellow Sea

Pacific Ocean

28°N

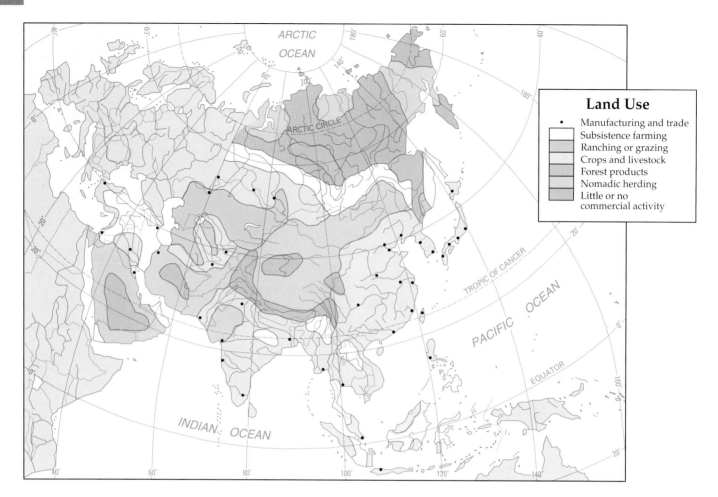

Land Use

- • Manufacturing and trade
- Subsistence farming
- Ranching or grazing
- Crops and livestock
- Forest products
- Nomadic herding
- Little or no commercial activity

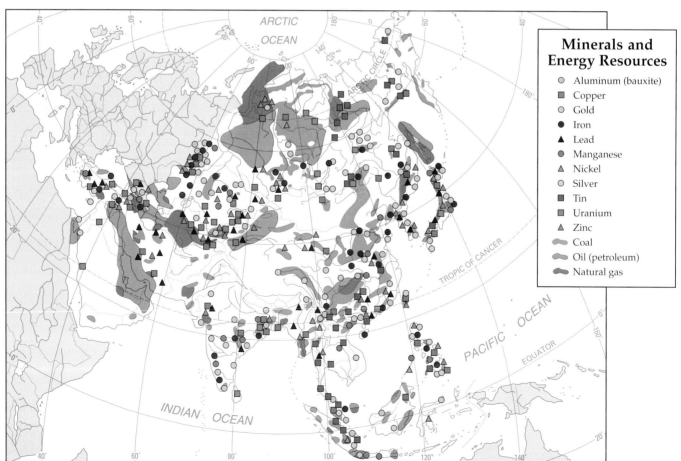

Minerals and Energy Resources

- ◯ Aluminum (bauxite)
- ▢ Copper
- ◯ Gold
- ⬤ Iron
- ▲ Lead
- ⬤ Manganese
- △ Nickel
- ◯ Silver
- ▢ Tin
- ▢ Uranium
- △ Zinc
- Coal
- Oil (petroleum)
- Natural gas

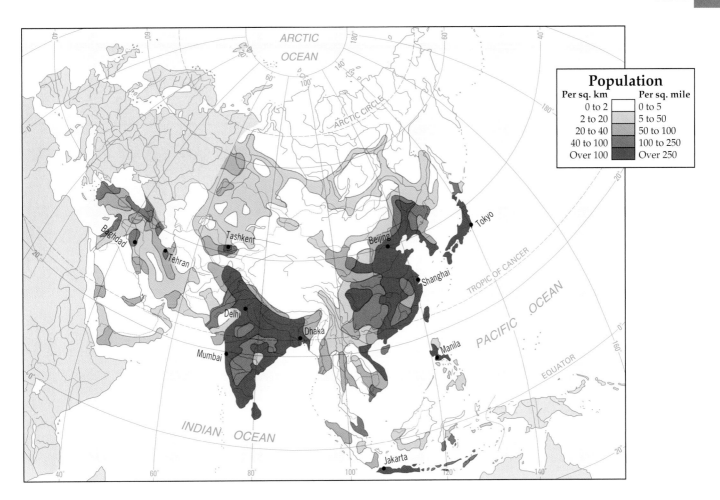

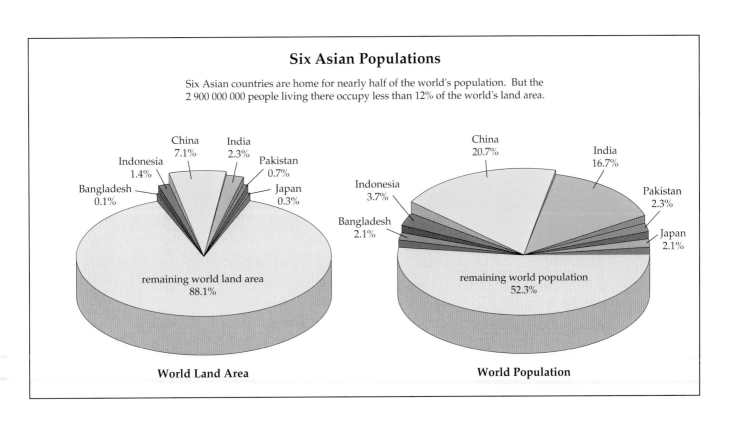

Six Asian Populations

Six Asian countries are home for nearly half of the world's population. But the 2 900 000 000 people living there occupy less than 12% of the world's land area.

World Land Area

- China 7.1%
- India 2.3%
- Indonesia 1.4%
- Pakistan 0.7%
- Bangladesh 0.1%
- Japan 0.3%
- remaining world land area 88.1%

World Population

- China 20.7%
- India 16.7%
- Indonesia 3.7%
- Bangladesh 2.1%
- Pakistan 2.3%
- Japan 2.1%
- remaining world population 52.3%

EQUATOR

PACIFIC OCEAN

Admiralty Is.

New Ireland

Bougainville

SOLOMON IS.

Homara

Guadalcanal

New Britain

Bismarck Sea

Solomon Sea

Espíritu Santo

Efate
Port-Vila VANUATU

Loyalty Is.

New Caledonia

Chesterfield Is.

Coral Sea

Tasman Sea

Norfolk I.

Lord Howe I.

Bay of Plenty

North Cape

Auckland
North Island

Cook Str.

Banks Pen.

Wellington

NEW ZEALAND

Mt. Cook
3764m

South Island

Southern Alps

Foveaux Strait

Stewart I.

PAPUA NEW GUINEA

Ms. New Guinea
Maoke

Java Pk.
5030m

Port Moresby

Gulf of Papua

Torres Strait

Great Barrier Reef

Townsville

Cape York

Cape York Pen.

Great Dividing Range

Great Dividing Range

Central

AUSTRALIA

Great Artesian Basin

Lowlands

Fraser I.

Brisbane

Sydney

Canberra
Australian Alps
Mt. Kosciuszko
2228m

Melbourne

Furneaux Group

King I.

Bass Strait

TASMANIA
Mt. Ossa
1617m

Biak

Halmahera

Sulawesi (Celebes)

I N D O N E S I A

Celebes Sea

Ceram Sea

Ceram

Buru

Banda Sea

Aru Is.

Tanimbar Is.

Dolak

Arafura Sea

Cobourg Pen.

Groote Eylandt

Gulf of Carpentaria

Wellesley Is.

Flinders

Tableland

Barkly

Arnhem Land

Melville I.

Darwin

Daly R.

Victoria R.

Joseph Bonaparte Gulf

Timor Sea

Wetar

EAST TIMOR

Timor

Flores

Savu Sea

Sumba

Flores Sea

Bali
Sumbawa
Mt. Tambora
2850m

Lombok

Java

Sumatra

Borneo

MALAYSIA

Kuala Lumpur

SINGAPORE

Jakarta

Bangka I.

Mentawai Is.

Nias

Mt. Krakatau
813m

Strait of Malacca

Karimata Strait

Makassar Strait

Java Sea

Macdonnell Ranges

Alice Springs

Musgrave Ranges

Simpson Desert

Lake Eyre

Lake Torrens

Lake Gairdner

Lake Frome

Flinders Ranges

Adelaide

Kangaroo I.

Spencer Gulf

Gulf St Vincent

Great Australian Bight

Plain

Nullarbor Plain

Kimberley Plateau

Roebuck Bay

Eighty Mile Beach

Great Sandy Desert

Western Plateau

Gibson Desert

Lake Disappointment

Great Victoria Desert

Lake Barlee

Hamersley Range

North West Cape

Shark Bay

Perth

Darling Range

Cape Leeuwin

INDIAN OCEAN

Christmas I.

INDIAN OCEAN

TROPIC OF CAPRICORN

N

AUSTRALIA
Physical

International boundary

Internal boundary

Jakarta   ⊛ National capital

Brisbane ● Major city

ELEVATION

Metres	Feet
Over 3000	Over 10,000
1500 to 3000	5,000 to 10,000
600 to 1500	2,000 to 5,000
300 to 600	1,000 to 2,000
150 to 300	500 to 1,000
0 to 150	0 to 500
Below sea level	Below sea level

WATER DEPTH

Less than 200 metres — Less than 600 feet
Greater than 200 — Greater than 600

0   250   500   750 Miles
0   250   500   750 Kilometres

Complete legend on page 7

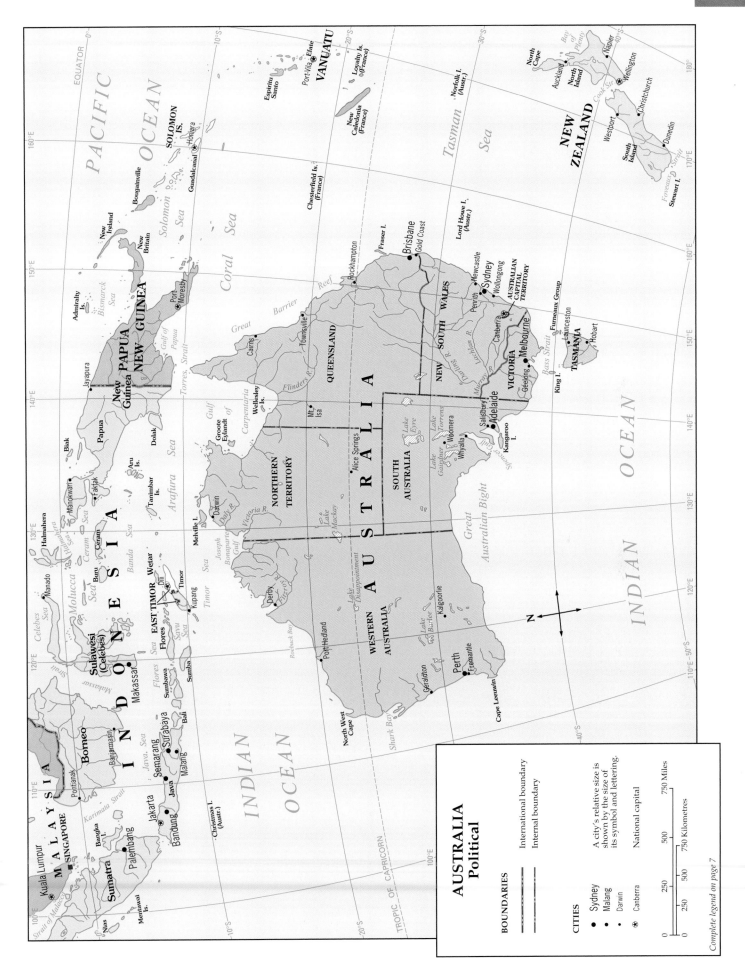

PACIFIC OCEAN

EQUATOR

Bougainville

New Ireland

SOLOMON IS.

New Britain

Bismarck Sea

Admiralty Is.

Honiara

Guadalcanal

VANUATU
Port-Vila Éfaté
Espíritu Santo

Loyalty Is. (France)

New Caledonia (France)

Chesterfield Is. (France)

Norfolk I. (Austr.)

Bay of Plenty

North Cape

North Island

Auckland

Napier

Wellington

NEW ZEALAND

Westport

Cook Str.

South Island

Christchurch

Dunedin

Foveaux Strait

Stewart I.

Tasman Sea

Lord Howe I. (Austr.)

Jayapura

New Guinea

PAPUA NEW GUINEA

Port Moresby

Gulf of Papua

Solomon Sea

Coral Sea

Torres Strait

Fraser I.

Brisbane
Gold Coast

Newcastle

Sydney
Penrith Wollongong

AUSTRALIAN CAPITAL TERRITORY

Canberra

Furneaux Group

Launceston

TASMANIA

Hobart

Bass Strait

King I.

Geelong Melbourne

VICTORIA

NEW SOUTH WALES

Rockhampton

Great Barrier Reef

Townsville

Cairns

QUEENSLAND

Flinders R.

Darling R.

Lachlan R.

Murray R.

Murrumbidgee R.

Adelaide
Salisbury

Woomera

Whyalla

Kangaroo I.

Lake Torrens

Spencer Gulf

Lake Gairdner

Great Australian Bight

Papua

Biak

Manokwari

Fakfak

Aru Is.

Tanimbar Is.

Dolak

Gulf of Carpentaria

Groote Eylandt

Wellesley Is.

Mt. Isa

Arafura Sea

Melville I.

Darwin

Daly R.

Victoria R.

NORTHERN TERRITORY

Alice Springs

Lake Mackay

SOUTH AUSTRALIA

Lake Eyre

AUSTRALIA

INDONESIA

Celebes Sea

Molucca Sea

Manado

Halmahera

Halmahera Sea

Ceram Sea

Ceram

Buru

Banda Sea

EAST TIMOR
Dili

Timor

Wetar

Kupang

Savu Sea

Flores

Timor Sea

Joseph Bonaparte Gulf

Derby

Roebuck Bay

Port Hedland

Lake Disappointment

WESTERN AUSTRALIA

Kalgoorlie

Lake Carnegie

Lake Barlee

INDIAN OCEAN

Sulawesi (Celebes)

Makassar Strait

Makassar

Java Sea

Surabaya

Semarang

Malang

Sumbawa

Bali

Sumba

Flores

Borneo

Banjarmasin

Pontianak

Karimata Strait

Java

Jakarta

Bandung

Christmas I. (Austr.)

North West Cape

Shark Bay

Geraldton

Perth
Fremantle

Cape Leeuwin

INDIAN OCEAN

TROPIC OF CAPRICORN

N

MALAYSIA

SINGAPORE

Kuala Lumpur

Sumatra

Palembang

Bangka I.

Mentawai Is.

Nias

Strait of Malacca

Halmahera

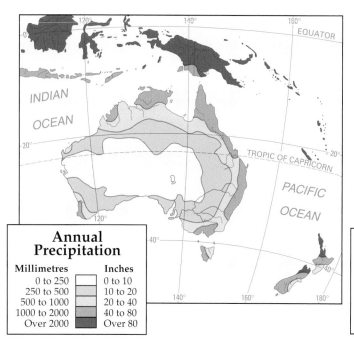

Annual Precipitation

Millimetres	Inches
0 to 250	0 to 10
250 to 500	10 to 20
500 to 1000	20 to 40
1000 to 2000	40 to 80
Over 2000	Over 80

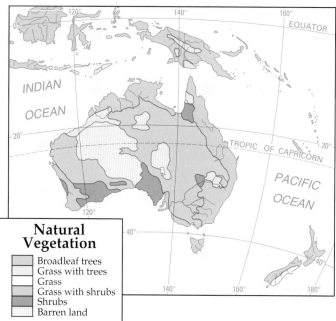

Natural Vegetation

- Broadleaf trees
- Grass with trees
- Grass
- Grass with shrubs
- Shrubs
- Barren land

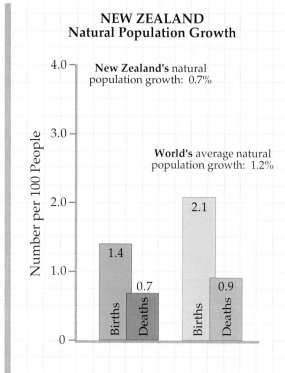

NEW ZEALAND Natural Population Growth

New Zealand's natural population growth: 0.7%

World's average natural population growth: 1.2%

Number per 100 People

- Births 1.4
- Deaths 0.7
- Births 2.1
- Deaths 0.9

Sydney is Australia's largest city. Its Opera House and Harbour Bridge are internationally recognized landmarks.

Isolated Australia is home to many unique animals, including marsupials such as the kangaroo.

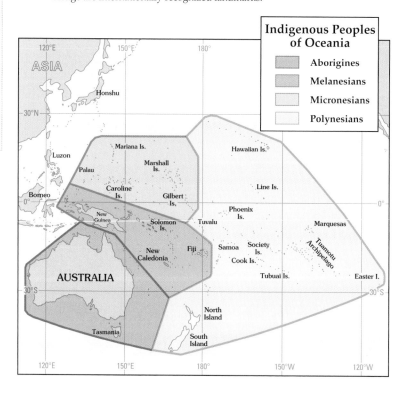

Indigenous Peoples of Oceania

- Aborigines
- Melanesians
- Micronesians
- Polynesians

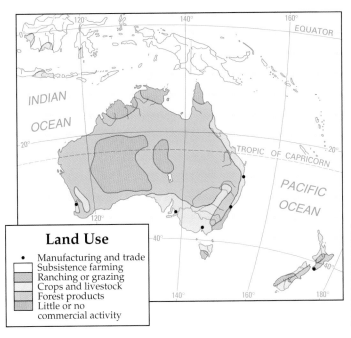

Land Use

- Manufacturing and trade
- Subsistence farming
- Ranching or grazing
- Crops and livestock
- Forest products
- Little or no commercial activity

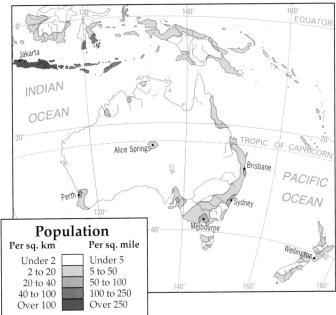

Population

Per sq. km	Per sq. mile
Under 2	Under 5
2 to 20	5 to 50
20 to 40	50 to 100
40 to 100	100 to 250
Over 100	Over 250

Australia's Isolation

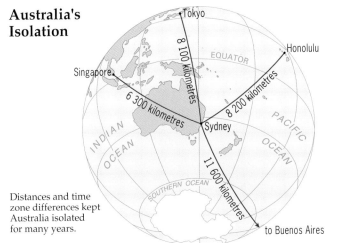

Tokyo
8 100 kilometres
Honolulu
Singapore
8 200 kilometres
6 300 kilometres
Sydney
EQUATOR
INDIAN OCEAN
PACIFIC OCEAN
SOUTHERN OCEAN
11 600 kilometres
to Buenos Aires

Distances and time zone differences kept Australia isolated for many years.

AUSTRALIA
Balance of Trade

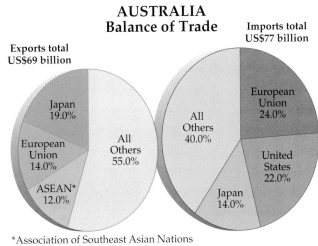

Exports total US$69 billion

- Japan 19.0%
- European Union 14.0%
- ASEAN* 12.0%
- All Others 55.0%

Imports total US$77 billion

- European Union 24.0%
- United States 22.0%
- Japan 14.0%
- All Others 40.0%

*Association of Southeast Asian Nations

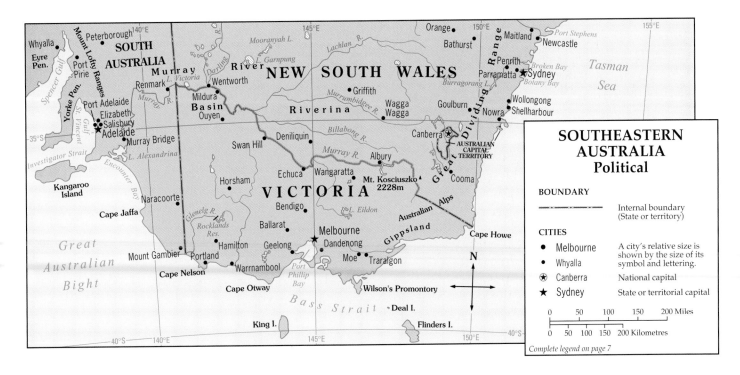

SOUTHEASTERN AUSTRALIA
Political

BOUNDARY

Internal boundary (State or territory)

CITIES

- Melbourne — A city's relative size is shown by the size of its symbol and lettering.
- Whyalla
- Canberra — National capital
- Sydney — State or territorial capital

0	50	100	150	200 Miles

0	50	100	150	200 Kilometres

Complete legend on page 7

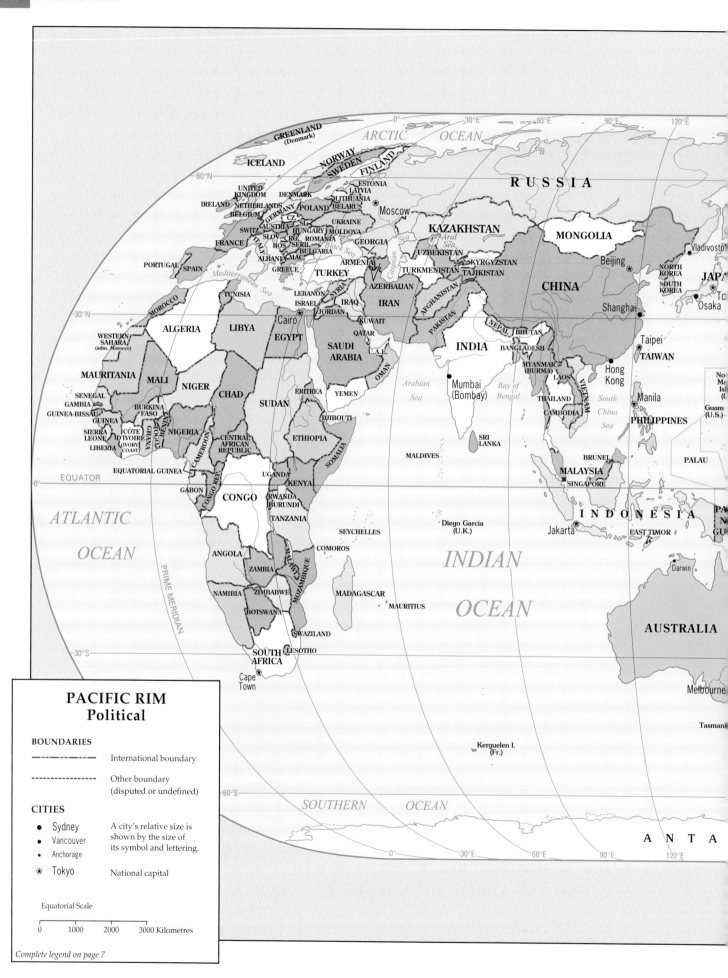

PACIFIC RIM
Political

BOUNDARIES

International boundary

Other boundary
(disputed or undefined)

CITIES

● Sydney   A city's relative size is
● Vancouver   shown by the size of
● Anchorage   its symbol and lettering.

⊛ Tokyo   National capital

Equatorial Scale

0   1000   2000   3000 Kilometres

Complete legend on page 7

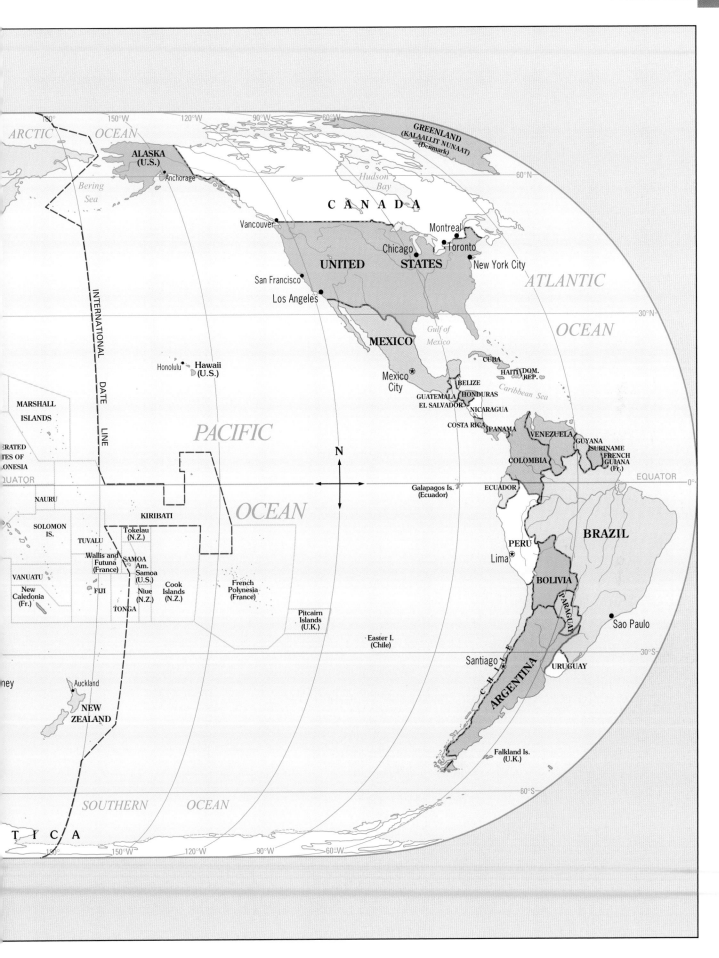

ARCTIC OCEAN

GREENLAND
(KALAALLIT NUNAAT)
(Denmark)

ALASKA
(U.S.)

Anchorage

Bering
Sea

Hudson
Bay

60°N

C A N A D A

Vancouver

Montreal

Chicago
Toronto

UNITED STATES

New York City

San Francisco

ATLANTIC

Los Angeles

30°N

INTERNATIONAL DATE LINE

MEXICO

Gulf of
Mexico

OCEAN

Honolulu

Hawaii
(U.S.)

CUBA

HAITI DOM.
REP.

MARSHALL
ISLANDS

Mexico
City

BELIZE

Caribbean Sea

GUATEMALA HONDURAS
EL SALVADOR
NICARAGUA

ERATED
TES OF
ONESIA

PACIFIC

COSTA RICA PANAMA

VENEZUELA

GUYANA
SURINAME
FRENCH
GUIANA
(Fr.)

N

EQUATOR

COLOMBIA

EQUATOR 0°

NAURU

Galapagos Is.
(Ecuador)

ECUADOR

KIRIBATI

OCEAN

BRAZIL

SOLOMON
IS.

Tokelau
(N.Z.)

TUVALU

PERU

Wallis and
Futuna
(France)

SAMOA
Am.
Samoa
(U.S.)

Lima

VANUATU

Cook
Islands
(N.Z.)

French
Polynesia
(France)

BOLIVIA

New
Caledonia
(Fr.)

FIJI

Niue
(N.Z.)

PARAGUAY

Sao Paulo

TONGA

Pitcairn
Islands
(U.K.)

Easter I.
(Chile)

30°S

ney

Auckland

Santiago

URUGUAY

NEW
ZEALAND

ARGENTINA

Falkland Is.
(U.K.)

60°S

SOUTHERN OCEAN

T I C A

180°

150°W

120°W

90°W

60°W

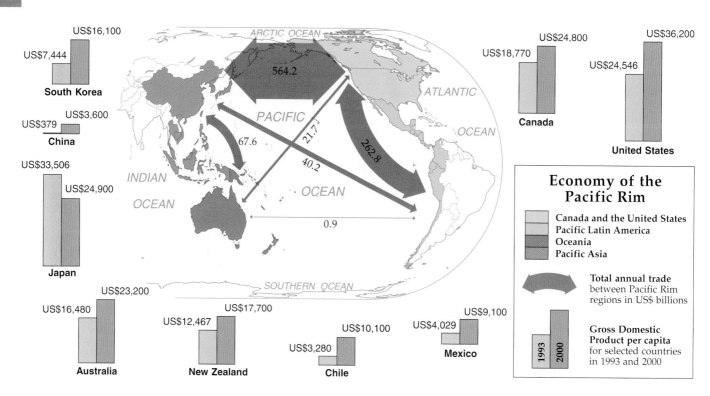

US$16,100
US$7,444
South Korea

US$3,600
US$379
China

US$33,506
US$24,900
Japan

US$23,200
US$16,480
Australia

US$17,700
US$12,467
New Zealand

US$10,100
US$3,280
Chile

US$9,100
US$4,029
Mexico

US$24,800
US$18,770
Canada

US$36,200
US$24,546
United States

564.2
PACIFIC
21.7
67.6
262.8
40.2
0.9

Economy of the Pacific Rim

Canada and the United States
Pacific Latin America
Oceania
Pacific Asia

Total annual trade between Pacific Rim regions in US$ billions

Gross Domestic Product per capita for selected countries in 1993 and 2000

1993
2000

Container ships loaded with trans-Pacific cargo are a common sight in Hong Kong and in other Asian and North American ports.

JAPAN Area Comparison

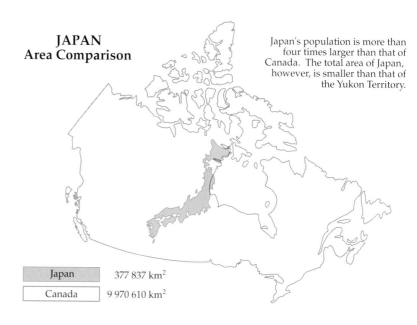

Japan's population is more than four times larger than that of Canada. The total area of Japan, however, is smaller than that of the Yukon Territory.

Japan	377 837 km²
Canada	9 970 610 km²

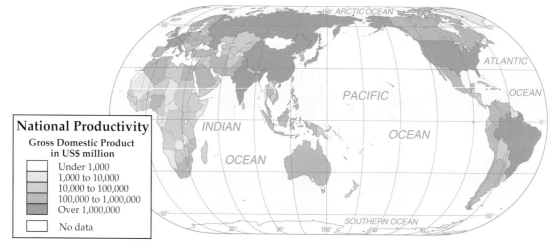

National Productivity

Gross Domestic Product in US$ million

Under 1,000
1,000 to 10,000
10,000 to 100,000
100,000 to 1,000,000
Over 1,000,000
No data

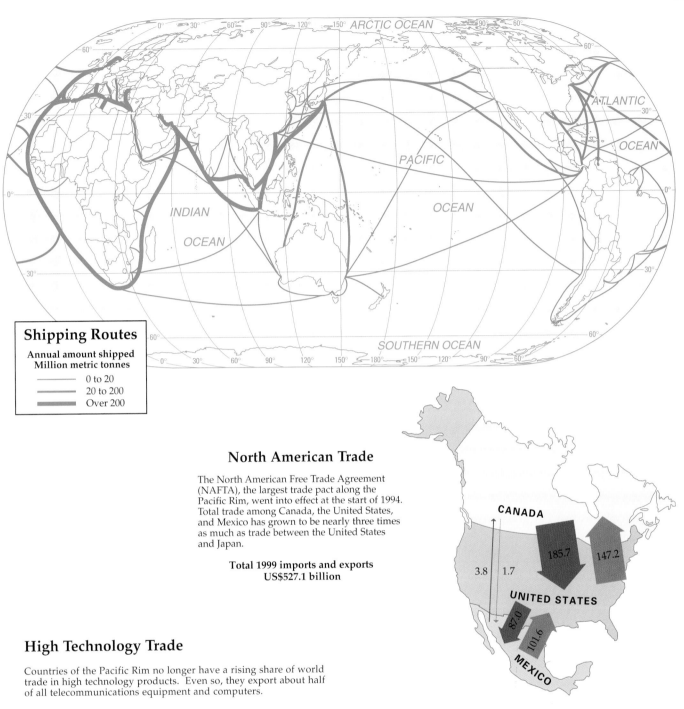

Shipping Routes

Annual amount shipped
Million metric tonnes

——	0 to 20
——	20 to 200
——	Over 200

North American Trade

The North American Free Trade Agreement (NAFTA), the largest trade pact along the Pacific Rim, went into effect at the start of 1994. Total trade among Canada, the United States, and Mexico has grown to be nearly three times as much as trade between the United States and Japan.

Total 1999 imports and exports
US$527.1 billion

High Technology Trade

Countries of the Pacific Rim no longer have a rising share of world trade in high technology products. Even so, they export about half of all telecommunications equipment and computers.

Telecommunications Equipment

Total exports:
US$117.9 billion

1999

Total exports:
US$169.3 billion

14.4%	United States
7.9%	Japan
6.2%	Hong Kong
4.7%	China
4.4%	South Korea
62.4%	All other countries

1995

Japan	15.5%
United States	15.1%
Hong Kong	7.7%
Singapore	5.8%
South Korea	3.6%
All other countries	52.3%

Percentage of total exports:
Top 5 Pacific Rim countries

Computers

Total exports:
US$123.8 billion

1999

Total exports:
US$166.7 billion

16.0%	United States
11.9%	Singapore
8.7%	Japan
4.8%	China
4.3%	South Korea
54.3%	All other countries

1995

United States	18.6%
Singapore	15.8%
Japan	13.9%
South Korea	3.2%
Thailand	2.3%
All other countries	46.2%

Percentage of total exports:
Top 5 Pacific Rim countries

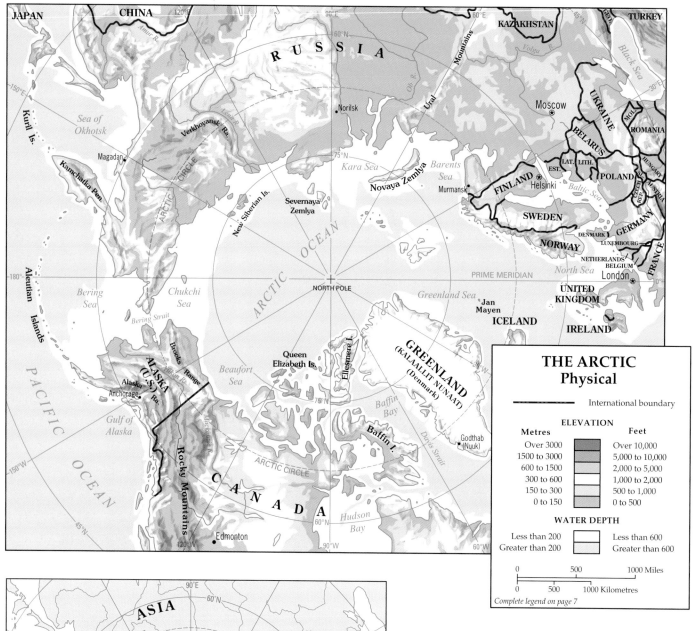

JAPAN
CHINA
RUSSIA
KAZAKHSTAN
TURKEY
Amur R.
Norilsk
Ural Mountains
Volga R.
Moscow
UKRAINE
Black Sea
ROMANIA
Sea of Okhotsk
Verkhoyansk Ra.
BELARUS
Kara Sea
Barents Sea
FINLAND
Helsinki
EST.
LAT.
LITH.
POLAND
Magadan
Kamchatka Pen.
New Siberian Is.
Severnaya Zemlya
Novaya Zemlya
Murmansk
SWEDEN
GERMANY
HUNGARY
Kuril Is.
ARCTIC CIRCLE
Baltic Sea
DENMARK
NORWAY
LUXEMBOURG
FRANCE
NETHERLANDS
BELGIUM
North Sea
London
Aleutian Islands
Bering Sea
Chukchi Sea
ARCTIC OCEAN
NORTH POLE
PRIME MERIDIAN
UNITED KINGDOM
PACIFIC OCEAN
Bering Strait
Greenland Sea
Jan Mayen
ICELAND
IRELAND
Brooks Range
ALASKA (U.S.)
Alaska Ra.
Anchorage
Beaufort Sea
Queen Elizabeth Is.
Ellesmere I.
GREENLAND
(KALAALLIT NUNAAT)
(Denmark)
Gulf of Alaska
Mackenzie R.
Rocky Mountains
Baffin Bay
Baffin I.
Godthab (Nuuk)
CANADA
ARCTIC CIRCLE
Hudson Bay
Davis Strait
Edmonton

THE ARCTIC
Physical

⎯⎯⎯⎯ International boundary

ELEVATION

Metres		Feet
Over 3000		Over 10,000
1500 to 3000		5,000 to 10,000
600 to 1500		2,000 to 5,000
300 to 600		1,000 to 2,000
150 to 300		500 to 1,000
0 to 150		0 to 500

WATER DEPTH

Less than 200		Less than 600
Greater than 200		Greater than 600

0   500   1000 Miles

0   500   1000 Kilometres

Complete legend on page 7

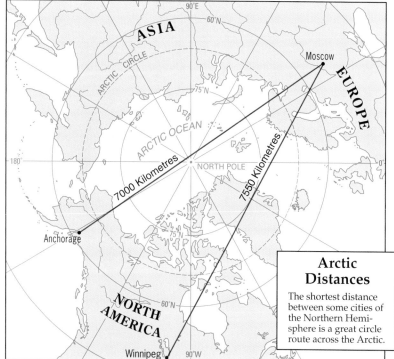

ASIA
EUROPE
NORTH AMERICA
ARCTIC CIRCLE
ARCTIC OCEAN
NORTH POLE
Moscow
Anchorage
Winnipeg
7000 Kilometres
7550 Kilometres

Arctic Distances

The shortest distance between some cities of the Northern Hemisphere is a great circle route across the Arctic.

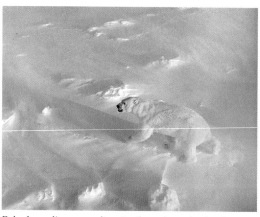

Polar bears live near salt water throughout the Arctic. These hunters can smell prey up to 15 km away.

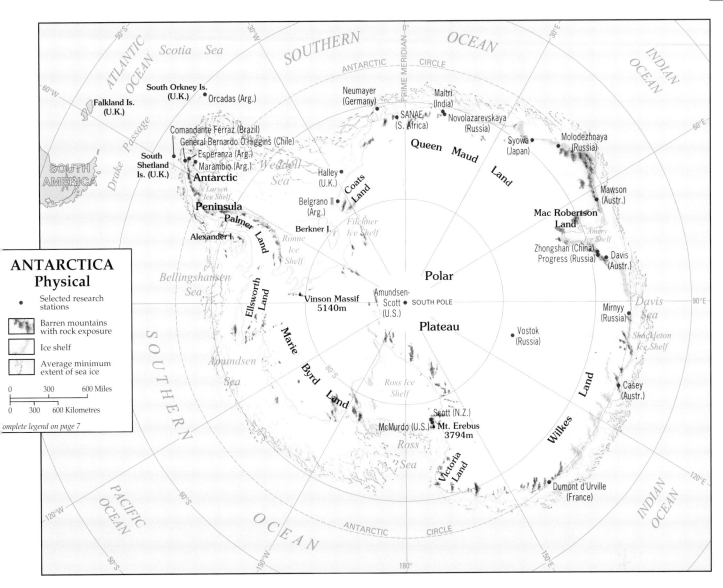

ANTARCTICA
Physical

- • Selected research stations
- Barren mountains with rock exposure
- Ice shelf
- Average minimum extent of sea ice

0   300   600 Miles

0   300   600 Kilometres

complete legend on page 7

Antarctica's Ice Cap

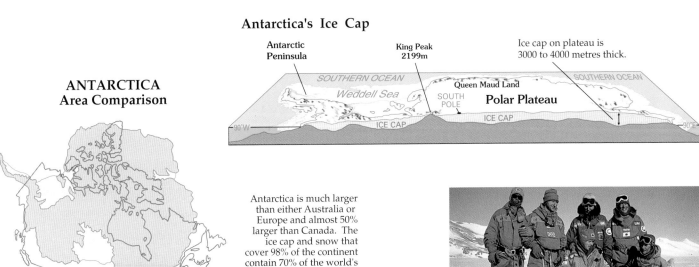

Antarctic Peninsula

King Peak 2199m

Ice cap on plateau is 3000 to 4000 metres thick.

SOUTHERN OCEAN

Weddell Sea

SOUTH POLE

Queen Maud Land

Polar Plateau

SOUTHERN OCEAN

ICE CAP   ICE CAP

90°W   90°E

ANTARCTICA
Area Comparison

Antarctica is much larger than either Australia or Europe and almost 50% larger than Canada. The ice cap and snow that cover 98% of the continent contain 70% of the world's supply of freshwater.

Antarctica	14 000 000 km²
Canada	9 970 610 km²

Expeditions to the interior of Antarctica provide scientists with information about the earth's coldest region.

MAP PROJECTIONS

Map projections are the means by which the curved surface of a globe is transferred to the flat surface of a map. Because the earth is a sphere, a globe is its only perfect model. Even though there are an infinite number of map projections, none can be as accurate as a globe. A globe simultaneously shows accurate shapes, sizes, distances, and directions. No single world map can show all four of these properties accurately. Every world map distorts one or more of them. For example, a world map that shows correct shapes cannot show correct sizes, and vice versa.

The projections illustrated here can be classified according to their map properties. *Conformal* projections show true shapes, but distort sizes. (You can remember this term's meaning by associating *shape* with the word *form* in *conformal*.) *Equal-area* projections show all areas in their true relative sizes, but distort shapes. *Compromise* projections allow some size distortions in order to portray shapes more accurately. For all types of world map projections, distortion is generally least near the center of the map and greatest at its edges.

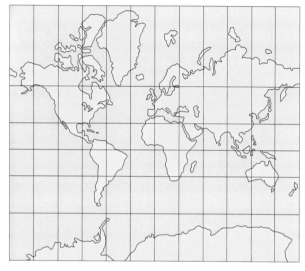

Mercator: First published in 1569, the Mercator is a conformal projection. North and South Poles are shown not as points, but as lines the same length as the Equator. The result is extreme size distortion in the higher latitudes. The Mercator map was designed for navigation, and the true compass direction between any two points can be determined by a straight line.

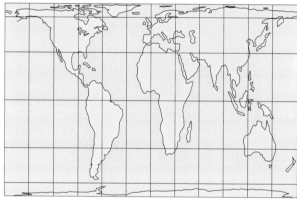

Gall-Peters: An equal-area projection first produced in the 1850s, the Gall-Peters greatly distorts shapes near the Equator as well as near the poles. Features near the Equator are stretched vertically, while features near the poles are flattened horizontally. The resulting shapes are quite different from those on the globe.

Armadillo: The Armadillo is a compromise projection that is intended to give young students the impression of a map being peeled from a globe. Because its unique appearance results in severe distortions, especially at the map's outer edges, it has seldom been used outside the classroom.

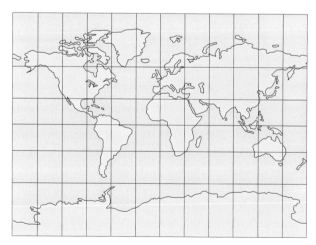

Miller Cylindrical: The Miller is a compromise projection based on the Mercator. Its shapes are not as accurate as those on the Mercator map, but it has much less size distortion in the higher latitiudes. The Miller cylindrical projection is frequently used when mapping world time zones.

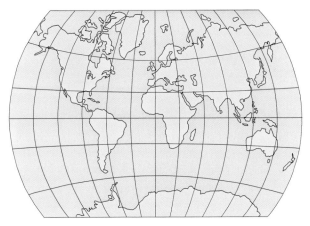

Van der Grinten: The Van der Grinten is a compromise between the Mercator and the Mollweide. The full projection is shaped like a circle, but the polar areas are normally not shown. Shapes, sizes, and directions are reasonably accurate between 60°N and 60°S, where most of the world's people live. The Van der Grinten has long been used for general reference maps.

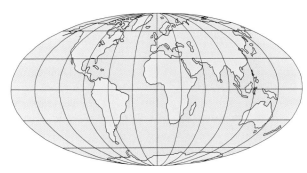

Mollweide: An equal-area projection, the Mollweide has an oval shape that reminds the viewer of a globe. The Mollweide projection is frequently used for world distribution maps. (A distribution map shows the relative location and extent of something—such as crops, livestock, or people—across the face of the earth.)

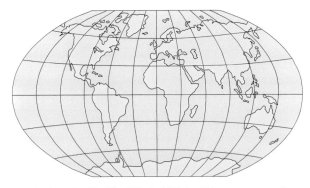

Winkel "Tripel": The Winkel "Tripel" is a compromise projection. Its oval shape and curving parallels result in a map with realistic shapes and minor size distortions at all latitudes. The Winkel has less size distortion than the Van der Grinten (above) and less shape distortion than the Robinson (below).

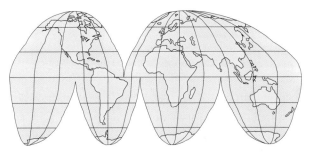

Goode's Homolosine: Goode's is an equal-area map that also shows shapes extremely well. Shapes can be shown more accurately than on most equal-area maps because the grid is *interrupted* or split in the ocean areas. The interruptions allow land areas to be shown with less stretch or distortion.

Robinson: First used in 1963, the Robinson is a compromise projection. Because it presents a reasonable overall picture of the world, it is often used for maps in educational materials. It looks similar to the Eckert IV (at right), but the Robinson is easily distinguished by its size distortion in the polar areas.

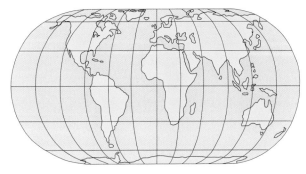

Eckert IV: An equal-area projection, the Eckert IV has relatively minor shape distortions near the Equator and the poles. The result is a map that is well-suited either for general reference or for showing world distributions. It has been used in several atlases to show world climates and other themes.

WORLD FACTS

Age and Dimensions of Earth

Age	4.6 billion years (4.6×10^9)
Mass	6 sextillion metric tonnes (6×10^{21})
Diameter	12 756.32 kilometres
Equatorial Circumference	40 075.16 kilometres
Polar Circumference	40 008.00 kilometres

Land Areas and Populations

Continent	Land Area km²	Percentage of World Land Area	Population	Percentage of World Population
Africa	30 251 000	20.2	828 487 666	13.5
Antarctica	14 000 000	9.3	0	0.0
Asia	44 009 000	29.4	3 729 663 850	60.6
Europe	10 445 000	7.0	728 822 900	11.8
North America	24 211 000	16.2	485 969 330	7.9
Oceania*	8 985 000	6.0	31 216 051	0.5
South America	17 832 000	11.9	350 819 346	5.7

Australia, New Zealand, and Pacific Islands

Largest Urban Areas

	Population	
City and Country	Actual in 2000	Projected for 2015
Tokyo, Japan	26 444 000	26 444 000*
Mexico City, Mexico	18 131 000	19 180 000
Mumbai (Bombay), India	18 066 000	26 138 000
São Paulo, Brazil	17 755 000	20 397 000
New York City, United States	16 640 000	17 432 000
Lagos, Nigeria	13 427 000	23 173 000
Los Angeles, United States	12 140 000	14 080 000
Kolkata (Calcutta), India	12 918 000	17 252 000
Shanghai, China	12 887 000	14 575 000
Buenos Aires, Argentina	12 560 000	14 076 000
Dhaka, Bangladesh	12 317 000	21 119 000
Karachi, Pakistan	11 974 000	19 211 000
Delhi, India	11 018 000	16 808 000
Jakarta, Indonesia	11 018 000	17 256 000
Osaka, Japan	11 013 000	11 013 000*
Manila, Philippines	10 870 000	14 825 000
Beijing, China	10 839 000	12 299 000
Rio de Janeiro, Brazil	10 582 000	11 905 000
Cairo, Egypt	10 552 000	13 751 000
Seoul, South Korea	9 888 000	9 923 000
Paris, France	9 624 000	9 677 000
Istanbul, Turkey	9 451 000	12 492 000
Moscow, Russia	9 321 000	9 353 000
Tianjin, China	9 156 000	10 713 000
London, England	7 640 000	7 640 000*
Lima, Peru	7 443 000	9 388 000
Bangkok, Thailand	7 281 000	10 143 000

No net population growth expected, 2000–2015

Extremes of Climate

Record Temperatures

Highest	57.7° C		
	Al Aziziyah, Libya	September 13, 1922
Lowest	−89.2° C		
	Vostok, Antarctica	July 21, 1983

Average Annual Precipitation

Highest	11 684.0 mm
	Mt. Waialeale, Hawaii, U.S.
Lowest	0.5 mm
	Arica, Chile

Maximum Precipitation

In 24 hours	1870.0 mm	
	Cilaos, Reunion Is.	March 16, 1952
In 1 hour	305.0 mm	
	Holt, Mo., U.S.	June 22, 1907

Ocean Areas and Maximum Depths

Ocean	Area km²	Maximum Depth m
Pacific Ocean	155 557 000	10 924
Atlantic Ocean	76 762 000	8 605
Indian Ocean	68 556 000	7 258
Southern Ocean	20 327 000	7 235
Arctic Ocean	14 056 000	4 665

Highest and Lowest Elevations

Continent	Highest Elevation	m above sea level	Lowest Elevation	m below sea level
Africa	Mt. Kilimanjaro, Tanzania	5 895	Lake Assal, Djibouti	156
Antarctica	Vinson Massif	5 140	Bentley Subglacial Trench	2 538
Asia	Mt. Everest, Nepal-China	8 850	Dead Sea, Israel-Jordan	411
Australia	Mt. Kosciuszko, Australia	2 228	Lake Eyre, Australia	16
Europe	Mt. Elbrus, Russia	5 642	Caspian Sea, Russia	28
North America	Mt. McKinley, U.S.	6 194	Death Valley, U.S.	86
South America	Mt. Aconcagua, Argentina	6 959	Valdes Peninsula, Argentina	40

Largest Lakes

Lake and Continent	Area km²
Caspian Sea, Asia and Europe	371 000
Superior, North America	82 103
Victoria, Africa	69 484
Huron, North America	59 570
Michigan, North America	57 760
Aral Sea, Asia	40 100
Tanganyika, Africa	32 900
Baikal, Asia	31 499
Great Bear, North America	31 328
Nyasa (Malawi), Africa	28 749
Great Slave, North America	28 568
Erie, North America	25 670
Winnipeg, North America	24 387
Ontario, North America	18 960
Balkhash, Asia	18 300
Ladoga, Europe	17 703
Chad, Africa	16 300
Maracaibo, South America	13 512
Onega, Europe	9 894
Bangweulu, Africa	9 800

Highest Waterfalls

Waterfall and Country	Total Height m
Angel (Churun Meru), Venezuela	979
Tugela, South Africa	948
Mtarazi, Zimbabwe	762
Yosemite, United States	739
Cuquenian, Venezuela	610
Sutherland, New Zealand	580
Kile, Norway	561
Kahiwa, United States	533
Mardal (Eastern), Norway	517
Ribbon, United States	491

Longest Rivers

River and Continent	Length km
Nile, Africa	6 650
Amazon, South America	6 437
Yangtze, Asia	6 300
Mississippi-Missouri system, North America	6 020
Yenisey, Asia	5 540
Huang, Asia	5 464
Ob, Asia	5 409
Parana, South America	4 880
Congo, Africa	4 700
Amur, Asia	4 444
Lena, Asia	4 400
Mekong, Asia	4 350
Mackenzie, North America	4 241
Niger, Africa	4 200
Zambezi, Africa	3 540
Volga, Europe	3 530
Madeira, South America	3 350
Jurua, South America	3 283
Purus, South America	3 211
Yukon, North America	3 185

COUNTRY TABLES

COUNTRY	CAPITAL(S)	PRINCIPAL LANGUAGE(S)	POPULATION	AREA KM²	POP. DENSITY PER KM²	NATURAL POP. GROWTH PER 100 PEOPLE BIRTHS	– DEATHS	= % GAIN
Africa								
ALGERIA	Algiers	Arabic, French, Berber dialects	31 736 053	2 381 741	13.3	2.3	0.5	1.8
ANGOLA	Luanda	Portuguese, Bantu, and other African languages	10 366 031	1 246 700	8.3	4.7	2.5	2.2
BENIN	Porto-Novo	French, Fon, Yoruba, tribal languages	6 590 782	14 760	446.5	4.4	1.4	3.0
BOTSWANA	Gaborone	English, Setswana	1 586 119	581 730	2.7	2.9	2.4	0.5
BURKINA FASO	Ouagadougou	French, Sudanic languages	12 272 289	274 400	44.7	4.5	1.7	2.8
BURUNDI	Bujumbura	Kirundi, French, Swahili	6 223 897	27 816	223.8	4.0	1.6	2.4
CAMEROON	Yaounde	24 major African language groups, English, French	15 803 220	475 442	33.2	3.6	1.2	2.4
CAPE VERDE	Praia	Portuguese, Crioulo	405 163	4 033	100.5	2.9	0.7	2.2
CENTRAL AFRICAN REPUBLIC	Bangui	French, Sangho, Arabic, Hunsa, Swahili	3 576 884	622 436	5.7	3.7	1.9	1.8
CHAD	N'Djamena	French, Arabic, Sara, Sango	8 707 078	1 284 000	6.8	4.8	1.5	3.3
COMOROS	Moroni	Arabic, French, Comoran	596 202	1 862	320.2	3.9	0.9	3.0
CONGO	Kinshasa	French, Lingala, Kingwana, Kikongo, Tshiluba	53 624 718	2 344 858	22.9	4.6	1.5	3.1
CONGO REPUBLIC	Brazzaville	French, Lingala, Monokutuba, Kikongo	2 894 336	342 000	8.5	3.8	1.6	2.2
CÔTE D'IVOIRE (IVORY COAST)	Abidjan, Yamoussoukro	French, Dioula	16 393 221	322 463	50.8	4.1	1.7	2.4
DJIBOUTI	Djibouti	French, Arabic, Somali, Afar	460 700	23 200	19.9	4.1	1.5	2.6
EGYPT	Cairo	Arabic	69 536 644	997 739	69.7	2.5	0.8	1.7
EQUATORIAL GUINEA	Malabo	Spanish, French, pidgin English, Fang, Bubi, Ibo	486 060	28 051	17.3	3.8	1.3	2.5
ERITREA	Asmara	Afar, Amharic, Arabic, Tigre, Kunama, Tigrinya	4 298 269	121 144	35.5	4.2	1.2	3.0
ETHIOPIA	Addis Ababa	Amharic, Tigrinya, Oromigna, Guaragigna, Somali, Arabic, English	65 891 874	1 133 882	58.1	4.5	1.8	2.7
GABON	Libreville	French, Fang, Myene, Bateke, Bapounou/ Eschira, Bandjabi	1 221 175	267 667	4.6	2.7	1.7	1.0
GAMBIA	Banjul	English, Mandinka, Wolof, Fula	1 411 205	10 689	132.0	4.2	1.3	2.9
GHANA	Accra	English, Akan, Moshi-Dagomba, Ewe, Ga	19 894 014	238 533	83.4	2.9	1.0	1.9
GUINEA	Conakry	French; each ethnic group has its own language	7 613 870	245 857	31.0	4.0	1.8	2.2
GUINEA-BISSAU	Bissau	Portuguese, Crioulo, African languages	1 315 822	36 125	36.4	3.9	1.5	2.4
KENYA	Nairobi	English, Kiswahili, numerous indigenous languages	30 765 916	582 646	52.8	2.8	1.4	1.4

Country: all independent countries, as well as selected dependencies. **Principal Language(s):** all official languages, as well as other primary languages spoken by a substantial proportion of the population. **Pop. Density:** population density, computed as population divided by area; given per square kilometre. **Natural Pop. Growth:** annual population increase per 100 people; does not include population change due to immigration or emigration.

COUNTRY	CAPITAL(S)	PRINCIPAL LANGUAGE(S)	POPULATION	AREA KM^2	POP. DENSITY PER KM^2	NATURAL POP. GROWTH PER 100 PEOPLE		
						BIRTHS	− DEATHS	= % GAIN
LESOTHO	Maseru	Sesotho, English, Zulu, Xhosa	2 177 062	30 355	71.7	3.1	1.6	1.5
LIBERIA	Monrovia	English, some 20 ethnic group languages	3 225 837	97 754	33.0	4.6	1.6	3.0
LIBYA	Tripoli	Arabic, Italian, English	5 240 599	1 757 000	3.0	2.8	0.4	2.4
MADAGASCAR	Antananarivo	French, Malagasy	15 982 563	587 041	27.2	4.3	1.3	3.0
MALAWI	Lilongwe	English, Chichewa	10 548 250	118 484	89.0	3.8	2.3	1.5
MALI	Bamako	French, Bambara, numerous African languages	11 008 518	1 248 574	8.8	4.9	1.9	3.0
MAURITANIA	Nouakchott	Hasaniya Arabic, Pular, Soninke, Wolof, French	2 747 312	1 030 700	2.7	4.3	1.4	2.9
MAURITIUS	Port Louis	English, Creole, French, Hindi, Urdu, Hakka, Bojpoori	1 189 825	2 040	583.2	1.7	0.7	1.0
MOROCCO	Rabat	Arabic, Berber dialects, French	30 645 305	458 730	66.8	2.4	0.6	1.8
MOZAMBIQUE	Maputo	Portuguese, indigenous dialects	19 371 057	812 379	23.8	3.7	2.4	1.3
NAMIBIA	Windhoek	English, Afrikaans, German, Oshivambo, Herero, Nama	1 797 677	825 118	2.2	3.5	2.1	1.4
NIGER	Niamey	French, Hausa, Djerma	10 355 156	1 267 000	8.2	5.1	2.3	2.8
NIGERIA	Abuja	English, Hausa, Yoruba, Igbo (Ibo), Fulani	126 635 626	923 768	137.1	4.0	1.4	2.6
RWANDA	Kigali	Kinyarwanda, French, English, Kiswahili (Swahili)	7 312 756	26 338	277.7	3.4	2.1	1.3
SAO TOME AND PRINCIPE	Sao Tome	Portuguese	165 034	1 001	164.9	4.3	0.8	3.5
SENEGAL	Dakar	French, Wolof, Pulaar, Jola, Mandinka	10 284 929	196 712	52.3	3.7	0.8	2.9
SEYCHELLES	Victoria	English, French, Creole	79 715	455	175.2	1.8	0.7	1.1
SIERRA LEONE	Freetown	English, Mende, Temne, Krio	5 426 618	71 740	75.6	4.5	1.9	2.6
SOMALIA	Mogadishu	Somali, Arabic, Italian, English	7 488 773	637 000	11.8	4.7	1.8	2.9
SOUTH AFRICA	Pretoria, Cape Town, Bloemfontein	Afrikaans, English, Ndebele, Pedi, Sotho, Swazi, Tsonga, Tswana, Venda, Xhosa, Zulu	43 586 097	1 219 090	35.8	2.1	1.7	0.4
SUDAN	Khartoum	Arabic, Nubian, Ta Bedawie, diverse dialects of Nilotic, Nilo-Hamitic, Sudanic languages, English	36 080 373	2 503 890	14.4	3.8	1.0	2.8
SWAZILAND	Mbabane, Lobamba	English, siSwati	1 104 343	17 364	63.6	4.0	2.2	1.8
TANZANIA	Dar es Salaam, Dodoma	Kiswahili or Swahili, Kiunguju, English, Arabic	36 232 074	945 090	38.3	4.0	1.3	2.7
TOGO	Lome	French, Ewe, Mina, Kabye (Kabiye), Dagomba	5 153 088	56 785	90.7	3.7	1.1	2.6

Country: all independent countries, as well as selected dependencies. **Principal Language(s):** all official languages, as well as other primary languages spoken by a substantial proportion of the population. **Pop. Density:** population density, computed as population divided by area; given per square kilometre. **Natural Pop. Growth:** annual population increase per 100 people; does not include population change due to immigration or emigration.

COUNTRY	CAPITAL(S)	PRINCIPAL LANGUAGE(S)	POPULATION	AREA KM²	POP. DENSITY PER KM²	NATURAL POP. GROWTH PER 100 PEOPLE BIRTHS – DEATHS = % GAIN		
TUNISIA	Tunis	Arabic, French	9 705 102	164 150	59.1	1.7	0.5	1.2
UGANDA	Kampala	English, Ganda or Luganda, other Niger-Congo languages, Nilo-Saharan languages, Swahili, Arabic	23 985 712	241 038	99.5	4.8	1.8	3.0
WESTERN SAHARA (Adm. Morocco)	El Aauin (Laayoune)	Hassaniya Arabic, Moroccan Arabic	250 559	252 120	1.0	2.4	0.6	1.8
ZAMBIA	Lusaka	English, Bemba, Kaonda, Lozi, Lunda, Luvale, Nyanja, Tonga	9 770 199	752 614	13.0	4.1	2.2	1.9
ZIMBABWE	Harare	English, Shona, Sindebele	11 365 366	390 757	29.1	2.5	2.3	0.2

Asia

COUNTRY	CAPITAL(S)	PRINCIPAL LANGUAGE(S)	POPULATION	AREA KM²	POP. DENSITY PER KM²	BIRTHS	DEATHS	% GAIN
AFGHANISTAN	Kabul	Pashtu, Afghan Persian (Dari), Uzbek, Turkmen, Balochi, Pashai	26 813 057	652 225	41.1	4.2	1.8	2.4
ARMENIA	Yerevan	Armenian , Russian	3 336 100	29 743	112.2	1.2	1.0	0.2
AZERBAIJAN	Baku	Azerbaijani (Azeri), Russian, Armenian	7 771 092	86 600	89.7	1.8	0.9	0.9
BAHRAIN	Manama	Arabic, English, Farsi, Urdu	645 361	694	929.9	2.0	0.4	1.6
BANGLADESH	Dhaka	Bangla (Bengali), English	131 269 860	147 570	889.5	2.5	0.8	1.7
BHUTAN	Thimphu	Dzongkha, various Tibetan dialects, various Nepalese dialects	2 049 412	47 000	43.6	3.6	1.4	2.2
BRUNEI	Bandar Seri Begawan	Malay, English, Chinese	343 653	5 765	59.6	2.0	0.3	1.7
CAMBODIA	Phnom Penh	Khmer, French, English	12 491 501	181 035	69.0	3.3	1.1	2.2
CHINA	Beijing	Standard Chinese or Mandarin (Putonghua), Yue (Cantonese), Wu (Shanghaiese), Minbei (Fuzhou), Minnan (Hokkien-Taiwanese), Xiang, Gan, Hakka dialects	1 273 111 290	9 572 900	133.0	1.6	0.7	0.9
CYPRUS	Nicosia	Greek, Turkish, English	762 887	9 251	82.5	1.3	0.8	0.5
EAST TIMOR	Dili	Tetum (Tetun), Portuguese	885 000	14 609	60.6	2.2	0.6	1.6
GEORGIA	Tbilisi	Georgian, Russian, Armenian, Azeri	4 989 285	69 700	71.6	1.1	1.4	-0.3
INDIA	New Delhi	Hindi, English, Bengali, Telugu, Marathi, Tamil, Urdu, Gujarati, Malayalam ,Kannada, Oriya, Punjabi, Assamese, Kashmiri, Sindhi, Sanskrit, Hindustani	1 029 991 145	3 165 596	325.4	2.4	0.9	1.5
INDONESIA	Jakarta	Bahasa Indonesia, English, Dutch, Javanese	227 552 870	1 907 961	119.3	2.2	0.6	1.6

Country: all independent countries, as well as selected dependencies. **Principal Language(s):** all official languages, as well as other primary languages spoken by a substantial proportion of the population. **Pop. Density:** population density, computed as population divided by area; given per square kilometre. **Natural Pop. Growth:** annual population increase per 100 people; does not include population change due to immigration or emigration.

COUNTRY	CAPITAL(S)	PRINCIPAL LANGUAGE(S)	POPULATION	AREA KM²	POP. DENSITY PER KM²	NATURAL POP. GROWTH PER 100 PEOPLE BIRTHS – DEATHS = % GAIN		
IRAN	Tehran	Persian and Persian dialects, Turkic and Turkic dialects, Kurdish, Luri, Balochi, Arabic, Turkish	66 128 965	1 633 841	40.5	1.7	0.5	1.2
IRAQ	Baghdad	Arabic, Kurdish, Assyrian, Armenian	23 331 985	435 052	53.6	3.4	0.6	2.8
ISRAEL	Jerusalem	Hebrew, Arabic, English	5 938 093	20 425	290.7	1.9	0.6	1.3
JAPAN	Tokyo	Japanese	126 771 662	377 837	335.5	1.0	0.8	0.2
JORDAN	Amman	Arabic	5 153 378	89 326	57.7	2.6	0.3	2.3
KAZAKHSTAN	Astana	Kazakh (Qazaq), Russian	16 731 303	2 724 900	6.1	1.7	1.0	0.7
KUWAIT	Kuwait	Arabic, English	2 041 961	17 818	114.6	2.2	0.2	2.0
KYRGYZSTAN	Bishkek	Kirghiz (Kyrgyz), Russian	4 753 003	199 900	23.8	2.6	0.9	1.7
LAOS	Vientiane	Lao, French, English	5 635 967	236 800	23.8	3.8	1.3	2.5
LEBANON	Beirut	Arabic, French, English, Armenian	3 627 774	10 400	348.8	2.0	0.6	1.4
MALAYSIA	Kuala Lumpur	Bahasa Melayu, English, Cantonese, Mandarin, Hokkien, Hakka, Hainan, Foochow, Tamil, Telugu, Malayalam, Panjabi, Thai, Iban, Kadazan	22 229 040	329 735	67.4	2.5	0.5	2.0
MALDIVES	Male	Maldivian Dhivehi, English	310 764	298	1 042.8	3.8	0.8	3.0
MONGOLIA	Ulaanbaatar	Khalkha Mongol, Turkic, Russian	2 654 999	1 564 116	1.7	2.2	0.7	1.5
MYANMAR (BURMA)	Yangon (Rangoon)	Burmese	41 994 678	676 577	62.1	2.0	1.2	0.8
NEPAL	Kathmandu	Nepali, English	25 284 463	17 181	1 471.7	3.3	1.0	2.3
NORTH KOREA	Pyongyang	Korean	21 968 228	112 762	194.8	1.9	0.7	1.2
OMAN	Muscat	Arabic, English, Baluchi, Urdu, Indian dialects	2 622 198	309 500	8.5	3.8	0.4	3.4
PAKISTAN	Islamabad	Punjabi, Sindhi, Siraiki, Pashtu, Urdu, Balochi, Hindko, Brahui, English, Burushaski	144 616 639	796 095	181.7	3.1	0.9	2.2
PHILIPPINES	Manila	Filipino, English, Tagalog, Cebuano, Ilocan, Hiligaynon or Ilonggo, Bicol, Waray, Pampango, Pangasinense	82 841 518	300 076	276.1	2.7	0.6	2.1
QATAR	Doha	Arabic, English	769 152	11 437	67.3	1.6	0.4	1.2
SAUDI ARABIA	Riyadh	Arabic	22 757 092	2 248 000	10.1	3.7	0.6	3.1
SINGAPORE	Singapore	Chinese, Malay, Tamil, English	4 300 419	660	6 515.8	1.3	0.4	0.9
SOUTH KOREA	Seoul	Korean, English	47 904 370	99 373	482.1	1.5	0.6	0.9
SRI LANKA	Colombo, Sri Jayewardenepura Kotte	Sinhala, Tamil, English	19 408 635	65 610	295.8	1.7	0.7	1.0

Country: all independent countries, as well as selected dependencies. **Principal Language(s):** all official languages, as well as other primary languages spoken by a substantial proportion of the population. **Pop. Density:** population density, computed as population divided by area; given per square kilometre. **Natural Pop. Growth:** annual population increase per 100 people; does not include population change due to immigration or emigration.

COUNTRY	CAPITAL(S)	PRINCIPAL LANGUAGE(S)	POPULATION	AREA KM²	POP. DENSITY PER KM²	NATURAL POP. GROWTH PER 100 PEOPLE BIRTHS – DEATHS = % GAIN		
SYRIA	Damascus	Arabic, Kurdish, Armenian, Aramaic, Circassian, French, English	16 728 808	185 180	90.3	3.1	0.5	2.6
TAIWAN	Taipei	Mandarin Chinese, Taiwanese, Hakka dialects	22 370 461	36 985	604.9	1.4	0.6	0.8
TAJIKISTAN	Dushanbe	Tajik, Russian	6 578 681	143 100	46.0	3.3	0.8	2.5
THAILAND	Bangkok	Thai, English	61 797 751	513 115	120.4	1.7	0.8	0.9
TURKEY	Ankara	Turkish, Kurdish, Arabic, Armenian, Greek	66 493 970	779 452	85.3	1.8	0.6	1.2
TURKMENISTAN	Ashgabat	Turkmen, Russian, Uzbek	4 603 244	488 100	9.4	2.9	0.9	2.0
UNITED ARAB EMIRATES	Abu Dhabi	Arabic, Persian, English, Hindi, Urdu	2 407 460	83 600	28.8	1.8	0.4	1.4
UZBEKISTAN	Tashkent	Uzbek, Russian, Tajik	25 155 064	447 400	56.2	2.6	0.8	1.8
VIETNAM	Hanoi	Vietnamese, English, French, Chinese, Khmer, Mon-Khmer, Malayo-Polynesian	79 939 014	331 041	241.5	2.1	0.6	1.5
YEMEN	Sanaa	Arabic	18 078 035	555 000	32.6	4.3	0.9	3.4

Australia and Oceania

COUNTRY	CAPITAL(S)	PRINCIPAL LANGUAGE(S)	POPULATION	AREA KM²	POP. DENSITY PER KM²	BIRTHS	DEATHS	% GAIN
AUSTRALIA	Canberra	English, native languages	19 357 594	7 692 030	2.5	1.3	0.7	0.6
FIJI	Suva	English, Fijian, Hindustani	844 330	18 272	46.2	2.3	0.6	1.7
FRENCH POLYNESIA (Fr.)	Papeete	French, Tahitian	253 506	4 000	63.4	1.9	0.5	1.4
KIRIBATI	Tarawa	English, I-Kiribati	94 149	811	116.1	3.2	0.9	2.3
MARSHALL ISLANDS	Majuro	English, two major Marshallese dialects, Japanese	70 822	181	391.3	4.5	0.6	3.9
MICRONESIA	Palikir	English, Trukese, Pohnpeian, Yapese, Kosrean	134 597	701	192.0	2.7	0.6	2.1
NAURU	Yaren District (unofficial)	Nauruan, English	12 088	21	570.2	2.7	0.7	2.0
NEW CALEDONIA (Fr.)	Noumea	French, 33 Melanesian-Polynesian dialects	204 863	18 575	11.0	2.0	0.5	1.5
NEW ZEALAND	Wellington	English, Maori	3 864 129	270 534	14.3	1.4	0.7	0.7
PALAU	Koror	English, Palauan, Sonsorolese, Tobi, Angaur, Japanese	19 092	488	39.1	2.0	0.7	1.3
PAPUA NEW GUINEA	Port Moresby	English, pidgin English widespread, Motu, 715 indigenous languages	5 049 055	462 840	10.9	3.2	0.8	2.4
SAMOA	Apia	Samoan (Polynesian), English	179 058	2 831	63.2	1.5	0.6	0.9
SOLOMON ISLANDS	Honiara	Melanesian pidgin, English, 120 indigenous languages	480 442	28 370	16.9	3.4	0.4	3.0
TONGA	Nukualofa	Tongan, English	104 227	750	139.0	2.4	0.6	1.8

Country: all independent countries, as well as selected dependencies. **Principal Language(s):** all official languages, as well as other primary languages spoken by a substantial proportion of the population. **Pop. Density:** population density, computed as population divided by area; given per square kilometre. **Natural Pop. Growth:** annual population increase per 100 people; does not include population change due to immigration or emigration.

COUNTRY	CAPITAL(S)	PRINCIPAL LANGUAGE(S)	POPULATION	AREA KM²	POP. DENSITY PER KM²	NATURAL POP. GROWTH PER 100 PEOPLE BIRTHS	– DEATHS	= % GAIN
TUVALU	Funafuti	Tuvaluan, English	10 991	26	429.3	2.2	0.8	1.4
VANUATU	Port-Vila	English, French, pidgin (Bislama or Bichelama)	192 910	12 190	15.8	2.5	0.8	1.7

Europe

COUNTRY	CAPITAL(S)	PRINCIPAL LANGUAGE(S)	POPULATION	AREA KM²	POP. DENSITY PER KM²	BIRTHS	– DEATHS	= % GAIN
ALBANIA	Tirana	Albanian (Tosk), Greek	3 510 484	28 748	122.1	1.9	0.6	1.3
ANDORRA	Andorra la Vella	Catalan, French, Castilian	67 627	468	144.5	1.0	0.5	0.5
AUSTRIA	Vienna	German	8 150 835	83 858	97.2	1.0	1.0	0.0
BELARUS	Minsk	Byelorussian, Russian	10 350 194	207 595	49.9	1.0	1.4	-0.4
BELGIUM	Brussels	Dutch, French, German	10 258 762	30 528	336.0	1.1	1.0	0.1
BOSNIA-HERZEGOVINA	Sarajevo	Croatian, Serbian, Bosnian	3 922 205	51 129	76.7	1.3	0.8	0.5
BULGARIA	Sofia	Bulgarian	7 707 495	110 994	69.4	0.8	1.4	-0.6
CROATIA	Zagreb	Croatian	4 334 142	56 542	76.7	1.3	1.2	0.1
CZECH REPUBLIC	Prague	Czech	10 264 212	78 866	130.1	0.9	1.1	-0.2
DENMARK	Copenhagen	Danish, Faroese, Greenlandic, German, English	5 352 815	43 096	124.2	1.2	1.1	0.1
ESTONIA	Tallinn	Estonian, Russian, Ukrainian, English, Finnish	1 423 316	45 227	31.5	0.9	1.4	-0.5
FINLAND	Helsinki	Finnish, Swedish, small Lapp- and Russian-speaking minorities	5 175 783	338 145	15.3	1.1	1.0	0.1
FRANCE	Paris	French	59 551 227	543 965	109.5	1.2	0.9	0.3
GERMANY	Berlin	German	83 029 536	357 021	232.6	0.9	1.0	-0.1
GREECE	Athens	Greek, English, French	10 623 835	131 957	80.5	1.0	1.0	0.0
HUNGARY	Budapest	Hungarian	10 106 017	93 030	108.6	0.9	1.3	-0.4
ICELAND	Reykjavik	Icelandic	277 906	102 819	2.7	1.5	0.7	0.8
IRELAND	Dublin	English, Irish (Gaelic)	3 840 838	70 273	54.7	1.5	0.8	0.7
ITALY	Rome	Italian, German, French, Slovene	57 679 825	301 337	191.4	0.9	1.0	-0.1
LATVIA	Riga	Latvian or Lettish, Lithuanian, Russian, other	2 385 231	64 589	36.9	0.8	1.5	-0.7
LIECHTENSTEIN	Vaduz	German, Alemannic dialect	32 528	160	203.3	1.2	0.7	0.5
LITHUANIA	Vilnius	Lithuanian, Polish, Russian	3 610 535	65 300	55.3	1.0	1.3	-0.3
LUXEMBOURG	Luxembourg	Luxembourgish, German, French	442 972	2 586	171.3	1.2	0.9	0.3
MACEDONIA	Skopje	Macedonian, Albanian, Turkish, Serbo-Croatian	2 046 209	25 713	79.6	1.4	0.8	0.6
MALTA	Valletta	Maltese, English	394 583	316	1 248.7	1.3	0.8	0.5
MOLDOVA	Chisinau	Moldovan, Russian, Gagauz	4 431 570	33 700	131.5	1.3	1.2	0.1
MONACO	Monaco	French, English, Italian, Monegasque	31 842	1.95	16 329.2	1.0	1.3	-0.3
NETHERLANDS	Amsterdam, The Hague	Dutch	15 981 472	41 526	384.9	1.2	0.9	0.3

Country: all independent countries, as well as selected dependencies. **Principal Language(s):** all official languages, as well as other primary languages spoken by a substantial proportion of the population. **Pop. Density:** population density, computed as population divided by area; given per square kilometre. **Natural Pop. Growth:** annual population increase per 100 people; does not include population change due to immigration or emigration.

COUNTRY	CAPITAL(S)	PRINCIPAL LANGUAGE(S)	POPULATION	AREA KM²	POP. DENSITY PER KM²	NATURAL POP. GROWTH PER 100 PEOPLE BIRTHS − DEATHS = % GAIN		
NORWAY	Oslo	Norwegian	4 503 440	323 758	13.9	1.3	1.0	0.3
POLAND	Warsaw	Polish	38 633 912	313 027	123.4	1.0	1.0	0.0
PORTUGAL	Lisbon	Portuguese	10 066 253	92 365	109.0	1.1	1.0	0.1
ROMANIA	Bucharest	Romanian, Hungarian, German	22 364 022	237 500	94.2	1.1	1.2	-0.1
RUSSIA	Moscow	Russian	145 470 197	17 075 400	8.5	0.9	1.4	-0.5
SAN MARINO	San Marino	Italian	27 336	61	448.1	1.1	0.8	0.3
SERBIA-MONTENEGRO	Belgrade	Serbian, Albanian	10 677 290	102 173	104.5	1.3	1.1	0.2
SLOVAKIA	Bratislava	Slovak, Hungarian	5 414 937	49 035	110.4	1.0	0.9	0.1
SLOVENIA	Ljubljana	Slovenian, Serbo-Croatian	1 930 132	20 273	95.2	0.9	1.0	-0.1
SPAIN	Madrid	Castilian Spanish, Catalan, Galician, Basque	40 037 995	505 990	79.1	0.9	0.9	0.0
SWEDEN	Stockholm	Swedish	8 875 053	449 969	19.7	1.0	1.1	-0.1
SWITZERLAND	Bern	German, French, Italian, Romansch	7 283 274	41 284	176.4	1.0	0.9	0.1
UKRAINE	Kiev	Ukrainian, Russian, Romanian, Polish, Hungarian	48 760 474	603 700	80.8	0.9	1.6	-0.7
UNITED KINGDOM	London	English, Welsh, Scottish form of Gaelic	59 647 790	244 101	244.4	1.2	1.0	0.1
VATICAN CITY	Vatican City	Italian, Latin, French	800	0.44	1 818.2	0.0	0.0	0.0

North America

COUNTRY	CAPITAL(S)	PRINCIPAL LANGUAGE(S)	POPULATION	AREA KM²	POP. DENSITY PER KM²	BIRTHS	DEATHS	% GAIN
ANTIGUA AND BARBUDA	Saint John's	English	66 970	442	151.5	2.0	0.6	1.4
ARUBA (Neth.)	Oranjestad	Dutch, Papiamento, English, Spanish	70 007	193	362.7	1.3	0.6	0.7
BAHAMAS	Nassau	English, Creole	297 852	13 939	21.4	1.9	0.7	1.2
BARBADOS	Bridgetown	English	275 330	430	640.3	1.4	0.9	0.5
BELIZE	Belmopan	English, Spanish, Mayan, Garifuna (Carib), Creole	256 062	22 965	11.2	3.2	0.5	2.7
CANADA	Ottawa	English, French	31 592 805	9 970 610	3.2	1.1	0.7	0.4
COSTA RICA	San Jose	Spanish, English	3 773 057	51 100	73.8	2.0	0.4	1.6
CUBA	Havana	Spanish	11 184 023	110 861	100.9	1.2	0.7	0.5
DOMINICA	Roseau	English, French patois	177 562	750	94.4	1.8	0.7	1.1
DOMINICAN REPUBLIC	Santo Domingo	Spanish	8 581 477	48 671	176.3	2.5	0.5	2.0
EL SALVADOR	San Salvador	Spanish, Nahua	6 237 662	21 041	296.5	2.9	0.6	2.3
GREENLAND (KALAALLIT NUNAAT) (Den.)	Godthab (Nuuk)	Greenlandic, Danish, English	56 352	2 166 066	0.0	1.7	0.8	0.9
GRENADA	Saint George's	English, French patois	89 227	344	259.4	2.3	0.8	1.5
GUADELOUPE (Fr.)	Basse-Terre	French, Creole patois	431 170	1 705	252.9	1.7	0.6	1.1
GUATEMALA	Guatemala City	Spanish, Quiche, Cakchiquel, Kekchi, Mam, Garifuna, Xinca	12 974 361	108 889	119.2	3.5	0.7	2.8
HAITI	Port-au-Prince	French, Creole	6 964 549	27 700	251.4	3.2	1.5	1.7

Country: all independent countries, as well as selected dependencies. **Principal Language(s):** all official languages, as well as other primary languages spoken by a substantial proportion of the population. **Pop. Density:** population density, computed as population divided by area; given per square kilometre. **Natural Pop. Growth:** annual population increase per 100 people; does not include population change due to immigration or emigration.

COUNTRY	CAPITAL(S)	PRINCIPAL LANGUAGE(S)	POPULATION	AREA KM²	POP. DENSITY PER KM²	NATURAL POP. GROWTH PER 100 PEOPLE BIRTHS − DEATHS = % GAIN		
HONDURAS	Tegucigalpa	Spanish, Amerindian dialects	6 406 052	112 492	56.9	3.2	0.6	2.6
JAMAICA	Kingston	English, Creole	2 665 636	10 991	242.5	1.8	0.5	1.3
MARTINIQUE (Fr.)	Fort-de-France	French, Creole patois	418 454	1 128	371.0	1.6	0.7	0.9
MEXICO	Mexico City	Spanish, various Mayan, Nahuatl, and other regional indigenous languages	101 879 171	1 958 201	52.0	2.3	0.5	1.8
NETHERLANDS ANTILLES (Neth.)	Willemstad	Dutch, Papiamento, English, Spanish	212 226	800	265.3	1.6	0.6	1.0
NICARAGUA	Managua	Spanish, English, indigenous language	4 918 393	131 812	37.3	2.8	0.5	2.3
PANAMA	Panama City	Spanish, English	2 845 647	75 517	37.7	1.9	0.5	1.4
PUERTO RICO (U.S.)	San Juan	Spanish, English	3 937 316	9 104	432.5	1.5	0.8	0.7
ST. KITTS AND NEVIS	Basseterre	English	38 756	269	144.1	1.9	0.9	1.0
ST. LUCIA	Castries	English, French patois	158 178	617	256.4	2.2	0.5	1.7
ST. VINCENT AND THE GRENADINES	Kingstown	English, French patois	115 942	389	298.1	1.8	0.6	1.2
TRINIDAD AND TOBAGO	Port-of-Spain	English, Hindi, French, Spanish, Chinese	1 169 682	5 128	228.1	1.4	0.9	0.5
UNITED STATES OF AMERICA	Washington, D.C.	English, Spanish	278 058 881	9 529 063	29.2	1.4	0.9	0.5

South America

COUNTRY	CAPITAL(S)	PRINCIPAL LANGUAGE(S)	POPULATION	AREA KM²	POP. DENSITY PER KM²	BIRTHS	DEATHS	% GAIN
ARGENTINA	Buenos Aires	Spanish, English, Italian, German, French	37 384 816	2 780 092	13.4	1.9	0.8	1.1
BOLIVIA	La Paz, Sucre	Spanish, Quechua, Aymara	8 300 463	1 098 581	7.6	2.7	0.8	1.9
BRAZIL	Brasilia	Portuguese, Spanish, English, French	174 468 575	8 547 404	20.4	1.8	0.9	0.9
CHILE	Santiago	Spanish	15 328 467	756 626	20.3	1.7	0.6	1.1
COLOMBIA	Bogota	Spanish	40 349 388	1 141 568	35.3	2.3	0.6	1.7
ECUADOR	Quito	Spanish, Quechua	13 183 978	272 045	48.5	2.6	0.5	2.1
FRENCH GUIANA (Fr.)	Cayenne	French	177 562	86 504	2.1	2.2	0.5	1.7
GUYANA	Georgetown	English, Amerindian dialects, Creole, Hindi, Urdu	697 181	215 083	3.2	1.8	0.9	0.9
PARAGUAY	Asuncion	Spanish, Guarani	5 734 139	406 752	14.1	3.1	0.5	2.6
PERU	Lima	Spanish, Quechua, Aymara	27 483 864	1 285 216	21.4	2.4	0.6	1.8
SURINAME	Paramaribo	Dutch, English, Sranang Tongo, Hindustani, Javanese	433 998	163 820	2.6	2.1	0.6	1.5
URUGUAY	Montevideo	Spanish, Portunol, Brazilero	3 360 105	176 215	19.1	1.7	0.9	0.8
VENEZUELA	Caracas	Spanish, numerous indigenous dialects	23 916 810	916 445	26.1	2.1	0.5	1.6

Country: all independent countries, as well as selected dependencies. **Principal Language(s):** all official languages, as well as other primary languages spoken by a substantial proportion of the population. **Pop. Density:** population density, computed as population divided by area; given per square kilometre. **Natural Pop. Growth:** annual population increase per 100 people; does not include population change due to immigration or emigration.

acid rain Rain or snow that carries acids formed from chemical pollutants in the atmosphere.

Antarctic Circle An imaginary line of latitude located at 66½°S, approximately 1,630 miles (2620 kilometres) from the South Pole.

Arctic Circle An imaginary line of latitude located at 66½°N, approximately 1,630 miles (2620 kilometres) from the North Pole.

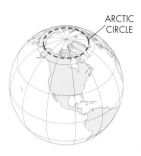
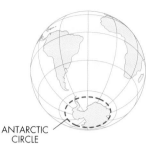

balance of trade The difference between how much a country exports and how much it imports, commonly measured in U.S. dollars. A country that exports more than it imports has a positive balance of trade, or *trade surplus*. A country that imports more than it exports has a negative balance of trade, or *trade deficit.*

Census Metropolitan Area (CMA) One or more cities with more than 100 000 residents, as well as the adjacent municipalities and parts of townships, as recognized for purposes of the census.

climate The usual weather conditions for a large area over a long period of time and through all seasons. Climate is affected by latitude, elevation, topography, ocean currents, and wind.

climograph Graph showing annual patterns of temperature and precipitation.

commodity One of the goods sold on the world market. Commodities may be agricultural products, manufactured items, or such natural resources as minerals.

deforestation Massive removal of trees from a forest.

elevation Height above sea level.

emigration Movement of people away from their native country or region to a new home elsewhere. The people moving away are called *emigrants.*

Equator An imaginary line that divides the earth into the Northern and Southern Hemispheres. All points along the Equator have a latitude of 0°.

European Union (EU) A group of European nations whose main goal is to establish themselves for trading purposes as a single market. The EU grew out of the European Economic Community.

export The sale of goods to a foreign country.

fossil fuels Natural fuels that were formed from the remains of plants and animals over millions of years. Principal fossil fuels are petroleum, natural gas, and coal.

gross domestic product (GDP) Annual value of all goods and services produced within a country's borders. GDP includes production by foreign-owned facilities.

gross national product (GNP) Annual value of all goods and services produced by companies that are owned by a country's citizens. GNP includes production in facilities operated by the nation's citizens in other countries.

immigration Movement of people into a new country of residence. The people moving in are called *immigrants.*

imperialism Action taken by one country to control or influence another country or territory in order to gain economic or political advantage.

import The purchase of goods produced in a foreign country.

indigenous Native to a particular region. Indigenous peoples are related to the earliest inhabitants of a region.

land use How people use the earth's surface and natural resources for economic purposes. Regions are identified by the dominant form of economy, such as farming, herding, or manufacturing.

latitude Distance from the Equator measured in degrees. Lines of latitude, or *parallels,* are numbered north and south from the Equator and appear on maps as east-west lines.

life expectancy The average number of years that a group of people may expect to live based on the prevailing death rates for that population. Life expectancy reflects the group's general health and welfare.

literacy The ability to both read and write. The percentage of literate people is a good indicator of a country's educational level, although literacy standards vary by country.

longitude Distance from the Prime Meridian measured in degrees. Lines of longitude, or *meridians,* are numbered east and west from the Prime Meridian and appear on maps as north-south lines.

map projection Any system for drawing lines of latitude and longitude onto a map. Projections are never completely accurate, distorting either sizes or shapes of the earth's land and water features.

natural population growth Annual population increase for a region or country. It is the difference between the number of births and the number of deaths and does not include change due to population movement.

natural vegetation The type of vegetation that can grow in a specific region's climate and soil without benefit of human intervention or cultivation.

Oceania Collective name for islands of the central and southern Pacific Ocean, usually including New Zealand and sometimes also including Australia.

Organization of Petroleum Exporting Countries (OPEC) Association of 11 nations that control most of the world's known oil reserves. OPEC members are Algeria, Indonesia, Iran, Iraq, Kuwait, Libya, Nigeria, Qatar, Saudi Arabia, United Arab Emirates, and Venezuela.

ozone A form of oxygen that occurs naturally in the atmosphere in small amounts. The layer of ozone in the upper atmosphere blocks most of the sun's harmful ultraviolet rays.

permafrost Permanently frozen soil. In some areas an *active layer* at the surface melts during the short summer, then freezes again in the autumn.

precipitation Water from the atmosphere that accumulates on the earth's surface as dew, rain, hail, sleet, or snow. For annual measures, ten millimetres of snow, sleet, or hail are counted as one millimetre of rain.

Prime Meridian The 0° meridian, which passes through Greenwich, England.

Sahel The drought-ridden area south of Africa's Sahara and extending east-west between Somalia and Senegal.

staple food A foodstuff that constitutes a major part of the diet for a region's population.

taiga A cold, mostly coniferous forest located just south of the tundra in North America, Europe, or Asia.

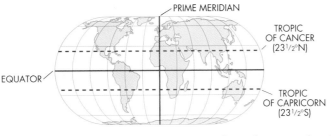

Tropic of Cancer An imaginary line of latitude located at 23½°N. It marks the northern boundary of the earth's tropical zone.

Tropic of Capricorn An imaginary line of latitude located at 23½°S. It marks the southern boundary of the earth's tropical zone.

tundra A treeless Arctic region of North America, Europe, or Asia; also, the short, frost-resistant vegetation or the cold, dry climate of this region.

wetlands A transition zone between land and water where the water level remains near or above the ground's surface for most of the year. Wetlands include swamps, marshes, and bogs.

Abbreviations

adm.	administered by	It.	Italy	Pop.	Population
AIDS	Acquired Immune Deficiency Syndrome	km	kilometres	Port.	Portugal
		L., l.	Lake, Lac	poss.	possession
Alb.	Albania	Lat.	Latvia	P.P.	Provincial Park
Alta.	Alberta	lat.	latitude	Prov., prov.	Province
Am. Samoa	American Samoa	Liech.	Liechtenstein	Pt.	Point
Ang.	Angola	Lith.	Lithuania	P.W.P.	Provincial Wilderness Park
Arg.	Argentina	long.	longitude		
Aus.	Austria	Lux.	Luxembourg	Que.	Quebec
Austr.	Australia	m	metres	R., r.	River, Riviere
Azer.	Azerbaijan	Mac.	Macedonia	Ra.	Range
B.C.	British Columbia	Man.	Manitoba	Res., res.	Reservoir
Bos.	Bosnia-Herzegovina	Mex.	Mexico	S. Afr.	South Africa
		mi.	miles	Sask.	Saskatchewan
Bur.	Bureau	Mont.	Montana	Serb.	Serbia-Montenegro
C.	Cape	Mt., Mts.	Mount, Mont, Mountain, Mountains	Sl., Slovak.	Slovakia
C. Afr. Rep.	Central African Republic			Slov.	Slovenia
		NAFTA	North American Free Trade Agreement	Sp.	Spain
Congo Rep.	Congo Republic			sq.	square
Cro.	Croatia	N.B.	New Brunswick	St., Ste.	Saint, Sainte
Cz., Cz. Rep.	Czech Republic	Neth.	Netherlands	Str.	Strait
D.C.	District of Columbia	Nfld.	Newfoundland	Switz.	Switzerland
Den.	Denmark	Nor.	Norway	Terr., terr.	Territory
Dom. Rep.	Dominican Republic	N.P.	National Park	U.A.E.	United Arab Emirates
Eq. Guinea	Equatorial Guinea	N.S.	Nova Scotia	U.K.	United Kingdom
Est.	Estonia	Nun.	Nunavut	UN	United Nations
Fk.	Fork	N.W.T.	Northwest Territories	UNAIDS	Joint United Nations Program on HIV/AIDS
Fr.	France, French	N.Z.	New Zealand		
ft.	feet	O.	Ocean	U.S.	United States
HIV	Human Immunodeficiency Virus	Ont.	Ontario	US$	United States dollars
		P.E.I.	Prince Edward Island	U.S.S.R.	Union of Soviet Socialist Republics
I., Is.	Island, Islands	Pen., pen.	Peninsula		
Intl.	International	Pk., pk.	Peak	Yukon	Yukon Territory

INDEX

The index lists all the place names that appear in the book. Each entry includes a brief description of what or where it is, its latitude and longitude, and its main page reference. Many of the entries also include phonetic pronunciations. The key to the system of phonetic respelling is given on page 168, facing the inside back cover.

The entry for a physical feature is alphabetized by the proper part of its name, not by the descriptive part. For example, Lake Superior is listed as *Superior, L.*, and Mount Etna is listed as *Etna, Mt.* The entry for a city, however, is alphabetized by the first word in its name, no matter what it is, so that the city of Lake Charles, Louisiana, is listed as *Lake Charles*. Similarly, foreign names such as Rio Grande are alphabetized by the first word in the name.

Names beginning with *St.* are spelled *Saint* in the index. Abbreviations that are used in the index and in other parts of the book are listed on page 145.

N

SOURCES

Populations and areas in thematic maps, graphs, and tables are the most recent available at the time of publication. All other statistics are averages over the three most recent years for which information is available, unless otherwise described where they appear.

"Acid Rain" web page, *Air and Water,* Environment Canada, 2000

Annual Statistical Bulletin, Organization of Petroleum Exporting Countries, 2001

Annual Time Series, United Nations Population Information Network, Food and Agricultural Organization, 2000

Atlas of Canada, Department, of Mines and Technical Surveys, 1957

Birds of West Africa, W. Searle and G.J. Morel, Stephen Greene Press, 1988

Book of the Year, Encyclopedia Britannica, 2001, 2000, 1996

Canada's Mineral Production, Statistics Canada, 2002

Canadian Landings Information, Canadian Department of Fisheries and Oceans, 2000

Census of Agriculture, Statistics Canada (earlier Bureau of Statistics) 2001, 1991, 1971, 1951, 1931

Census of Canada, Statistics Canada (earlier Bureau of Statistics) 2001, 1996, 1991, 1981, 1971, 1951

Census of Population, Bureau of the Census, U.S. Department of Commerce, 2000

"Coal Map of North America," U.S. Geological Survey, 1988

The Daily, Statistics Canada

Direction of Trade Statistics Yearbook 2001, International Monetary Fund

"Economic Conditions: National Accounts" Statistics Canada, 2001

Economic Overview of Farm Incomes, Volume 2, Agriculture and Agri-Food Canada, 2002

"Economy: Manufacturing and Construction" Statistics Canada, 2002

Electrical Power Generating Stations, Statistics Canada, 1998, 1994

Elephant Trade Information System Summary Report, Convention on International Trade in Endangered Species of Wild Flora and Fauna, 2002

Enterprise Reforms in a Centrally planned Economy: The Case of the Chinese Bicycle Industry, Xui-Hai Zhang, St. Martin's Press, 1992

Essentials of Physical Geography, G.T. Trewartha, McGraw-Hill, 1957.

"Generalized Land Vegetation map of the World," A.W. Kuchler, in *Introduction to Plant Geography,* N. Polunin, McGraw-Hill, 1957

Glacial Geology, N. Eyles, Pergamon Press, 1983

Historical Atlas of Canada I, II, III, University of Toronto Press, 1987, 1993, 1990

Indian Ocean Atlas, U.S. Central Intelligence Agency, 1976

International Energy Annual, Energy Information Administration, U.S. Department of Energy, 2002

"International Data Bank," U.S. Census Bureau, 2000

International Petroleum Monthly, Energy Information Administration, U.S. Department of Energy, 2002

International Trade Statistics Yearbook, Ecosoc Statistical Office, 1999

"Management of Water" web pages, Environment Canada, 2002

NAFTA Agriculture Fact Sheets, Foreign Agriculture Service, U.S. Department of Agriculture, 2000

National Air Pollutant Emissions Trends: 1900–1998, U.S. Environmental Protection Agency, 2000

The National Atlas of Canada, 5th and on-line editions

The National Atlas of the United States, 1970

National Transportation Statistics 2000, Bureau of Transportation Statistics, U.S. Department of Transportation, 2000

The Navigator Magazine, Feb. 2002

1998 Energy Yearbook, UN Statistical Division, 2002

The Nystrom Atlas of Our Country's History, Nystrom, 2002

The Nystrom Desk Atlas, Nystrom, 2003, 1994

Oxford Economic Atlas of the World, 4th edition, Oxford University Press, 1972

"Preliminary Metalogenic Map of North America," U.S. Geological Survey, 1981

"Profile: Economic Community of Central African States," Organization of African Unity

Regional Economic Observer, Industry Canada, 2001, 2000

"Southern Ontario Employment by Industry," Human Resources Development Canada, 2000

Trade Data Online, Industry Canada, 2002

"Traffic," Marine Statistics, Transport Canada, 2001

Transportation Infrastructure, Transport Canada, 1999

"Uranium Production Figures: 1995–2001," World Nuclear Association, 2002

"Valeur des expéditions manufacturiéres selon le Systém de classification des industries de l'Amérique du Nord, Canada, 1990–1997," Institut de la statisique Québec, 2001

Weekly Epidemiological Report, World Health Organization

WHO Estimates of Health Personnel, World Health Organization, 1998

The World Almanac and Book of Facts, 2002

World Book Encyclopedia, 2000

The World Factbook, U.S. Central Intelligence Agency, 2001

"World Nuclear Power Reactors, 2001–2002," Uranium Information Centre, 2002

World Population Prospects, United Nations Population Division, 2001

World Urbanization Prospects: The 1999 Revisions, Population Division, UN Department of Economic and Social Affairs, 1999

The index of *The Nystrom Atlas of Canada and the World* provides phonetic pronunciations for many of the names that appear on the maps. The names are divided into syllables and respelled the way they sound. For example:

Barranquilla (BAHR uhn KEE uh)

The syllable that gets the strongest emphasis when spoken is shown in capital letters (KEE). If another syllable receives secondary emphasis, it appears in small capitals (BAHR).

The system of phonetic respelling is the same as the one used in *The World Book Encyclopedia,* and the key to the system is reproduced here with permission of World Book.

- Dictionaries use special letters and diacritical marks to indicate word sounds. The first column in the key shows the letters and marks used by *The World Book Dictionary.*
- The second column, titled "As in," lists words that include the sounds indicated in the first column.
- The third column, titled "Respelling," shows how the word sounds are phonetically respelled.
- The two columns under "Example" list words that include the sounds and show them respelled.

Letter or Mark	As in	Respelling	Example	
a	h*a*t, m*a*p	a	**alphabet**	Al fuh beht
ā	*a*ge, f*a*ce	ay	**Asia**	AY zhuh
ã	c*a*re, *air*	ai	**bareback**	BAIR bak
ä	f*a*ther, f*a*r	ah	**armistice**	AHR muh stihs
ch	*ch*ild, mu*ch*	ch	**China**	CHY nuh
e	l*e*t, b*e*st	eh	**essay**	EHS ay
ē	*e*qual, s*ee*	ee	**leaf**	leef
	ma*ch*ine, cit*y*		**marine**	muh REEN
ėr	t*er*m, l*ear*n			
	s*ir*, w*or*k	ur	**pearl**	purl
i	*i*t, p*i*n, h*y*mn	ih	**system**	SIHS tuhm
ī	*i*ce, f*i*ve,	y	**Ohio**	oh HY oh
	*i*con	eye	**iris**	EYE rihs
k	*c*oat, loo*k*	k	**corn**	kawrn
o	h*o*t, r*o*ck	ah	**Ottawa**	AHT uh wuh
ō	*o*pen, g*o*, gr*o*w	oh	**rainbow**	RAYN boh
	châ*t*e*au*		**tableau**	TAB loh
ô	*o*rder, *a*ll	aw	**orchid**	AWR kihd
			allspice	AWL spys
oi	*oi*l, v*oi*ce	oy	**coinage**	KOY nihj
ou	h*ou*se, *ou*t	ow	**fountain**	FOWN tuhn
s	*s*ay, ni*c*e	s	**spice**	spys
sh	*sh*e, aboli*ti*on	sh	**motion**	MOH shuhn
u	c*u*p, b*u*tter,	uh	**study**	STUHD ee
	fl*oo*d		**blood**	bluhd
u̇	f*u*ll, p*u*t, w*oo*d	u	**Fulbright**	FUL bryt
			wool	wul
ü	r*u*le, m*o*ve, f*oo*d	oo	**Zulu**	ZOO loo
	m*u*sic	yoo	**Muses**	MYOOZ ehz
zh	plea*s*ure	zh	**Asia**	AY zhuh
ə	*a*bout, *a*meb*a*	uh	**Burma**	BUR muh
	tak*e*n, purpl*e*	uh	**fiddle**	FIHD uhl
	pen*c*il	uh	**citizen**	SIHT uh zuhn
	lem*o*n	uh	**lion**	LY uhn
	circ*u*s	uh	**cyprus**	SY pruhs
	lab*y*rinth	uh	**physique**	fuh ZEEK
	curt*ai*n	uh	**mountain**	MOWN tuhn
	Egypt*ia*n	uh	**Georgia**	JAWR juh
	se*c*tion	uh	**legion**	LEE juhn
	fabul*ou*s	uh	**anonymous**	un NAHN uh muhs